DRAWING FROM LIFE:

BEAUTY
As we proceed through this kaleidoscope
DRAWING FROM LIFE

DRAWING FROM LIFE:
THE JOURNAL AS ART

JENNIFER NEW

PRINCETON ARCHITECTURAL PRESS, NEW YORK

Published by
Princeton Architectural Press
37 East Seventh Street
New York, New York 10003

For a free catalog of books, call 1.800.722.6657.
Visit our web site at www.papress.com.

Printed and bound in China
09 08 07 06 5 4 First edition

Editing: Jennifer N. Thompson
Design: Min Lew and Manuel Miranda

Special thanks to:
Nettie Aljian, Nicola Bednarek, Janet Behning, Megan Carey, Penny (Yuen Pik) Chu, Russell Fernandez, Jan Haux, Clare Jacobson, John King, Mark Lamster, Nancy Eklund Later, Linda Lee, Katharine Myers, Lauren Nelson, Molly Rouzie, Jane Sheinman, Scott Tennent, Joe Weston, and Deb Wood of Princeton Architectural Press —Kevin C. Lippert, publisher

Library of Congress Cataloging-in-Publication Data
New, Jennifer.
Drawing from life : the journal as art / Jennifer New.
p. cm.
ISBN 1-56898-445-6 (pbk. : alk. paper)
1. Drawing—Themes, motives. 2. Notebooks. 3. Diaries. I. Title.
NC53.N49 2005
760—dc22
2004025202

To Isabella and Tobias
—May you always be beautiful, inquisitive creatures.

G·R·E·E·N··S·E·A··T·U·R·T·L·E··
Chelonia mydas
just a brief glimpse of the turtle.
osed to be related to molluscs.
·A··A·N·G·E·L··
teropod. Curious!
sparent like a jelly.
ent told me to move out
the way of the signs.
one shrinks up
other can stay extended
2.
1.
two long feat
tentacles fi
water for f
body silmultaneously
begins to spin,
reeling in plankton.
3.
Pleurobrachia bachei
S·E·A··G·O·O·S·E·B·E·R·R·I·E·S··
(these look too "furry" — feathered tentacles actually less dense).

CONTENTS

PREFACE

Journals are unsung heroes, the working stiffs of creative life. They live in the pockets and shoulder bags of all sorts of people. A birder on a morning walk, a scientist in the field, a film director delayed in a foreign airport, a fashion designer musing over next season's collection, a teenager avoiding schoolwork: all keep journals as trusted confidantes and reliable workhorses.

This book celebrates these seemingly humble tools, beautiful objects in and of themselves. Like old Shaker chairs grown smooth from supporting so many bodies, or a handmade quilt faded from decades of laundering and human contact, journals are utilitarian objects transformed by repeated and fond use. They hold life in them, which is why we cannot let them go. And yet they are ubiquitous to the point of invisibility.

One day while I was working on this book my friend John, a building contractor, came over to see about adding a wall to our upstairs. As he tried to visualize just what I wanted, he took a small spiral notebook from his shirt pocket and began making notes. Of course I was curious (I have been known of late to beeline into cafes when I see someone in the window working on a journal, and I have accosted at least one person on an airplane drawing in her sketchbook). He was happy to put aside our planning and talk about his notebooks. "Oh, I don't know," he said and smiled when I asked how many notebooks he had. "Hundreds, I guess. They go back to about '79. I throw them in a box when I'm done. They're all up in the attic of my shop."

I found most people, like John, pleased when I asked about their journals. A few demurred, saying their books were too private or too pointless. But mainly they were happy to share and reminisce as they flipped through pages. Living in a shirt pocket, after all, makes a book an extension of oneself. Pride is to be expected. The ones that intrigued me—journals filled with drawings, photos, collages, charts, and detritus taped or folded into pages—were visual, and that made them more pragmatic, less confessional, and better fit for public viewing.

My interest begins with my own journals, the earliest of which dates back to childhood when I kept a single book from the ages of nine through twelve. Salmon in color, it was made by my mother who was studying book arts. I scrawled my competitive swimming times and goals on thick, handmade paper better suited for watercolors or poetry. It was a book with a purpose, a tool in what I imagined might be my rise to Olympic heights. I did not take up a journal again until college, when a period of intense dreaming compelled me to start one. Nearly two decades of continuous journals have followed, though months sometimes pass between entries. Rarely visual in nature,

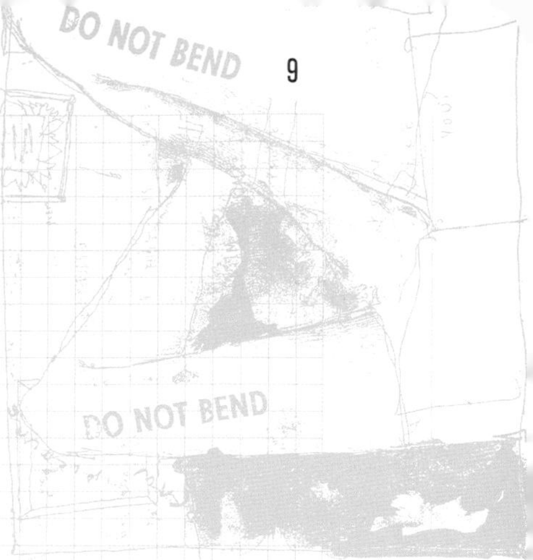

they do not even amount to a writer's journal. Rather, they contain the emotional stuff of everyday life, a young woman's search for self: some whining and self-pity, a lot of fretting, and occasional joy.

Unceremoniously, I keep the books—no two are alike in size or color—in a cardboard box along with old calendars and address books, which serve their own journal-like purposes. But only rarely do I open them. Their pages makes me squirm. There goes Blindly in Love at 19, followed by Depressed and Searching at 24, and Confused about the Motherhood Decision at 31. Yet no matter how discomforting it is to revisit these earlier selves, I'm pulled into the narrative and read on in order to remember what it was like to be me at those different junctures.

In her pitch-perfect essay, "On Keeping a Notebook," Joan Didion says a journal has no use for anyone except its keeper; who else would care about an overheard conversation at a hotel hatcheck some twenty years earlier? Much of a journal's information is lost even to its author. And yet, Didion argues, it is crucial in the way it helps us to reconnect with our former selves. "I think we are well advised to keep on nodding terms with the people we used to be," she writes. "Whether we find them attractive company or not. Otherwise they turn up unannounced and surprise us, come hammering on the mind's door at 4 A.M. of a bad night and demand to know who deserted them, who betrayed them, who is going to make amends. We forget all too soon the things we thought we could never forget."

When I visit my old journals, what attracts me most are the random images stuck into the pages. Usually these are free-floating, loosely folded, and tucked between pages rather than glued. A newspaper photo of a homeless man circa 1991 plants my feet back on the Seattle streets of my early twenties, passing the empty-eyed men and women panhandling outside my apartment building. A tissue-thin bag from a patisserie in Aix falls out of another book, and a cream-filled cake blooms in my mouth. But I did not so much as mention the pastry or even the shop in my written entry of that day in France.

I came to realize the full potential of visual journals when, in 2000, I wrote a book about Dan Eldon, a photojournalist killed on assignment. Though his legacy is complex, he is most remembered for his collage-style journals, which he began early in high school. As his biographer, I depended greatly on the journals and was forced to interpret their mosaic story lines, sorting truth from half-truth from flight of fancy. Even when Eldon proved an unreliable narrator (most of us are), I returned to the journals again and again. The pull was magnetic. Not only were they beautiful, but they contained his

breath and spirit. From them, much more than via any photograph or friend's recollection, I could feel his presence.

Because Eldon was such a visual person, the journals served as a window into his creative process. I could glimpse how he saw his world: a telephone looked like the horns of a water buffalo; an old man in East Berlin the Devil. As all young artists do, he was developing a language of symbols largely impenetrable to casual viewers. The journal held the key.

This is the appeal of visual journals to outside viewers—the opportunity to see how a person operates. As one contributor to this book, Thomas Oslund, told me about his own readings of master architects' sketchbooks, "You're looking into somebody's life. It's a lot different than looking at a finished drawing. You can start to see and almost understand how the ideas evolved into the building."

This book seeks to take advantage of the opaque quality of the visual journal and to shed light on the complex creative process of their diverse authors. Rather than being organized by genre or vocation, such as artists' books, travel journals, and scientists' field books, the order magnifies parallels between seemingly unrelated kinds of authors. It asks: What can be derived from viewing the pages of a physicist and a songwriter side by side? A quilt maker and a cartoonist? In part, what came into focus for this author after looking at hundreds of journals was a four-pointed hierarchy of reasons for keeping such a book.

At the top of the circle (and it is circular, since a journal keeper can enter the process at any point) is observation. The journal keepers in this section are engaged in close observation of the self or the natural world, looking at the color of clothing on a city sidewalk or the cloud formations over a Western mountain range. Observation quickly moves into reflection, the consideration of the significance of the thing observed: I know what it looks like, now what does it mean?

Observation and reflection are the primary kernels of nearly every visual journal. They are followed by journals of exploration and creation. Journals of exploration may be literal (a record of a trip) or figurative (a playful investigation). Either way, they help an author to look outside his or her usual confines and to revive the senses. Filled with colors and collage, these are often the most vivid journals. By comparison, journals of creation tend to be a tangle of black and white lines, hastily drawn in the midst of realizing an idea.

Many visual journals can be placed in more than one of these categories. Obviously, we move through the stages fluidly. The journal keepers here are

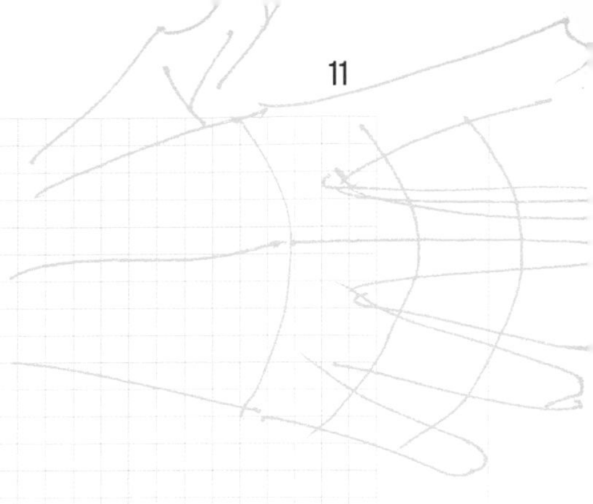

arranged according to which reason for journal keeping most strongly propels their book. And while this is not intended as a how-to—most of these books are much too personal and pragmatic for replication—there are certainly many creative seeds to inspire readers.

My own journals have evolved, both since writing about Eldon and interviewing the contributors to this book. I have become interested in what a journal can help me learn about how I view my world, and what trace it can leave for others. Having children has made me acutely aware of a journal's transparent, blueprint qualities. I have exiled my old, ranting entries; they did me little good for too long. In their place are three journals: one is work-related, a no-nonsense black book; another is for recording my children's everyday activities, moments I do not want to forget but know I will; and the third is digital, a project inspired by two contributors to this book, for which I take a daily photograph of our domestic life.

The latter two journals have taught me to look at my kids with different eyes. When I try to capture what these early days of childhood look like, I stand apart from them, outside my role as mother, becoming sociologist, artist, therapist, and documentarian. This idea of inspecting life's smallest details is the most vital role of the journal. Too often, we go blindly, numbly through our days, unable to recall the shape of a peach eaten at breakfast or the color of a co-worker's sweater. The people featured in this book spend considerable time observing and recording what so many of us never notice. They hone their sensitivity, allowing them to dig deeper into their craft. Great wisdom comes from looking closely at our world, and yet those engaged in it go largely unheralded. Perhaps because they are our Cassandras.

INTRODUCTION:

AND THE KITCHEN SINK

Visual journals are created in a secret language of symbols. Intentional or not, they are private maps only their makers can follow. No one else can look at a page and understand the specific meaning of a punching bag or a set of arrows. And no one else can remember the moment of its making. Joni Mitchell blaring on the stereo. Sage wafting in a hidden garden. The discomforting echo of last night's argument.

That said, visual journals may provide stronger records of the cultural milieu in which they were created than their purely written counterparts. Rather than describing the stuff of the day, they are often made from it. Anyone who has used primary source materials for research knows this. The difference between reading about someone's life and opening old, yellowed letters is startling. When pressed flowers and handwritten recipes escape from a tattered envelope, one can almost see hollyhocks growing in the garden and smell bread baking in the oven. Worn newspaper articles give a stronger sense of the day's values than any historian-digested primer can.

But all of these things are found in scrapbooks, letters, and even calendars. So, what is a journal? Several people related that their journals had been supplanted by email. One man who keeps dream journals on individual sheets of paper, some of them poster-size, argued convincingly that his work constitutes a journal, as did another who keeps computer spreadsheets of his daily activities. When asked for definitions, people's responses were varied and metaphoric: A habit. A map of consciousness. Internal maps. A security blanket. Memory banks. A one-stop shop. One man who keeps a variety of journals—large ones for recording things of interest from the newspaper, tiny ones that operate as to-do lists, medium ones kept by the telephone for doodling—asked, "Doesn't everyone keep a journal?" Meaning, whether we call it a journal or not, don't we all keep something that serves its purpose?

Naturalist Hannah Hinchman has kept a journal for more than thirty years. Her daily ritual of writing and drawing anchors her investigation of both internal and external landscapes.

If we work with the broadest possible definition of a journal—a place where we record personal reflections, observations of our world, playful meanderings, and plans—then datebooks, notebooks, sketchbooks, wall calendars, letters, and address books can all serve as journals. As Alexandra Johnson writes in *Leaving a Trace: On Keeping a Journal,* "A journal is as much an intention to record and save as it is a physical form."

Journal is the widest term, encompassing *diary*, *sketchbook*, and *notebook*. In his exploration of written journals, *A Book of One's Own*, Thomas Mallon writes of the difference between *journal* and *diary*: "The two terms are in fact hopelessly muddled. They are both rooted in the idea of dailiness, but perhaps because of *journal's* links to the newspaper trade and *diary's* to *dear,* the latter seems more intimate than the former." He goes on to cite *Samuel Johnson's Dictionary,* which defines *diary* as "an account of the transactions, accidents and observations of every day; a journal."

Author and cartoonist Lynda Barry refers to the writing and illustrations she does on loose, yellow legal pages as a journal, though she still pines for the diaries she saw as a kid at Woolworth's. She hopes she might yet complete one of the three-sentence-a-day diaries and has two in her collection that she cannot bear to write in. "I don't think I've ever seen anything that looked as good to me as those tiny keys hanging on a string from the latch," she says. "I still get giddy when I see diaries. There is something so hopeful about them. Diaries assume there will be a future."

Painter John Copeland started his journal as an art student at the suggestion of a professor. Though the books still further his creative exploration, they also serve as confidante and emotional punching bag.

Because of its largeness of purpose, a journal can include anything and the kitchen sink. Serving as a collection point for life's contradictions, moments of intense feeling, and factoids that compel but seem without obvious use is one of the journal's greatest virtues. In *The Writer's Journal: 40 Contemporary Writers and Their Journals* by Sheila Bender, Naomi Shihab Nye remarks, "I've heard someone say that notebooks are the kitchen drawers into which we place all the little scraps of things—bits of string, ragged recipes, nails and screws, half-used birthday candles, coupons. Where is it? Oh, it must be in there. Where else could it be?" Or as illustrator John Clapp says of his journals, they "are a collection of things I'm curious about, like the Smithsonian: 'the attic of mankind.'"

In this way, journals serve as file folders for future works. Although Joan Didion disregarded the notion of using the journal as a savings account on which one can draw later with interest, it is clear that many artists *do* use their journals in this manner. Photographer Robert ParkeHarrison relies on his journal during every step of the creative process and values it above most of his professional tools because it contains so may unused ideas. "The journal is like the residue that goes into the making of a final thing," he comments. In the earliest stages of brainstorming, he tapes in photocopies and magazine advertisements and writes in lines of poetry and descriptions of film scenes. These items that resonate for him may never go further than the journal, while others become the foundation for his photographic narratives.

Scientist Erwin Boer fills a few notebooks a year (*notebook, lab book, and field book* are the terms of choice in the scientific community, though none of the scientists I interviewed balked at the term *journal*). Like ParkeHarrison, they are very dear to him as repositories of ideas. He does not return to them as often as the photographer, however, conceding that while the journals contain many publishable ideas, he rarely pursues them because after he has played with a thought it no longer holds fascination for him.

Which touches on another use of the journal: they are a place to play, a safe haven away from our embedded editor. We vent and brainstorm and try on different guises in our journals. They are seldom read by others—unless we invite someone in or our trust is broken. In them, we are released from the obligation to create polished work or to play nice. Architect Anderson

Kenny says that when he first began to keep a journal he found it liberating: "I was free between the pages."

Not surprisingly, several contributors talked about their journals as a meditative process. Kenny says, "I work in my journal every day. If I don't, I feel a void. It's like a prayer or meditation." Renato Umali finds the process of reviewing his day via his journal meditative and grounding, a connection to self that he might otherwise lose. Several contributors are students of Buddhism who commented on the similar attention to detail necessitated both by meditation and journal keeping. As Hinchman has written, "Buddhists and practitioners of yoga have made it their goal to get past the needlings of nervous energy to a deeper layer of stillness."

A journal can play the role of teacher when one allows it to, whether in slowing us down or in re-training our eye. It assists us in seeing the unexpected, to revel in incongruities. Illustrator Maira Kalman refers to this as "the serendipity of life." She always has a journal in hand to help her remember what she sees that might seem too fleeting to recall otherwise—the pigeon-toed girl in the purple pants clutching a pink notebook. Or, as she says, "what you're not supposed to be looking at," like the guard at the museum rather than the Rembrandt on the wall. Likewise, quilt maker Denyse Schmidt finds inspiration in unlikely places: the shapes on the backs of tractor trailers, the colors of ice cream.

During an eight-hour layover in San Francisco, director Mike Figgis noticed these nuns and quickly sketched them. Like many contributors, he says he does some of his best thinking in airports

Not surprisingly, journal keepers tend to have specific material requirements about their supplies. Lined paper versus unlined. The thickness of the paper. Softbound or hardbound. All can make or break the experience. Several contributors were not choosy, but they were the exceptions. Geologist Rick Hoblitt, for instance, has relied on brown Department of the Interior DI-6 field notebooks throughout his career. For someone associated with quirkiness, singer-songwriter David Byrne displays absolutely no finicky behavior when it comes to his journals. He uses datebooks, legal pads, or random blank books picked up on the road.

Others are more purposeful in their use of simple materials. Like writing guru Natalie Goldberg, who recommends plain-Jane spiral notebooks for their lack of import, Lynda Barry favors legal pads because they remind her that she's just messing around. "Some diaries seem too good to use," she says. "That's something that's always been a conflict for me. They seem so perfect until I write on the first page. Then somehow they seem ruined."

More often, avid journalers are on the brink of being book fetishists, collecting journals on trips and receiving them as gifts. They can recite names of companies that produce blank books the way some people know wines or shoe labels (care for a Daler-Rowney?) and are on more than nodding terms with a wide array of pens and art supplies; even the non-visual artists can be particular about their pens. They become excited and nostalgic when remembering stationery stores from past trips. *Do you know the store on the southwest corner of the mall in D.C. that sells European notebooks? I go to a paperie in Paris off the rue de Rivoli and stock up.* One serial journal keeper I spoke with panicked when the small-size notebooks he had been using were no longer available. He called the company and purchased the rest of their stock—all three hundred books—enough for the rest of his life.

Hinchman and painter Mike Roberts make their own books—no need to worry about their going out of style. Director Mike Figgis was rhapsodic about the perfect Italian journal he had recently purchased. Many people mentioned having Italian journals in their collections, but most were hesitant to use them: "Too confining." "Too beautiful."

Journal keepers are notably attached to the tactile quality of books as opposed to computers. "Show me a Palm [Pilot] you can glue stuff into," photographer Lyle Owerko says of his choice to keep a book rather than an electronic organizer. Though digital journals, especially blogs, are the fastest growing form of journal keeping, many visual thinkers prefer to work by hand. A pen and its slower pace ground them in the process more than the machinations of a computer. Among the artist contributors here, most believe important lessons can be learned from drawing. As Andrew Swift, a medical illustrator, explains of his field, "You can easily make atmospheric perspective on a computer, such as in illustrating a cell, but you wouldn't know to do that unless you'd solved that problem in traditional drawing first."

The journal helps us see. The act of putting something down in a book—sitting and drawing, finding the right words of description, mixing the truest colors—forces us to look so much more closely at a subject. Science illustrator Jenny Keller waits patiently at the window of an aquarium tank with a Pantone color book in hand to get just the right hue. Volancanologist Hoblitt makes cursory notes throughout the day when on assignment, then burns the midnight oil getting down the details as accurately as possible.

Unlike Keller, who is working for clients, or Hoblitt, whose science is relied upon by many others, most of us have only ourselves knocking on the door looking for material. Still, we'd rather retain vibrant, lush memories than watered-down, clichéd ones. During her year-and-a-half-long bicycle trip around the world, Sophie Binder finished seven journals. The process slowed her already unhurried pace, forcing her to dig deep into a place and absorb the lines of its buildings, the color of the clothing, the scent on the wind. Even traveling through her hometown in southwestern France she saw things she'd never noticed before: "You sit in one spot and you're paying attention to many things you wouldn't have seen otherwise."

Thoreau is often considered the patron saint of the written journal. *Walden*, based on the journal he kept during his famous sojourn near a lake in the Massachusetts woods, is a celebration of close observation and a model for generations of followers, from conservationist Aldo Leopold to essayist-poet Annie Dillard. Every writer who has followed in Thoreau's footsteps has done so with eyes wide open, intent on seeing things previously unnoticed. "How much virtue there is in simply seeing!" intones Thoreau, a line if ever there was one to tape on the inside cover of a journal.

Dating back to their earliest iterations, journals have been steeped in

Though many people are guarded with their journals, others welcome readers and even contributors. Anderson Kenny invited his five-year-old neighbor, Chase, to add to his book because it would leave a stronger "imprint" than a loose drawing.

John Muir, founding father of the American conservationist movement, made precise pencil drawings in his field books, like this one of Mt. Calder rendered during his first trip to Alaska in July 1879.

observation, giving them a visual nature even when they do not contain drawings. One of the earliest journals, *The Pillow Book of Sei Shonagon*, by a member of the Japanese court in the Heian Period at the end of the tenth century, is resplendent with impressionistic threads, such as "...clad in Court cloaks that look lighter than a cicada's wings." Though her book was not unusual at the time (Thomas Mallon writes, "Japanese women were confiding their emotions to 'pillow books,' kept in a slipcase and away from a husband's eyes, for centuries before there was anything like a tradition of diary-keeping in the West.") Shonagon's eye was notably sharp. Her journal was driven by a purposeful system, of which she explains: "I set about filling the notebooks with odd facts, stories from the past, and all sorts of other things, often including the most trivial material. On the whole I concentrated on things and people that I found charming and splendid; my notes are also full of poetry and observations on trees and plants, birds and insects."

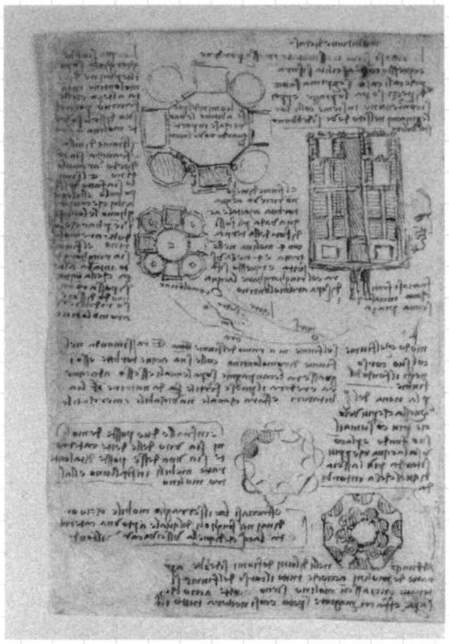

Around 1517, in his role as "first painter, engineer, and architect" to the King of France, Leonardo da Vinci made these sketches for a completely new city, Romorantin, to house the royal court.

Her purpose and method were not so dissimilar from that described by Leonardo da Vinci in one of his notebooks: "This will be a collection without order, made up of many sheets which I have copied here, hoping afterwards to arrange them in order in their proper places according to the subjects of which they treat; and I believe that before I am at the end of this I shall have to repeat the same thing several times; and therefore, O reader, blame me not, because the subjects are many, and the memory cannot retain them and say 'this I will not write because I have already written it.'"

Journal keepers with artistic and scientific bents acclaim da Vinci, much more so than Thoreau, for how widely he cast his sight and how magnificently he rendered what he saw, both real and imagined. Nothing was too small or too puzzling for his curiosity. He left behind thousands of sketches, many of them collected into codices by either da Vinci himself or his inheritors. Their subjects mirror his interest in anatomy, the nature of water, urban planning, flying machines, and the properties of color and light, to name a few.

Da Vinci valued sight above all other means of perception. "The eye, which is said to be the window of the soul, is the main organ whereby man's understanding can have the most complete and magnificent view of the infinite works of nature." Ironically, da Vinci partly grounded his science and art in firsthand observation, as opposed to the day's reliance on books by learned experts, because he could not read Latin proficiently.

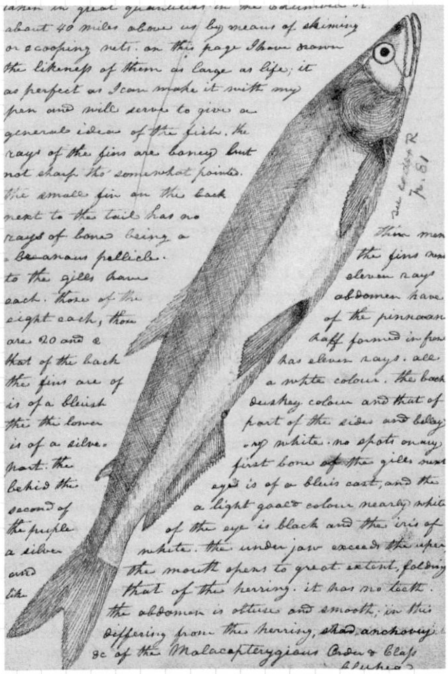

What has come to be known as Lewis and Clark's journals were contributed to by many of their party, as well as by the two explorers. Hand drawn maps, flora and fauna, and the occasional canoe all make appearances in the journals.

His practice of empirical observation, so apparent in his journals, revolutionized many areas of study. Centuries later, Thomas Jefferson was certainly under its sway when he wrote to Lewis and Clark as they organized their momentous journey: "Your observations are to be taken with great pains and accuracy to be entered distinctly, and intelligibly for others as well as yourself, to comprehend all the elements necessary, with the aid of the usual tables to fix the latitude and longitude of the places at which they were taken.... Several copies of these as well as of your other notes, should be made at leisure times and put into the care of the most trustworthy of your attendants, to guard by multiplying them against the accidental losses to which they will be exposed. A further guard would be that one of these copies be written on the paper of the birch, as less liable to injury from damp than common paper." Heeding Jefferson's instructions, Lewis and Clark's journals survive to this day, including notes from both men and five other members of their party. Lewis, who was prone to moodiness and melancholia, made particularly keen observations about flora and fauna. Clark's notes, which suffer from poor spelling and grammar, contain more sketches. The result of variously tempered and differently skilled authors keeping a lengthy record of one trip has allowed for a more composite picture of what was encountered on the historic exploration.

Exploration and its modern cousin, travel, have made for some of the greatest journals. Frank Hurley, for example, kept a journal of the harrowing 1914 Imperial Trans-Arctic Expedition led by Ernest Shackleton. Hired as a filmmaker-photographer, Hurley brought photographic plates and film canisters, the bulk of which had to be abandoned when the team's ship sank in frigid waters and supplies were pared to absolute essentials. His journal, then, provided an important window into the ill-fated trip.

The appeal many journals have for outside readers lies in voyeurism. A journal that lacks this eavesdropping characteristic can be disappointing. I remember finding a copy of a great-great grandfather's diary and being terribly let down when it recorded little more than the weather and the health of the cows on his farm. Unless one is interested in the style of a specific artist, sketchbooks often lack the personal element. Two notable exceptions, both cited frequently by artist journal keepers, are Delacroix's of his trip to Morocco and Frida Kahlo's visual diary. The former, resplendent with color, reminds modern readers of how sensually evocative travel was prior to frequent flyer miles and CNN. The artist returned to it for years, its themes and palate reoccurring in his canvases. Kahlo's journal, dense with psychological imagery, offers clues into the painter's highly autobiographical work. Maintained during the final decade of her life, it served as both artistic playground and personal sounding board.

While such historical examples are some of the inspirations cited by contributors to this book, others are more personal or less well known. The surrealists' game of the exquisite corpse and its emphasis on the subconscious were mentioned by several contributors, as was the work of designer Edward Tufte, artists Joseph Beuys and Anselm Kiefer, and composer John Cage—the latter not for any journals of his own but for his philosophy that art is more about perception and the way one interacts with the world than about what one makes.

Professors, colleagues, and family members were also frequently mentioned as models for journal keeping. The most important inspiration to Robert ParkeHarrison was his grandfather, a landscape painter in the Ozarks, who left behind journals that ParkeHarrison copied as a teenager. "I was so impressed by the constant observational notes he kept, the charting of his vision throughout his creative life," ParkeHarrison recalls. "I am drawn to

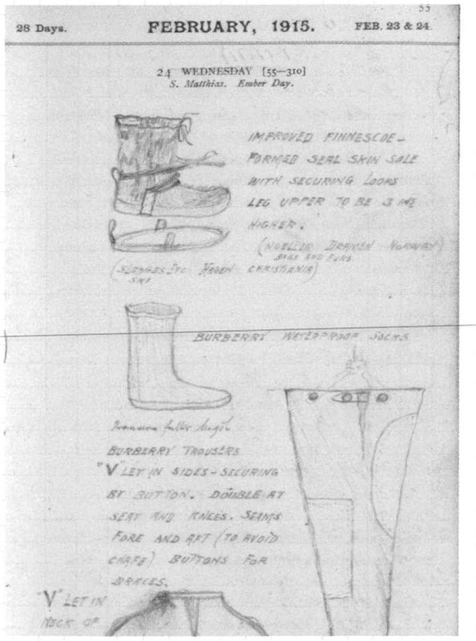

Frank Hurley, expedition photographer to an exploration of Antarctica, made drawings in his diary prior to leaving dock. When the *Endurance* and her crew became trapped in ice for ten months, eventually sinking, the diary proved more important than ever.

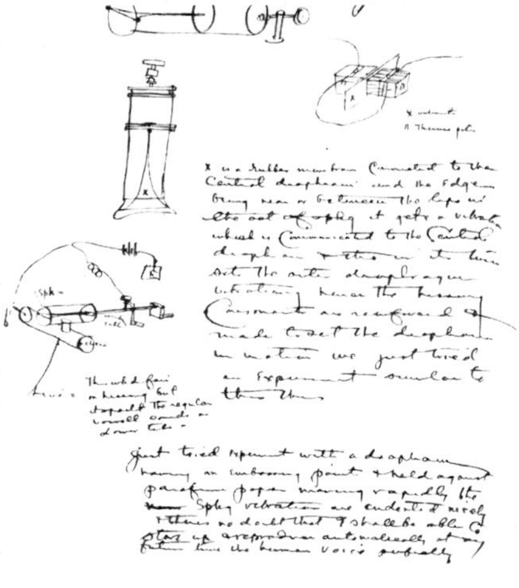

On July 17, 1877, Thomas Edison sketched and described a device that would record a telephone message and play it back slowly enough to write down. The next morning, writing again in his lab book, he realized he had not just invented the world's first answering machine but the first phonograph.

how someone's entire visual thinking lives on beyond them—all of those steps, those daily steps that led up to the finished work."

Once again it is the opaque nature of the journal that appeals to outside readers—the series of stepping stones laid out for us, the map with most but not all of the lines connected. Since da Vinci, creative thinkers have been producing these intimate, unpolished works for which an outside audience is either unanticipated or an afterthought. The journal's primary purpose is to serve as a place for its author to sort ideas and observations. An internal dialog runs through its pages, of which one contributor said, "It's the only truly frank conversation I can ever have." In the end, journals may show more fully than any finished piece what it has meant to be us.

01 / OBSERVATION

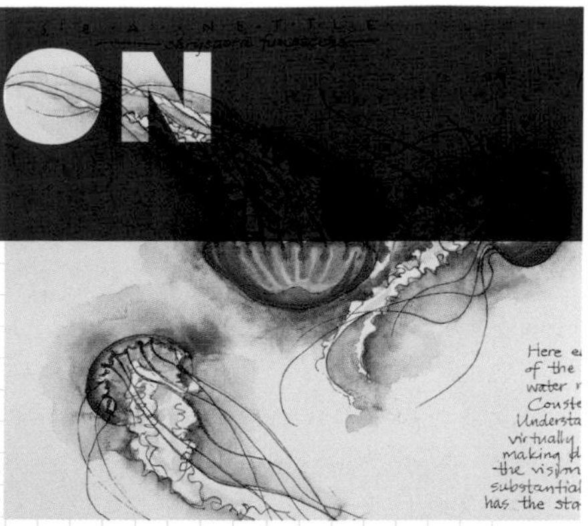

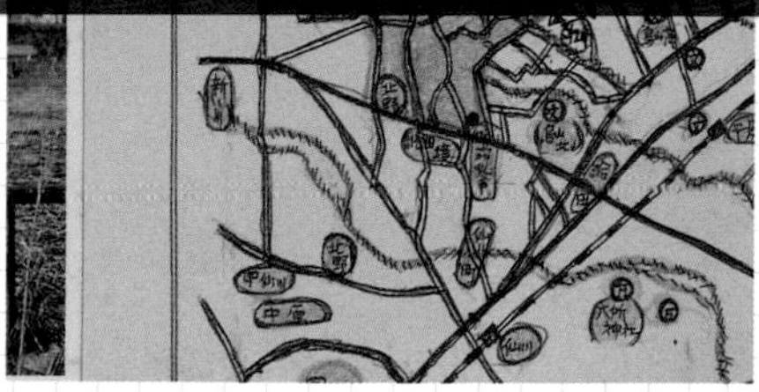

/ OBSERVATION

Close observation of a single subject, whether it is as tiny as Pasteur's microbes or as great as Einstein's universe, is the kind of work that happens less and less these days. Glued to computer and TV screens, we have forgotten how to look at the natural world, the original instructor on how to be curious about detail.

In the late 1940s, conservationist Aldo Leopold wrote about the eradication of a prairie plant called Silphium. Though it had once been as abundant as the buffalo, the last plants in central Wisconsin were being mowed down by road crews. Leopold mourned their demise, but he also mourned the uncurious and uninformed who drove by. "The Highway Department says that 100,000 cars pass yearly over this route during the three summer months when the Silphium is in bloom," he noted. "In them must ride at least 100,000 people who have 'taken' what is called history, and perhaps 25,000 who have 'taken' what is called botany. Yet I doubt whether a dozen have *seen* the Silphium [author emphasis], and of these hardly one will notice its demise. If I were to tell a preacher of the adjoining church that the road crew has been burning history books in his cemetery, under the guise of mowing weeds, he would be amazed and uncomprehending. How could a weed be a book?"

The most elemental purpose of a journal is to serve as a place to record observations, whether about the fate of the prairie or about the changes in our own bodies. Journals devoted to unadulterated observation tend to have a scientific bent, giving them an air of authority. It takes a certain premeditated dedication to get down just how things are; otherwise, the noise of editorializing sounds out the finer notes. A chart of when the birds returned reads much differently than a spring-induced epiphany of the cycle of life. Even when re-reading our work, we tend to find more merit in the former in terms of how it informs us of the outside world, though the latter can tell us plenty about who we were on that particular spring day.

There may seem to be some eccentricity in the undertakings of the contributors to this section; a level of compulsiveness and exactitude is necessary to keep a journal devoted largely to observation. But their patience for ongoing, lengthy examination and the acuity gained therein is humbling.

Illustrator Maira Kalman is dedicated to collecting the unexpected; her journals have the effect of a movie still in which the unknown actress laughing in the background is freeze-framed. On a similar note, Christopher Leitch says of his dream journals, "They aren't about qualifying an experience, but about discovering new things that I might not have seen." Science illustrator Jenny Keller's renderings of marine life are purposely not spontaneous; the results are precise, concentrated, and exquisite. Working largely in the field under emergency conditions, geologist Rick Hoblitt's journals strive to record as many details as he can get down: meticulousness in the face of chaos. Hannah Hinchman's journals marry her dual passions for science and art. In them she tries out geological theories and practices identifying cloud formations.

More intrigued by the human element are Martin Wilner, Renato Umali, and Masayoshi Nakano, each of whom has kept daily recordings of various aspects of urban existence. Wilner draws his fellow New York subway passengers, while Nakano's daily walks through Tokyo are a means for connecting with history. Umali has tracked his life since adolescence and, as is probably true of all these journal keepers, is heartened by the ebb and flow of the natural cycles he encounters. Life offers a myriad of patterns, but our eyes must be open to see them.

So begins
volume ten
in this continuing
tale!

/ MAIRA KALMAN

Maira Kalman's days are filled with visual-information gathering. As she once told a magazine, "I was out walking the dear dog and I saw five hundred things that made me want to make art." She finds beauty in simple items the rest of us are blind to: the long ice-cream spoon, square-toed shoes, tea pots. Her journals provide a glimpse of what it must be like to rove the world with such visual perspicuity. When crowds at a museum gawk at a famous painting, Kalman sketches the guard. Presented with tea, she draws the tray's contents before eating a morsel.

To replenish her visual diet, Kalman travels frequently. Recent trips have been to India, Israel, Japan, Russia, and France. In one journal, she recorded some of the items bought on recent excursions: "The odd fez, string, book, chair, vase, pair of shoes, pair of another shoes, a bag, another bag, different bag, a tumbleweed from Texas, a ball of twine, a doll's outfit from Tennessee, a polka-dot ball, a polka-dot plate, a model house, several sets of pillowcases, a flute, a clock, a lemon-yellow silk chaise, a stack of magazines, shampoo, conditioner (leave in and wash out), a relish spoon, a Queen Mary mug, photos of Russian dogs..." And that's only half the list.

Whether traveling abroad or by subway via her home in the West Village, Kalman makes quick pen-and-ink sketches. In recent years she's become an avid snapper of digital pictures. All of the images she creates go into the extensive catalog she keeps in her office, which, in addition to the chronologically shelved journals, includes "millions" of reference files filled with magazine tear sheets, postcards, photographs, and other scraps. The files have titles like Old Men with Canes or Fake Flowers, and Kalman can never anticipate how any of these items will work their way into one of her projects. A man she once drew from a restaurant window, for example, has since appeared in several books and illustrations.

Given her roving curiosity, it is not surprising that Kalman does not relish the confines of a quiet office. "I like to write in public places where there is action around me but I can also focus on my work," she says. She often works on the subway, which is, she notes, "a good place to think. It's a catalyst for sorting out my thoughts. People are zoning out, and almost everyone looks interesting and real." In fact, her children's book *Fireboat* was written almost entirely during one forty-five-minute ride between her home in Manhattan and the outer reaches of Brooklyn, filling much of a journal.

At heart, all of Kalman's projects, which include *New Yorker* covers, designs for the company started by her late husband, Tibor Kalman, and public murals, are about looking compassionately at the world and finding beauty in unexpected places. As she wrote in her journal in preparation for a public talk, "I am what I am because there is a never-ending parade of humanity that I can record, draw, engage in." Whether it is a Turkish bath in Paris, an old Spanish mission in California, or a Piggly Wiggly in Mississippi, Kalman captures what she calls "the serendipity of life."

ASKEW?
Lucky coffee cup
egg slicer
orange SODA
enamel bucket
mini cooper
Bertoia Chair
CHAISE?
chunky
super deluxe IRON
SHAKER SIEVE
SWAROVSKI CROWN
SHOE
IPOD
Elizabeth Taylor
Cleopatra BOBBY PIN
AMBIEN

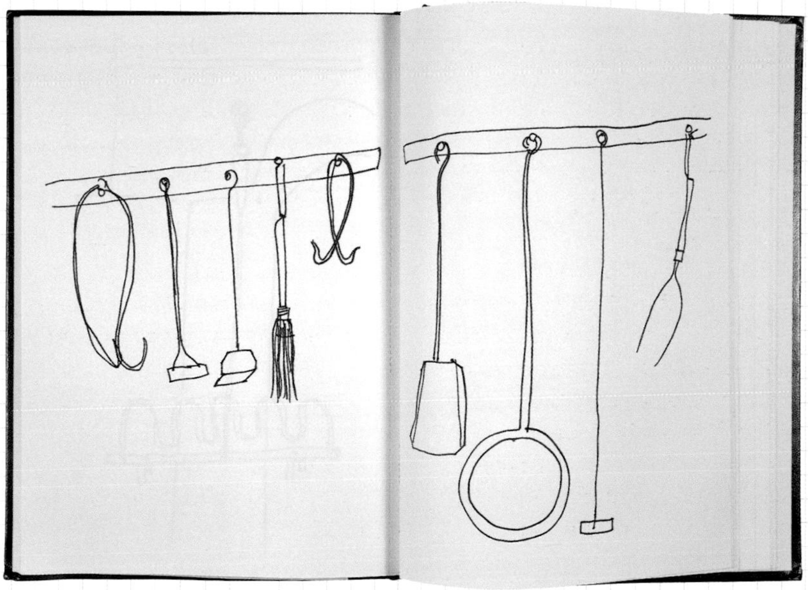

guard at museum

White Arches B&B

/ CHRISTOPHER LEITCH

Each morning Christopher Leitch writes down an objective, non-analytical summary of the previous night's dreams. It is a practice started when Leitch was seventeen and knew he wanted to be an artist but was not sure yet what that meant. Few members of his family had been to college, and most of what he knew about art came from his grandmother and mother. "My mom was a real craft queen," he remarks fondly. "If we needed something, we made it."

The ongoing dream journals have since served as an important cornerstone for his art. His daily descriptive texts provide images for drawings, collages, and constructions. He also makes suites of drawings that feature images of a given person or object from a dream.

The drawings are done on a variety of media, including large panels, found booklets, and other paper scraps he finds. Despite their unbound quality, he considers both the written dream text and the drawings to be part of a journal: "They formally adhere to the traditions of bookmaking. They are works on paper. There is a well-established history in the fine arts of various and diverse works being collected into folio, suite, or booklike formats for viewing and preservation, and my efforts grow from an awareness of that tradition."

Leitch's renditions of specific dreams are often hard to decipher. He purposefully makes text illegible, not out of a sense of privacy but more to mimic the gauzy quality of dreams. "Looking at text you can't read is very frustrating. It's meant to be," he says of the works. "We sense that our dreams—even our waking life—must mean something, but as we live, I think we figure out we can never know what."

After so many years of writing down his dreams, Leitch's aptitude for recalling details from them has been finely honed. No element is too small for mention. He notes which side of a room he was standing on and what he was wearing. Of special interest to him are the juxtapositions conjured in dreams, the mundane coupled with the intensely magical. "I'm always intrigued by how the chemical soup of consciousness can stir this up," he says of the unlikely content of dreams.

The discipline Leitch has built in keeping the journals has seeped into his work with textiles and cloth objects. Just as he never interprets a dream but rather documents it as faithfully as possible, he believes his fabric design is not personality-driven. "I consider my fabric to be diaries in themselves," he explains. "I'm printing with natural dyes, made by organisms that live on the surface of fabrics. I try to remember that I don't always need to be doing something. I set up the conditions and then step aside."

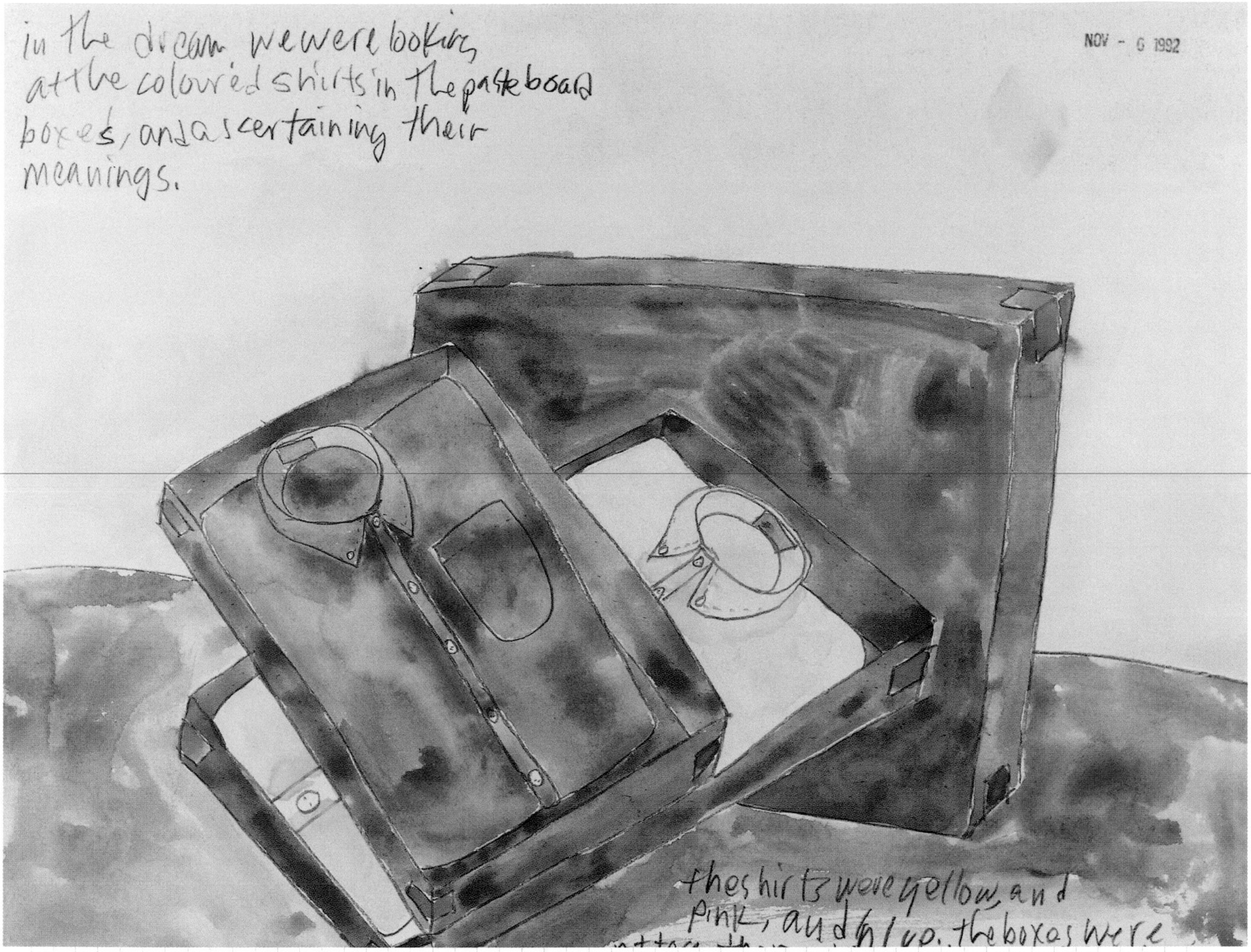
in the dream we were looking
at the coloured shirts in the pasteboard
boxes, and ascertaining their
meanings.
NOV - 6 1992
the shirts were yellow, and
pink, and blue. the boxes were

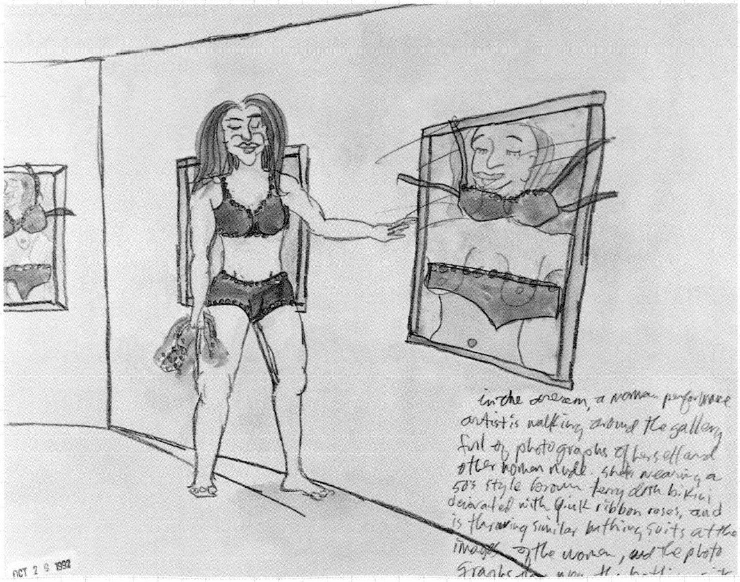
in the dream, a woman performance
artist is walking around the gallery
full of photographs of herself and
other women nude. she's wearing a
50's style brown terry cloth bikini
decorated with pink ribbon roses, and
is throwing similar bathing suits at the
images of the women, and the photo
OCT 2 8 1992

the scientist sits at the head of the table. he is wearing a brown suit, wool or something, that is wiry and coarse like mohair. he is becoming bald, he is fat, well stocky, and has short fat fingers with gold rings on them. does he wear glasses. i think so, but he seems not to. he is rolling the ping-pong balls around on the table in front of him, as if what he were doing were some sort of game. the polo mallet is also in his hand. he is showing us how he pounds the ping-pong balls into the heads of the children. the children are horribly altered. their heads have changed shape - they are amorphous blobs, almost like those balloons at fairs and carnivals that have ears on them and are inside other balloons. their heads are different colours - red, orange, green, and purple. their heads have changed shapes be- cause of the experimental implants the scientist has installed in them. they do not seem to be able to hear us, or speak to us, their ideas and speech are muff- led and suffocated under the implanted dev- ices.they are punished for non-compli- ance with the wishes of the docter by having ping-pong balls knocked into the pain centers in the backs of their misshape heads. they bob about at the end of the table, unable to cry or even breathe. the scientist is proud of his achie- vements and wishes us to con- gratulate him. i am more than a little stunned and wish to retire from the room, in order to find help of some sort - i think of my nephew jason and of how horrible it would be for something like this to happen to him. i go out into the hallway and find my brother ben. i am glad to see him, as i feel i can trust him with the horrible secret of the institute. we are talking in the hall, i am furtively whispering in his ear, there are children running to and fro, they seem unaware of the fate which has befallen their comrades. the matron is their. she is short and stocky, like the scientist, she wears a plain business like suit and a white blouse, her hair is swept up into one of those rolly-polly jelly-roll boufant things on top of her forehead. she

notices that i am speaking to ben, and becomes very angry. she goes down the hallway to get the scientist, and tells him that i am a subversive influence who should be quieted. the scientist concurs, and sets about his plan to silence me, by taking retribution against my brother. the woman syas to me - he is on the verge of a breakthrough in his research in data storage and retrieval - his work is very important that is why we allow him to do these seemingly evil things to the children - their sacrific will serve us all. i do not belive she is saying this to me. then i go into the school room at the side of the hall. the ~~light in the room is faded and~~ sad, it comes from the windows at the left. in the room i encounter ben. he has bleached part of his hair at thr front and is allowing it to grow longer. he is very afraid that they have taken jason for the experiments. i am talking to him about this. he is dejected and forlorn looking. his face shows unutterable sorrow at this possible fate for his son. he cannot cry, the burden of the pain is so great upon him. as he relates to me his fear for jason, he also says - but he [the scientist] is on the verge of a breakthrough in the area of data retrieval and storage, and his experiments should be allowed to continue, i suppose. this grieves me. i cannot accept that ben actually believes this, as the pain in his face reveals the truth of his feeling for the experiments in the lab. there are men with machine guns in the halls, looking for us, they are about to find us in the room with the sad light. the evil matron is in the hall, she knows where we are and must allow the guards to find us of their own. we must find jason before it is too late. we set out separately insearch of the boy.

MAR 1 0 2003

in a dark interior space. it appears to be similar to the office space at the Belger arts center, a row of industrial-looking work stations against a wall. there is the usual administrative clutter. lights from overhead in the stations, standing files, rolodexes, papers et al. down the line, to the right, the space opens up and becomes lighter. have come from that direction to have conversation with someone. it's jason p. he is seated at the last station on the left, the head of the line. he is wearing brown and green, it seems. talking about some upcoming ... ent. it is large and complicated, and important to him. he ... gossiping about this and that, mostly with ... ant import, as not involved with the planning. however in the course of talking jason comes to the conclusion that he should purchase a scarf from the studio display, for the guest of honor, some important woman. while somewhat surprised, express pleasure to j.p. have been leaning over his left shoulder to speak with him. now disengage right arm from around him and go around behind his chair and head down the line to the lighter area, the display area of the expo, to get him a good one. he is coming with, following somewhat behind. on the way, spy something on the floor to the right, it is a scarf dropped there at some point, it has not been stepped on. it has kimono fabric lining on the ends, contrasting with mold printed fabric in the middle. it is only mildly dusty, and a favorite, so gladly scoop it up, trying to disguise the gesture with the walking, so that jason doesn't see that it was on the floor. return to the display, on the same wall orientation as the work stations, up on the left, past the heavy metal shelves. ... of the scarf ensuring the creased bit is on the underside as it is placed atop all the others there, on the wooden bar.

wandering back through the building, through echoing stairwells, through corridors... having taken belongings to the new room, determine to return them to that just vacated. making a first trip with some things — mostly clothes ... return later with boxes and ... the room. it is ... apparent it is ... a couple of guys. they ... old. they are ... brushing their ... return to ... the ... hall...

... aut sec

in the house with melissa, and ... the proportions of the house at ... one another, in a white-painted ... often found in basements. the ... are uninsulated drywall on ... are cinderblock. it is clean ... pack up some things — getting ready ... down the hall from the room ... light is brighter here. a washer ... facing the door, perhaps on ... in the far left corner of the ... on the floor, gather around ... all laughing and talking, ... mom says something in a deli... let's get to work — exaggeratedly ... black shorts, a short-sleeved ... and a head-band or scarf. ... ever. very tanned with ...

driving in the country ... there ... looking for the right house.

MAR 1 6 2003

...'s apartment he has bought a new lamp for ... place in D.C. he has asked to make a new shade ... examining the thing while he is busy with ... ing else. circling, circumambulating it. it is maybe 7 or eight feet tall. painted industrial grey. sits on a tripod and arches over, like a flower pod. the lamp itself is bell-shaped, ... 24–30 inches deep ... 18" across ... round the whole, clockwise. Todd ... ht, next to the windows of ... his small apartment ... it is right. the lamp illuminates ... in the room. it is so big. can ... iowa new lampshade can be made to ... existing. maybe he means he wants some ... completely different. where the tripod base ... arm of the lamp, about 18" from the floor ... price tag. Todd has been going on about ... bargain ... as it is. the tag reads: "$1200." this is ... raising, even if the clunky medical-industrial style does have some campy charm.

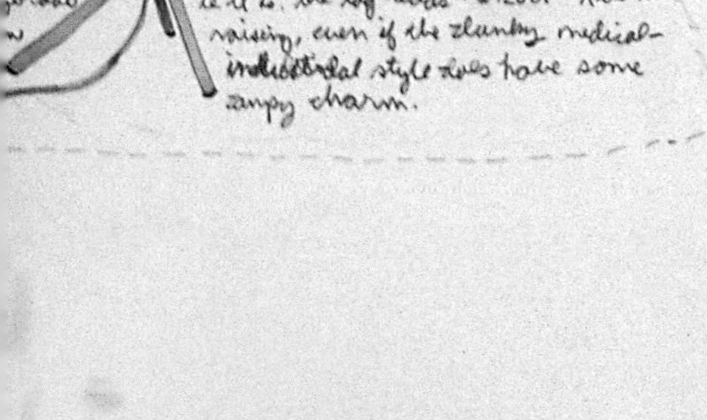

MAR 1 7 2003

... are bushes and plantings. although ... day is sunny and bright ... it is ... the window frames ... a rustic limestone ... windows are loose in their frames ... building is threatened with demo... as a studio or something. ... on the right, ... on the left ... out the building ... several of the ... are open for inspection ... looking through pamphlets ... the ... with other auction-goers ... wooden floor echoes ... old ... that must have been ... a ... through the ... stoves and work stations ... they have ... all cleaned. they have six ... eight ... stove handles are ... a ... griddle ... grease. maybe they are ... but they are attractive.

... on hills ... at the base ... point, in the ... steep, toward rolling, thick and green with trees. the houses are ... toward the road and ... on ebay to be auctioned. apparent ... buy them and give them to the ... are rapt to the conversation ... of these branded pieces, these ... so nice in the center of the ... over the ... on a table ... can be seen ... talking ... with cream ... rounded ... like that and there this left. he is cerulean blue with simple and no ... baldoa ebay seen. abra and ...

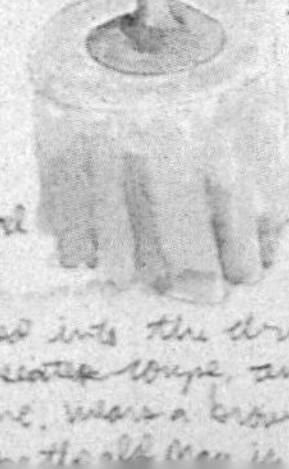

sitting in a car waiting for people to arrive home. ... a ... beard, and matching wig, made of ... how the ... it is obviously artificial but makes up for this in the ... proportions. the beard falls across the chest, and the wig below the shoulders. seated on the passenger side of the ... orange-brown sedan, leaning against the glass, staring into the front yard. the house is behind, to the right ... far side of the single story white and grey ranch ... weather is warm ... grey ... light, for some reason ... found that the ... family house ... the truck with camper, on the left, pulled up on the driver side ... the truck is silver, grey ... the whole family is the ... the wig and beard ... W.E.B. Dubois ... passenger door ...

then seated in a car across the street from the apartment buildings, facing west in the driver seat ... truck, pulled and park opposite, at the curb: this is mike and ... through the tinted glass, there ... to cool the passengers in the ... he gets out of the driver seat, wearing ... shirt and ... aviator-style sunglasses. he laughs ... still wearing the wig and beard. mike and ... say everyone else is already here, ... the beard and wig ... that the wig is made atop a ... baseball cap, for ease in handling.

walking around now inside, all the family are there, ... seated in family groups at ... tables ... white tile ... floor ... to make dinner for everyone ...

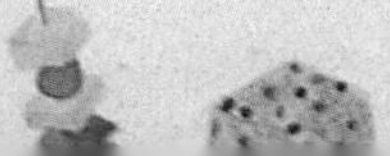

an image of ... someone else, at night, in a car — the driver has pulled into the drive, ... the car ... his ... raised from his 2-seater coupe, and he ... out, ... confused at not knowing anyone, wears a brown ...

in new room, don't like it as the new roommate.

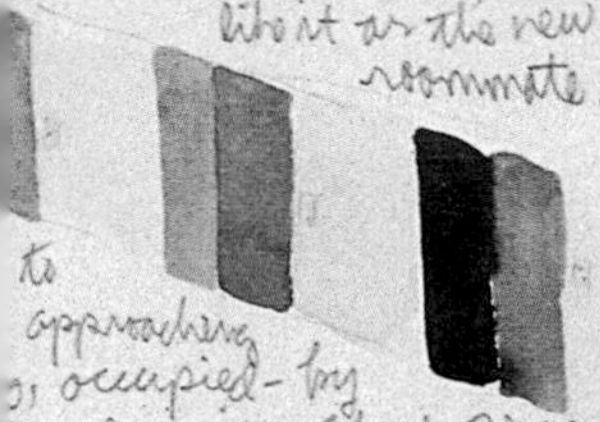

to approaching ... occupied - by ... very nice, about 20 years and settling in. somewhat chagrined ... "new" room, through the ... crowded with moving families and residents, someone in a red sweater, another in a wide brown rib knit. then discover the new room is already occupied, with 2 new ten... and had given up the new with another! this is foolish.

waist high. escalators left visitors up to these levels. in a seating group just ahead and to the left is a mother and her two children. she is blonde, thin, twenties, and her children are toddlers. they obviously wait for one of the residents - brother? husband? ... a banner stretched across the atrium, in front of the walkway just one storey up, says: Welcome dr. jane (with an ill-read last name). she is very famous and is scheduled, very affectionately, for some speech or session, like a conference. the elevators on the right, black doors and closer than imagined, go up to the residential levels.

then in the room with R. he is reclining on the day-bed, against the wall, leaning on his right or left side. he is doodling on a paper he holds in his lap, reading it upside down. he is talking and laughing, does not seem at all surprised to be together again. he is drawing a picture which, he says, "describes you beautifully. he is making many loose hatch-marks and overlapping previously drawn areas with a blue pen. it is a portrait with an over-caption, he says - its so funny - this - is - you, it so perfectly resembles me of you. he is outlining the hatched letter forms in the drawing (solid outlined forms with rounded edges, upper case) and its surrounding balloon. it says Seinfeld and he giggles in his wonderful way.

MAR X 7 2003

... are cleaning or straightening. the house has ... a bit more cramped. in two rooms next ... with light of a cheap and diffused quality ... low, 7 feet or so. the walls in the rooms ... the surrounding walls of the house ... if inexpensive ... Helping mom ... none? or just organizing. Moving to the room on the left. the ... in the room, perhaps ... and as entering ... - sized room ... things ... while working ... voice: OK, ... fully. she is wearing ... button-up blouse, ... and beautiful as ... and shiny earrings.

mom is kneeling on the floor on the left, near the corner, she is holding a vintage garment and calling to join her. something of grandma's? or a surprise from an auction? joining her, mom facing the wall to the left, melissa on mom's right, across the box. looking a little from behind and to the left. mom is handling an antique smock discovered in the box. she holds it tenderly in both hands, under the shoulders. it is made with front and back yokes of small patchwork, mostly blue and red but some green and yellow and pink, too. the bodice in back and at the front bottom are blue cotton. the top front bodice is a flesh color. at first it looks like a soft matte jersey. there is a pocket. mom exclaims: look at this work - you just don't see that any more. holding it closer to examine, say - oh, my. this is - really made. upon a closer look, it turns out the fabric is actually a fine vintage cotton netting. it's in good shape, lovely, old and charming. the pocket evidences quickly rendered stitches and flawlessly tied knots. mom's finger traces the stitches. she folds the garment and places it in a brown paper sack. there, smiling and pleasant, mom finds a black stretch satin tube-hat in a box, it has white polka dots. she is giggling and having a fine time. she puts on the hat, pulling it down over her eyes. it is so funny; so pleasant to see her. realize one reason it is so enjoyable is that have missed her, her sense of humor, her delight in everything. Because.

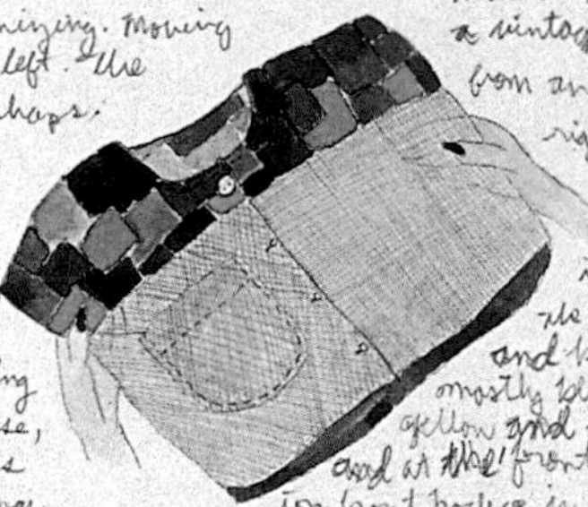

... is simultaneously aerial ... as of a dimensional map ... and street-level, ob... serving the qualities and characters of the passing homes ... the map ... with stone or cedar, many with white trim and composite roof, or often and the same. no luck find... ing the right place. view from the passenger seat.

MAR 1 2 2003

... auction them so a donor can ... so that Dick can use them. all ... i have a ... fair number ... and they ... would look ... in a ... grouping, to his right ... pictures ... room, to ... the ceramics ... a nice interior ... proportion ... be ... cups may be ... must have bought the candle ... the whitehouse, here.

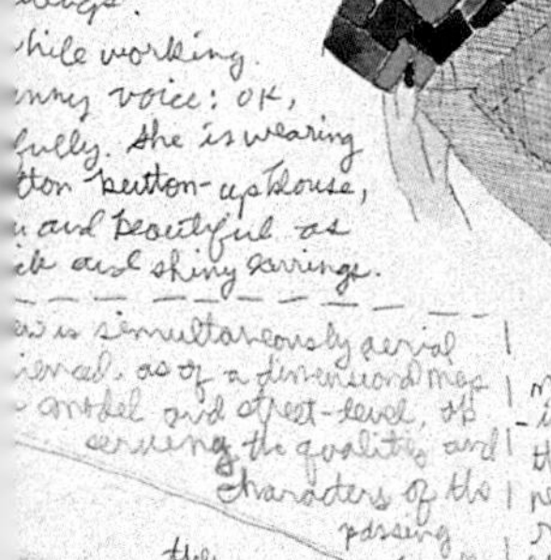

stopped at a station, it is small and old, barely a room, glass-fronted, dusty and grimy, although not evil. two old country guys are there. one behind the small counter, the other to the left, on this side. blue jeans or overalls, barn jackets, a dirty red baseball cap. of indeterminate old age. they argue about a question just asked of them, about which road to take. it is an old country-codger argument: that was old brown's road, wasn't it? oh no yer thinking of old postal route 10. and so forth. this sparks a remembrance, and ask: looking for road #6231 and the man behind the counter begins to trace it with his finger on the map in front of him, upside down. as he traces, seem to be in the car, on the route he indicates. then, there, finally, seated at the long formal dining table for a big feast. although in the country, at the lake, seated not in a rustic but an urbane table. the interior is the white house, the yellow reception room, looking toward the door from the opposite corner. bright yellow walls, clean white mouldings and trim. all are vociferously discussing favorite recipes for stuffing to put in a roast turkey - gravy? sage? cornbread? the questions and opinions are numerous. dick belzer, who is the

MAR 1 5 2003

... ing when we left the ... to smell it - will ... to others like it? this ... likely, although it is ...

Look across at melissa. now resting herself back in the corner. she is wearing dark ... blue short sleeved button-up shirt, crying, tears meandering across her ... red downcast eyes, her exhausted ... instantly why. taking too much ... being there, when all know her to ... mom knows this. it is unwise to ... to such a figure - among ... for her family. the realization sinks like ... groups. mom's giggling now becomes ... mumble, as she rocks on her heels ... rumbled hat, covering her eyes ... want to - ever - be without this, her. and - this is the harshly simple ... laughed, now, after this realization, ... turn - for melissa, mom. extend ... ding mom, to mom's shoulder, ... ging down for a last, long, infinitely ... moment ... turn and leave the room, can do it, knowing what will be. mom's laughter drifts to the air ... hallway and re-enter the room, ... the door revealing my sister sitting ... the corner, where mom was now ... bare spots of pale tile where her brown ... arranged some clutter. she was ... and now she is so definitely ... not. want to cry. do not want to distur... light seems duller, now.

/ JENNY KELLER

"What color was the ring around the eye?" Jenny Keller will prod a marine biologist. "How much branching was there in the rays of the tail fin?" Many scientists are not able to answer her questions, at least not with the kind of specificity it would take to create a realistic illustration. Keller is dismayed by such paucity of visual information. She is reminded, not for the first time, of Darwin, who said of the famed *Beagle* expedition, "From not being able to draw, a great pile of the manuscript from the voyage has proved almost useless." If he had had Jenny Keller along, there would not have been a problem. In her drawings you can smell the salt and feel the force of a slippery, coral-hued fin as it darts through shallow waters.

Keller grew up in the mountains of Southern California with a scientist father and an artist mother. From a young age, she carried a travel art pack with her everywhere, content to curl up with her book and "leave the adults to their conversing." In college, stymied by the choice of a major, she tailored her own degree in science illustration at the University of California, Santa Cruz, and now teaches in the certified program that was born from it. Eighteen years later, she also works for clients that include the Monterey Bay Aquarium and *National Geographic*.

Keller mainly illustrates creatures who reside near her coastal home. Rarely does she draw exclusively from photos, because important details are invariably cut off. "If you draw it," she explains, "you'll see the whole thing. You're more thorough, you're thinking in a different way." So, she takes her journals with her on initial site visits, making notes. After discussing the project with an art director, she sketches the creature.

Regarding the necessity of those initial drawings, she says, "Even if I do a sketch that is not that wonderful or detailed, the practice of seeing it move, the contrast between colors, what a fin looks like when it's extended—all of this helps me to get the gist of it in a really important way." During these visits, Keller also gets out her Pantone color swatches and holds them up to the tank's window with the aquarist and art director looking on. She says it is her "insurance" if someone disputes a color she uses.

When she needs a break from the minutiae of her professional work, Keller often takes a journal outside. Though she considers her personal drawing relaxed and sloppy, which is like imagining Emily Dickinson on a wordy day, she also understands its value to her art as a whole: "I adore the facts of nature and do not want to escape them, but I also need to spill my guts sometimes and explore my heart. As I tell my students, this can make you a better absorber when you return to a project."

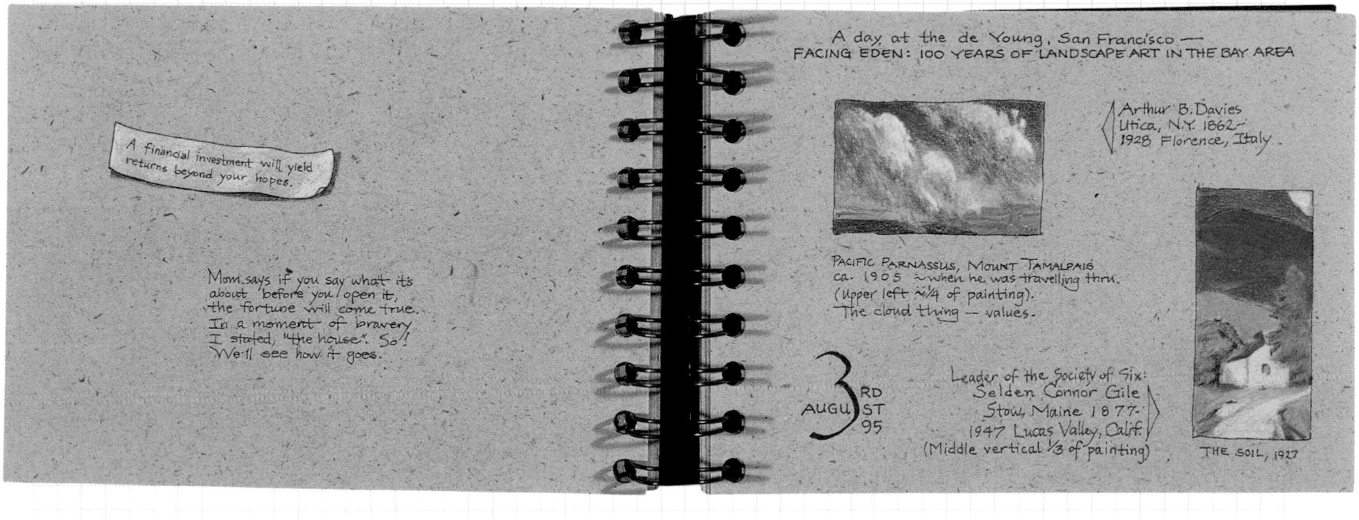

A financial investment will yield returns beyond your hopes.
Mom says if you say what its about before you open it, the fortune will come true. In a moment of bravery I stated, "the house". So! We'll see how it goes.
A day at the de Young, San Francisco —
FACING EDEN: 100 YEARS OF LANDSCAPE ART IN THE BAY AREA
Arthur B. Davies
Utica, N.Y. 1862-
1928 Florence, Italy.
PACIFIC PARNASSUS, MOUNT TAMALPAIS
ca. 1905 ~when he was travelling thru.
(Upper left 1/4 of painting).
The cloud thing — values.
3RD AUGUST 95
Leader of the Society of Six:
Selden Connor Gile
Stow, Maine 1877-
1947 Lucas Valley, Calif.
(Middle vertical 1/3 of painting)
THE SOIL, 1927

JENNY KELLER

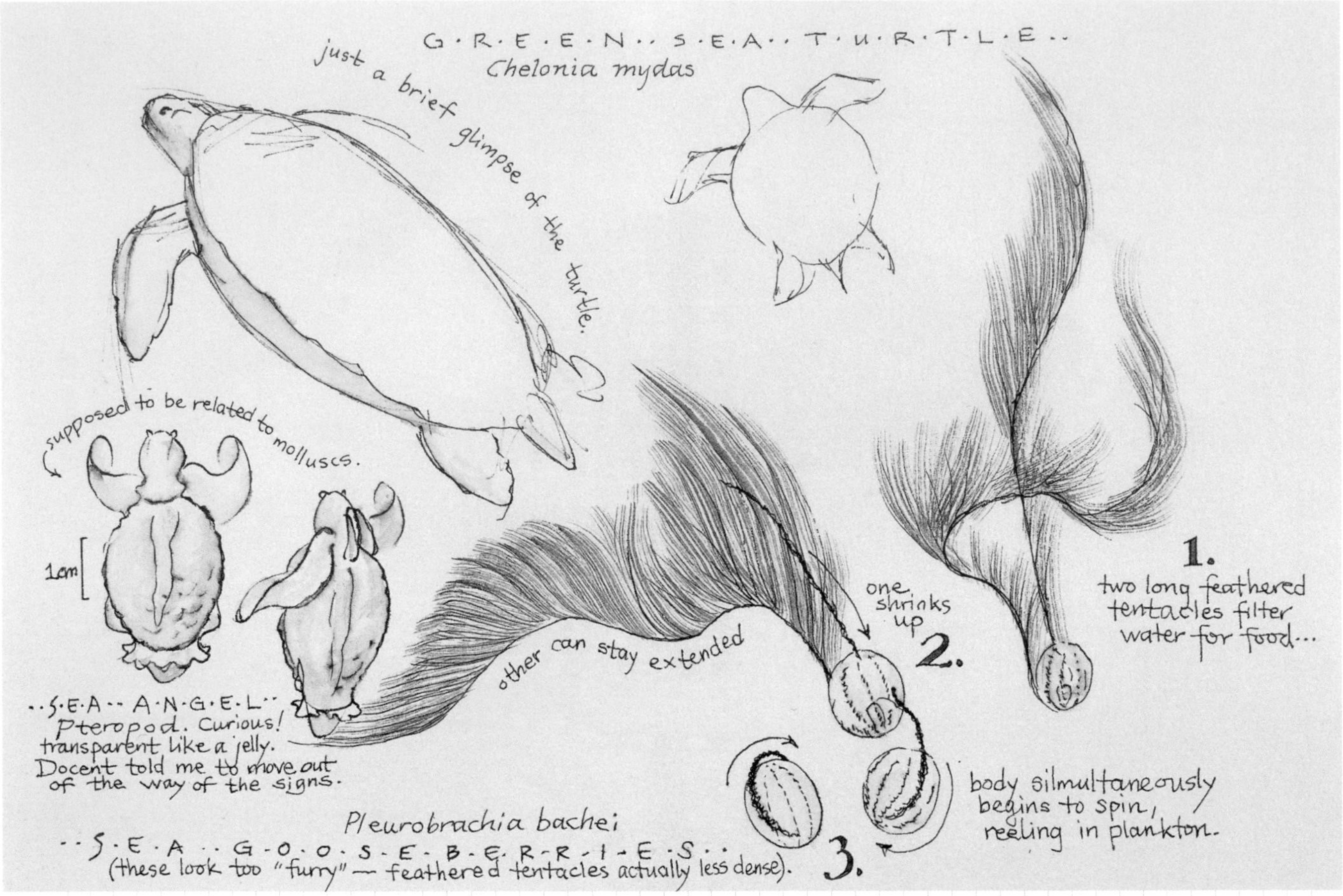
G·R·E·E·N··S·E·A··T·U·R·T·L·E··
Chelonia mydas
just a brief glimpse of the turtle.
supposed to be related to molluscs.
1cm
··S·E·A··A·N·G·E·L··
Pteropod. Curious!
transparent like a jelly.
Docent told me to move out of the way of the signs.
other can stay extended
one shrinks up
1.
two long feathered tentacles filter water for food...
2.
3.
body silmultaneously begins to spin, reeling in plankton.
Pleurobrachia bachei
··S·E·A··G·O·O·S·E·B·E·R·R·I·E·S··
(these look too "furry" — feathered tentacles actually less dense).

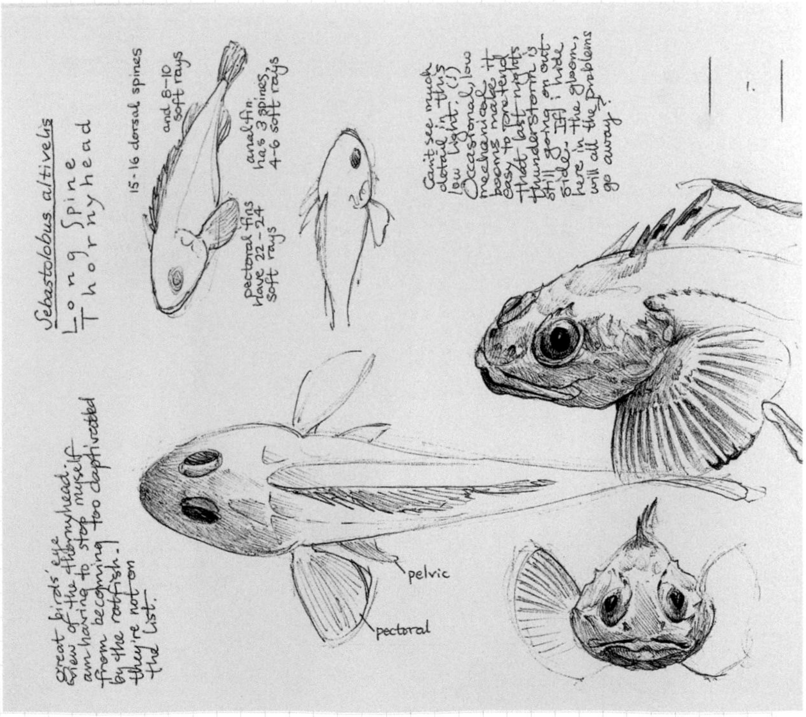
Sebastolobus altivelis
Long Spine Thornyhead
15-16 dorsal spines
and 8-10 soft rays
pectoral fins have 22-24 soft rays
anal fin has 3 spines, 4-6 soft rays
Can't see much detail in this low light. (!) Occasional, low mechanical booms make it easy to pretend that last night's thunderstorm is still going on outside. If i hide here in the gloom, will all the problems go away?
great birds' eye view of the thornyhead. am having to stop myself from becoming too captivated by the ratfish. they're not on the list.
pelvic
pectoral

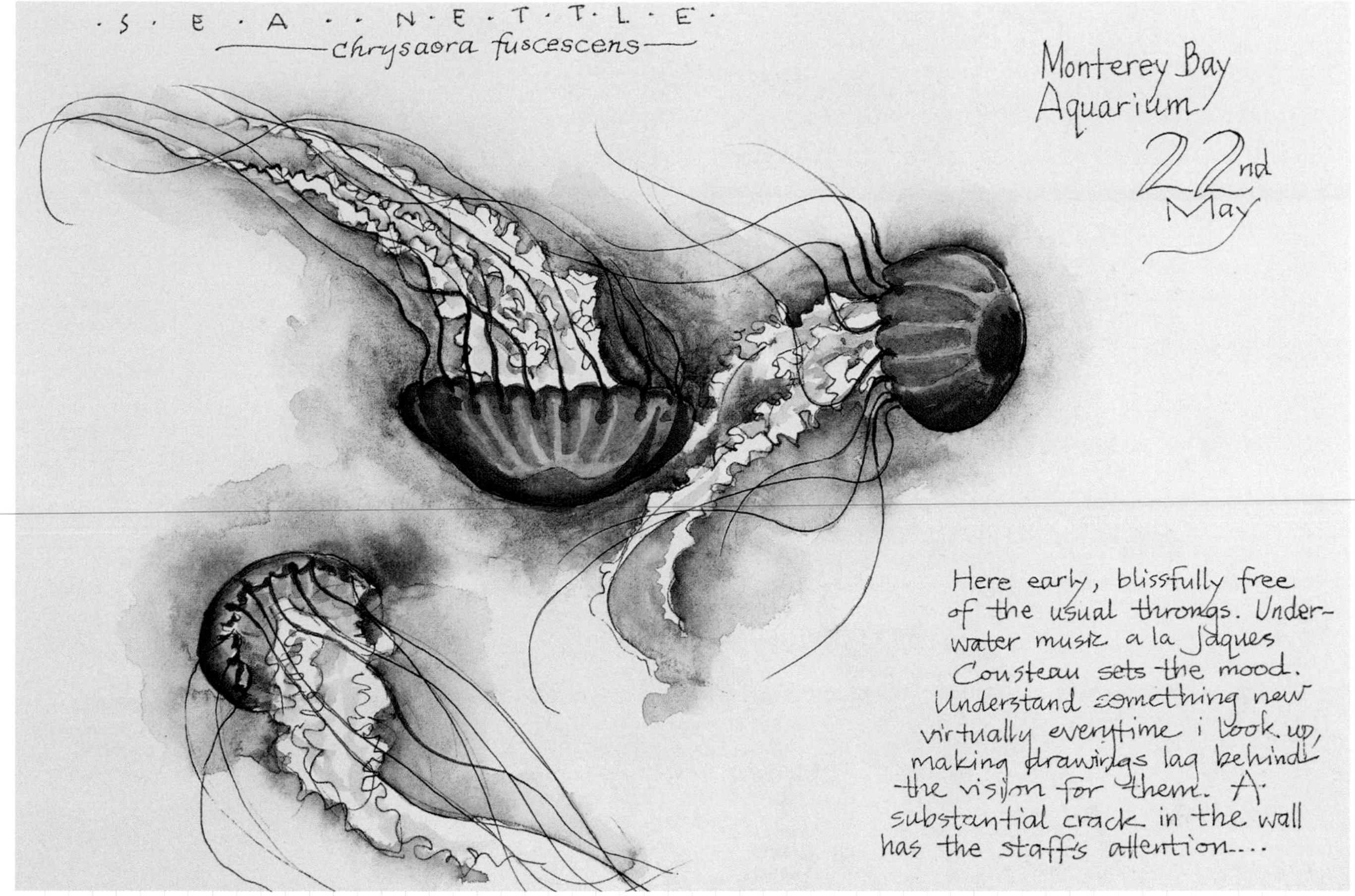
S E A N E T T L E
Chrysaora fuscescens
Monterey Bay Aquarium
22nd May
Here early, blissfully free of the usual throngs. Underwater musik a la Jaques Cousteau sets the mood. Understand something new virtually everytime i look up, making drawings lag behind the vision for them. A substantial crack in the wall has the staff's attention....

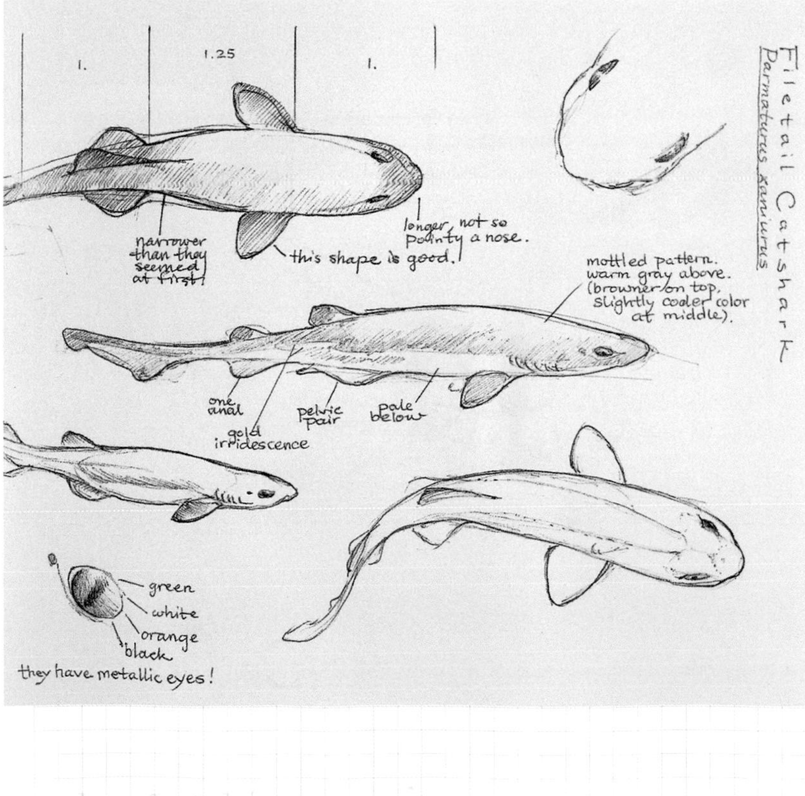

JENNY KELLER

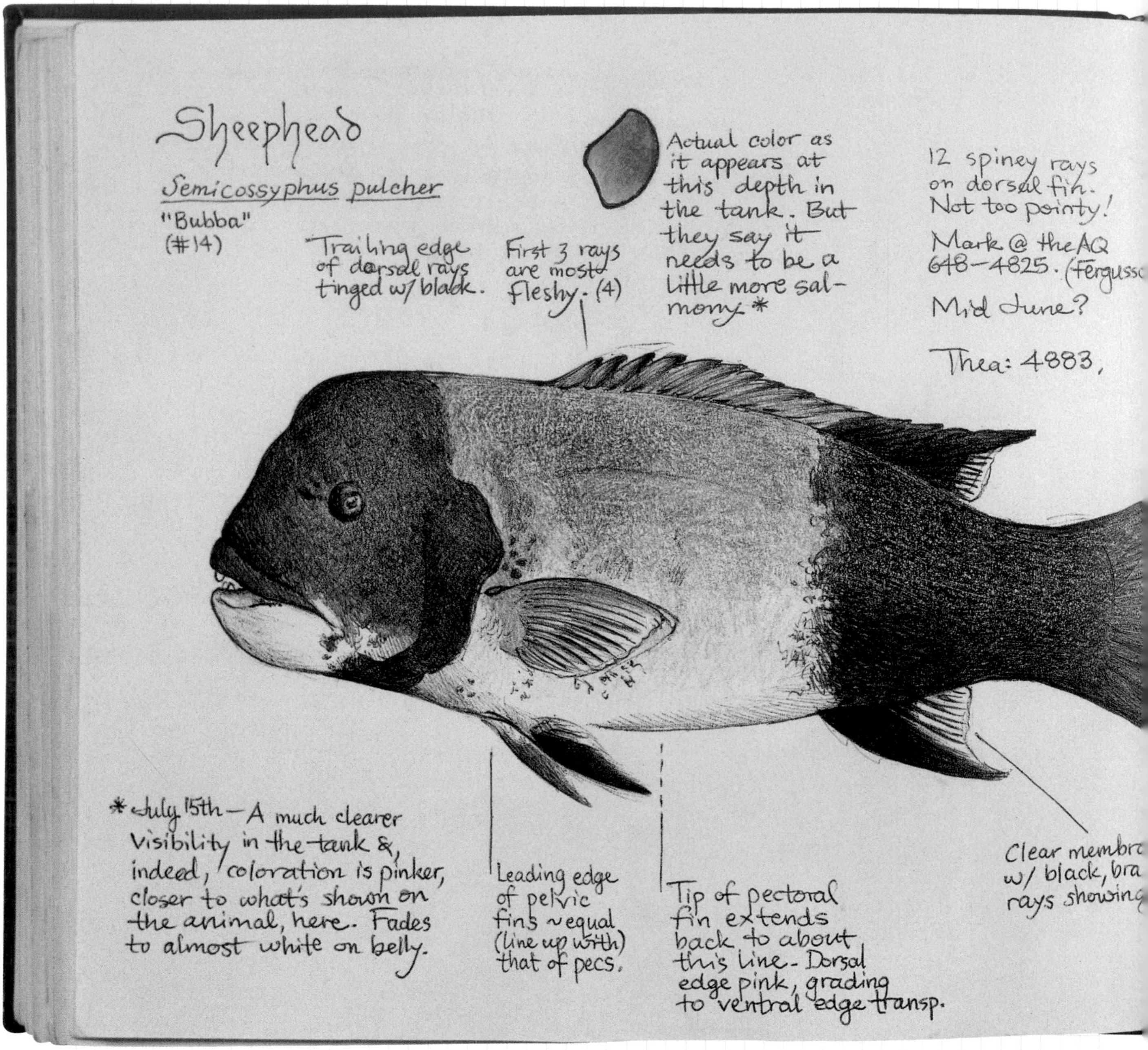
Sheephead
Semicossyphus pulcher
"Bubba"
(#14)
Trailing edge of dorsal rays tinged w/ black.
First 3 rays are most fleshy. (4)
Actual color as it appears at this depth in the tank. But they say it needs to be a little more salmony *
12 spiney rays on dorsal fin. Not too pointy!
Mark @ the AQ 648-4825. (Fergusso
Mid June?
Thea: 4883,
* July 15th – A much clearer visibility in the tank &, indeed, coloration is pinker, closer to what's shown on the animal, here. Fades to almost white on belly.
Leading edge of pelvic fins ~ equal (line up with) that of pecs.
Tip of pectoral fin extends back to about this line. Dorsal edge pink, grading to ventral edge transp.
Clear membra w/ black, bra rays showing

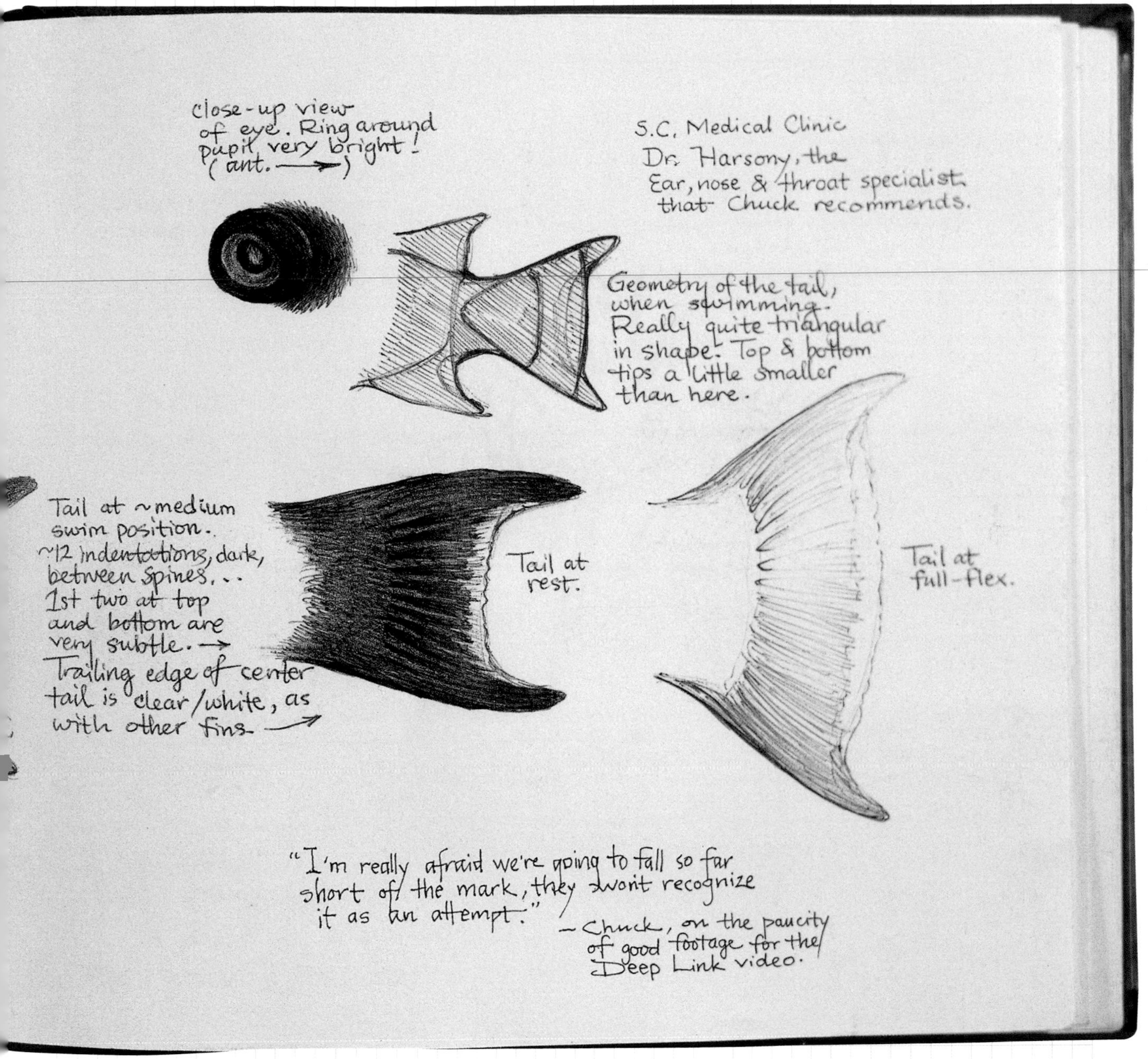
close-up view of eye. Ring around pupil very bright! (ant. →)
S.C. Medical Clinic
Dr. Harsony, the Ear, nose & throat specialist that Chuck recommends.
Geometry of the tail, when swimming. Really quite triangular in shape. Top & bottom tips a little smaller than here.
Tail at ~medium swim position. ~12 indentations, dark, between spines... 1st two at top and bottom are very subtle. →
Trailing edge of center tail is clear/white, as with other fins →
Tail at rest.
Tail at full-flex.
"I'm really afraid we're going to fall so far short of the mark, they won't recognize it as an attempt."
– Chuck, on the paucity of good footage for the Deep Link video.

/ RICK HOBLITT

In 1980, Rick Hoblitt was a junior member of the United States Geological Survey (USGS) in Washington State. He would have been considered too green to be included on a team for a volcanic eruption except that he happened to have done his dissertation on the volcano in question: Mount St. Helens. So when the long-dormant volcano began to reawaken in March and on May 18 produced the largest eruption on the U.S. mainland in recent history, Hoblitt was there.

More than twenty years later, Hoblitt has been to the biggest eruptions of our time: Pinatubo, Montserrat, Popcatepetl. Usually he has gone as a member of the Volcano Disaster Assistance Program (VDAP), a USGS program initiated after more than 23,000 people died at Nevado del Ruiz, in Colombia, where villagers living on the volcano's flanks were insufficiently warned of the danger of mudflows caused by an eruption.

Among his colleagues, whose notebooks rarely see the light of day beyond their own research needs, Hoblitt's journals are renowned for their thoroughness. They're rife with facts and impressions but make no pretense at being artful. During an eruption, he can fill one of his USGS-issued notebooks in less than a month. He tries to chronicle every event of his day, making skeletal notes and then filling in the gaps when time allows. The results are what he calls "myopic" views of these significant but relatively rare events.

He was not always so meticulous. St. Helens made his journals what they are. Although the beautifully symmetrical volcano was crawling with geologists once it rumbled to life, no one kept good notes, not even Hoblitt, who calls his notebook of the event "inadequate." And yet, more than two decades later, Hoblitt still gets requests for his St. Helens notes from other scientists, government officials, urban planners, and journalists, all of whom can gain from understanding the series of events.

When Hoblitt was deployed to the Philippines eleven years later to help set up an emergency monitoring station of Mount Pinatubo, a volcano with no historical eruption, he did not make the same mistake twice. When the first major eruption occurred. Hoblitt was somehow able to scrawl, "8:50. The fucker blows!" while driving away in a car. For several days, he and his VDAP colleagues charted the volcano's eruptive reawakening around the clock, often with the most rudimentary of tools—their senses. "At the height of the climactic eruption all but one of our instruments had been destroyed by the volcano," he recalls. "I was sitting there in the dark recording times of earthquakes, holding a flashlight in my mouth so I could write in my field book."

The drama at Pinatubo was extreme. At many eruptions, Hoblitt has "more time for geologizing." In Montserrat in 1995, for example, he was able to examine deposits, the evidence of previous activity that tells stories too old for written history. Geologists can not easily locate the charcoal necessary for Carbon-14 dating on Montserrat because the Caribbean island's vegetation is so dense. Luckily for Hoblitt, a hurricane cleaned out a gully, allowing him to sketch a stratigraphic section and collect deposits, which turned out to be four to five hundred years old.

In recent years Hoblitt has given his passport a rest for a position at the Hawaiian Volcano Observatory. Without the adrenaline of an emergency eruption, he finds it hard to keep up the necessary pace and attention for daily note-taking. In order to produce his VDAP notebooks, something always had to give. "Sleep. Food. Free time," he ticks off his sacrifices with a laugh. "It's quite a burden to keep a detailed journal."

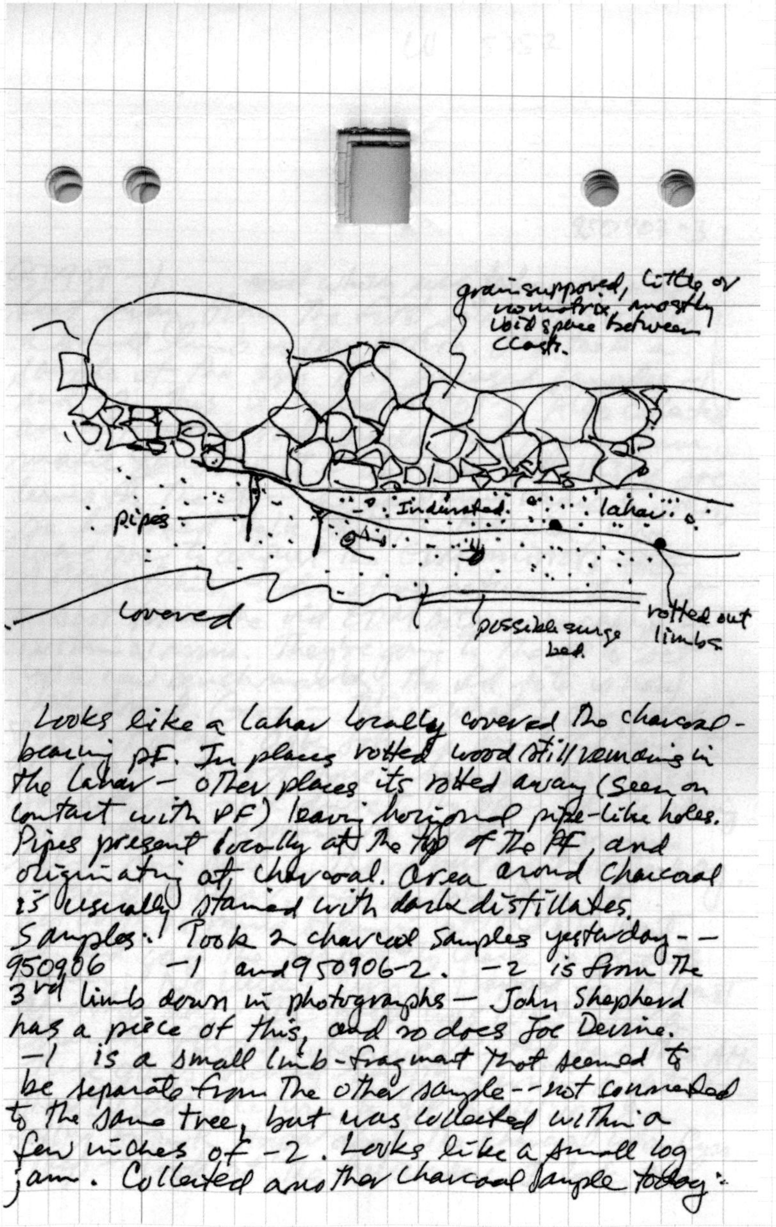

Looks like a lahar locally covered the charcoal-bearing PF. In places rotted wood still remains in the lahar — other places its rotted away (seen on contact with PF) leaving horizontal pipe-like holes. Pipes present locally at the top of the PF, and originating at charcoal. Area around charcoal is usually stained with dark distillates.
Samples: Took 2 charcoal samples yesterday -- 950906-1 and 950906-2. -2 is from the 3rd limb down in photographs — John Shepherd has a piece of this, and so does Joe Devine. -1 is a small limb-fragment that seemed to be separate from the other sample -- not connected to the same tree, but was collected within a few inches of -2. Looks like a small log jam. Collected another charcoal sample today:

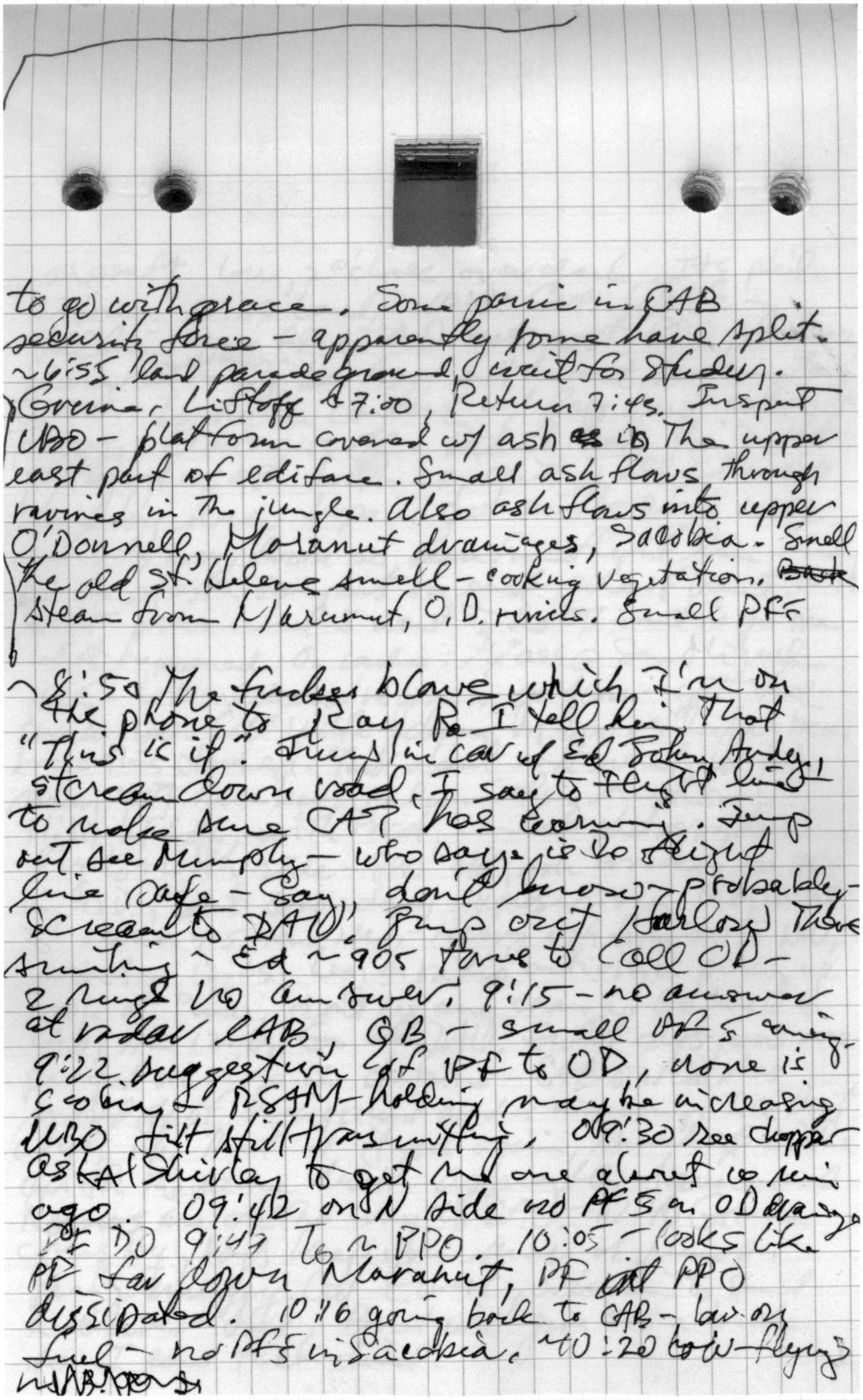

to go with grace. Some panic in CAB
security force – apparently some have split.
~6:55 land parade ground, wait for Studer.
Greening, Liftoff ~7:00, Return 7:45. Inspect
UBO – platform covered w/ ash in the upper
east part of edifice. Small ash flows through
ravines in the jungle. Also ash flows into upper
O'Donnell, Marunut drainages, Sacobia. Smell
the old St. Helens smell – cooking vegetation. ~~Back~~
Steam from Marunut, O.D. rivers. Small PFs

~8:50 The fudges blows which I'm on
the phone to Ray Pa I tell him that
"This is it". Jump in car w/ Ed, John, Andy,
scream down road. I say to flight line
to make sure CAT has coming. Jump
out see Murphy – who says is to flight
line safe – Say don't know – probably –
Scream to DAV, Jump out Harlow There
running ~ Ed ~905 have to call OD –
2 rings no answer. 9:15 – no answer
at radar CAB, QB – small PFs coming.
9:22 suggestion of PF to OD, dome is
cooking. RSAM holding maybe increasing
UBO tilt still transmitting. 09:30 see chopper
ask Al Shirley to get me one about 10 min
ago. 09:42 on N side no PFs in OD drainage.
PF DO 9:47 to ~ PPO. 10:05 – looks like
PF far down Marunut, PF at PPO
dissipated. 10:16 going back to CAB – low on
fuel – no PFs in Sacobia. ~10:20 low flying
[illegible]

2/23/92 UTM 28605 79835

Return to 2-21-92 ① to sample blast more carefully – Sampled units 1-6

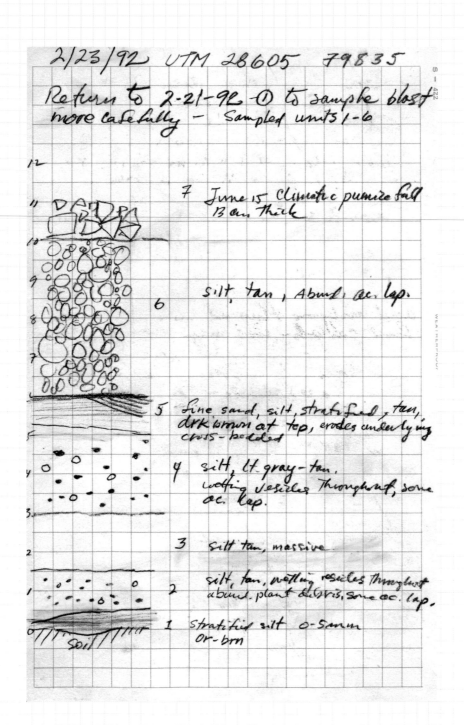

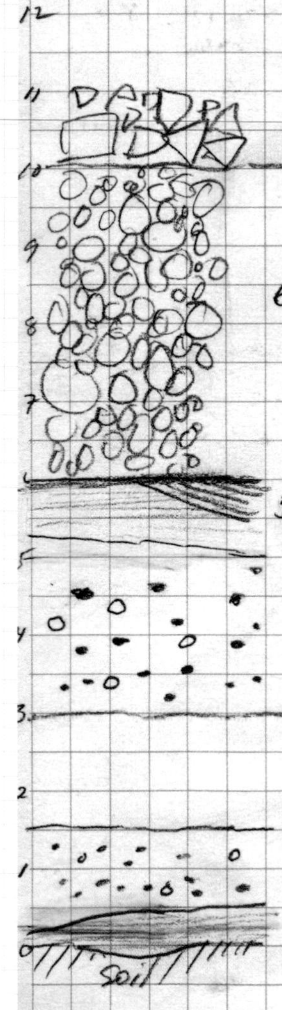

7 June 15 Climactic pumice fall 13 cm thick

6 silt, tan, Abund. ac. lap.

5 fine sand, silt, stratified, tan, drk brown at top, erodes underlying cross-bedded

4 silt, lt gray-tan.
wetting vesicles throughout, some ac. lap.

3 silt tan, massive

2 silt, tan, wetting vesicles throughout abund. plant debris, some ac. lap.

1 Stratified silt 0-5mm or-brn

S – 422

WEATHERPROOF

/ HANNAH HINCHMAN

The life of a freelance illustrator, workshop teacher, and self-professed amateur naturalist does not come with fringe benefits, at least not the monetary kind. Hannah Hinchman is characteristically candid about the drawbacks of such an existence: "I've never thought much about money in the bank. As long as I had enough for cat food and coffee, that was plenty. But now here I am at fifty with no appreciable assets."

And yet she has accumulated assets that many people would envy. Since she was seventeen, Hinchman has been keeping journals. She's now approaching volume seventy. The books provide wry critiques and sun-dappled illustrations of a life led largely in rural and wild places. Some are worn with silver electric tape holding their spines ("I don't take very good care of them," she admits). Several have blowsy covers that look like they were purchased at a stationery store in the mid-eighties. Newer ones are handmade by Hinchman of thick, creamy paper and silken bindings. All of the journals have carefully made title pages with Hinchman's name and usually a dedication, a date, and a return address.

The earliest books are attributed to Hannah Woodthrush, the name she took as a teenager while trying to hammer out an identity for herself apart from her family and peers. "It was a bulwark, keeping out the messy common world," she says of her nascent journal. "I fought within myself so as not to get sucked into adolescent stuff, ambition, grades, having life mapped out." Inspired by Thoreau and Emerson, as well as by a book of illustrated woods lore by Ernest Thompson Seton, Hinchman dedicated herself to immersion in the natural world and "soul-filled experience." The journals were more than just a place to record back-to-nature experiments. They imbued experiences such as camping trips and bird watching with meaning, helping her to understand what she was seeing.

Though Hinchman has since filled plenty of pages with soul-searching prose, she is proudest of the pages resembling a scientist's field book. "The most excitement I get from the journal is from on-the-spot recording of things that are happening," she says passionately. "I think of myself as an amateur scientist and take pleasure in the artistic, scientific, and intellectual convergence." Indeed, Hinchman has the rare ability to capture the power and grace of nature's details in her art. She dives into the sublime without coming out the other side covered in sap.

Read as single, continuing oeuvre, Hinchman's trove of journals provides a beautiful visual example of a woman growing older. Over time, she's become less self-absorbed and more self-reliant. She is increasingly more interested in what the journals can help her learn about the world than about herself. Today, her observations are surgically precise, the work of one who has honed the skill for decades. Her pen-and-ink sketches and watercolors, combined with graceful calligraphy, remind one of illuminated manuscripts. Rather than being saturated with the spirit and hues of religious scripture, though, her pages glorify a spring meadow or the multi-hued stones collected from a cold, western river.

Aware of the evolution, Hinchman revisits her old volumes sparingly. "When I actually look over the juvenile pages, I cringe to appear so bloated with clichés, so obviously running on pure idiot idealism," she confesses. Perhaps this is why so many people start journals but do not continue them: ghosts of younger selves are not always pleasant company. Hinchman knows, though, that the attention to detail she so values in the field has undoubtedly been sharpened through her unyielding, ongoing personal examination. The two are now tangled symbiotically.

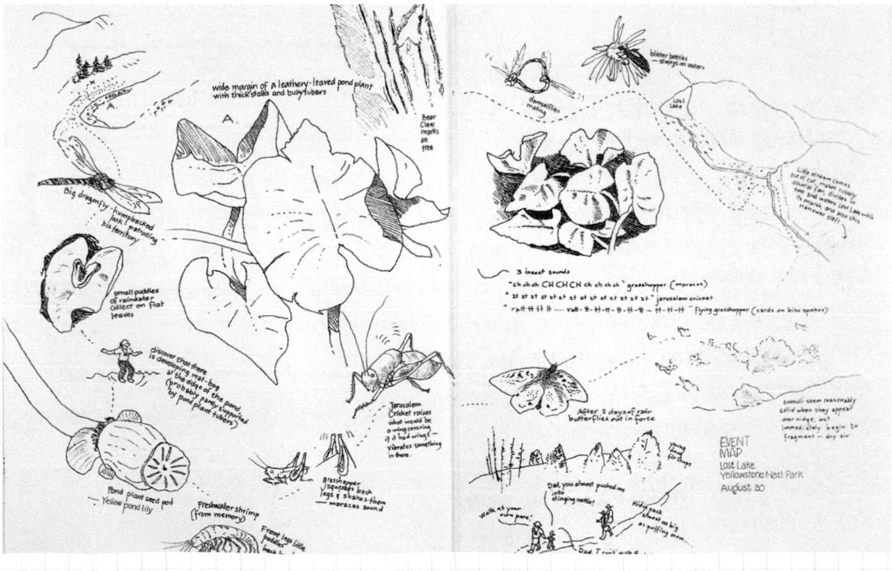

ADVANCE and of retreat SPRING

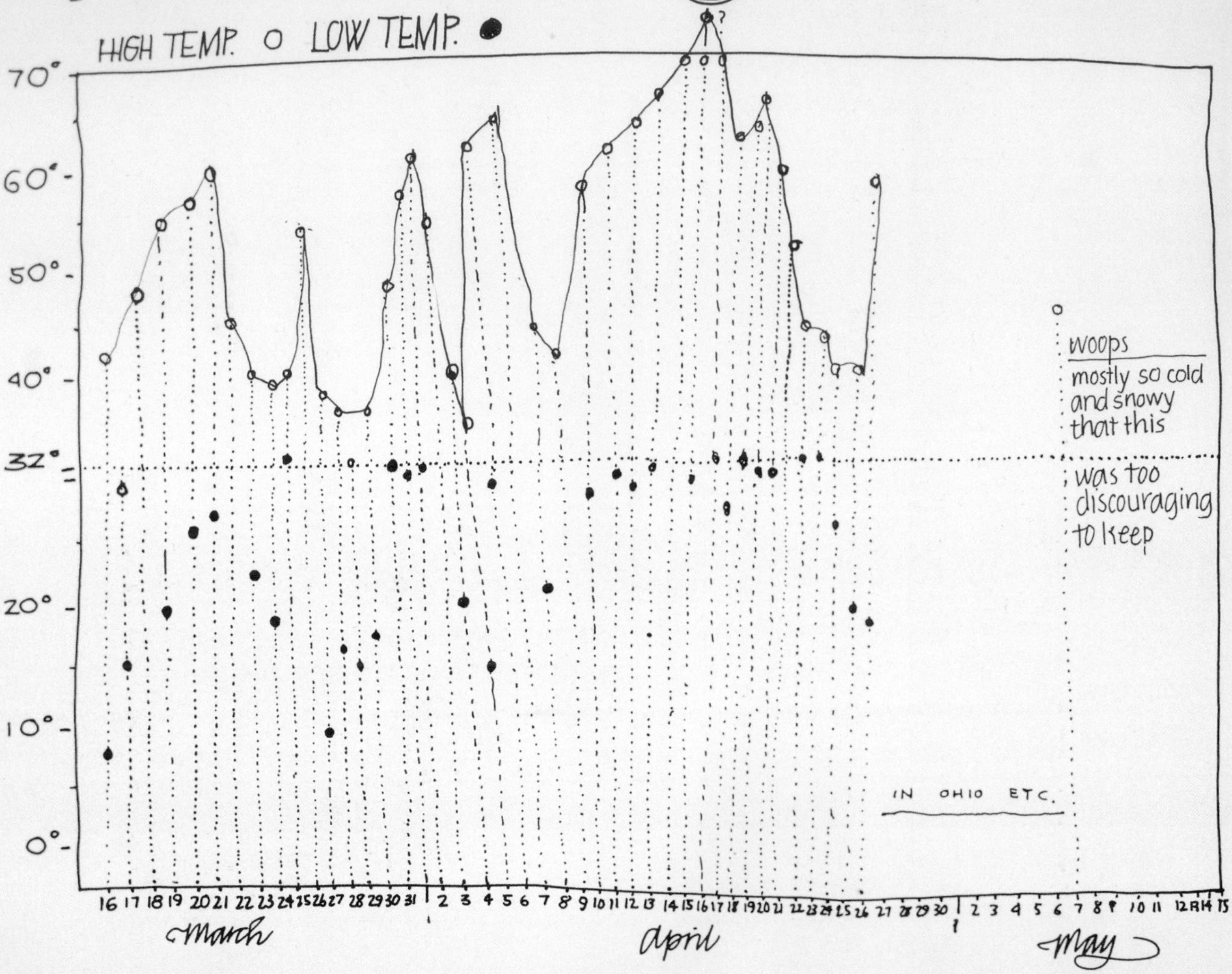

March 16: Storm clearing, 2" snow, still clouds on mountains
March 17: Shreds of clouds a.m. – p.m. all clear, windy, cold
March 18: Clear, breezy, milder, few small clouds
March 19: High clouds, windy, mild – clouds coming & going – jetstream pullouts
March 20: Very warm, very windy, sparse, long cirrus 10%, winds of 25-30 mph.
March 21: A.M. warm sunny, P.M. high sheet clouds, windy, still warm – dusk: all clouds, rain threatening
March 22: Still clouds from front passing; skiff of snow, wind, cooler. P.M. mostly cleared, clouds over mountains, windy
March 23: Snow flurries morning, mild – colder in pm & blizzard conditions – 3" in 2 hours – strong winds
March 24: Still clouds coming over from storm. Mostly clear. Blizzard-squall 9:30 am. Part squalls pt. clear all day
March 25: Awake to blizzard (spring everywhere else in U.S.) squalls all day; little clearing at evening – warming in eve.
March 26: Clear, ragged cumuli – warm, very windy
March 27: Snow squalls. colder (Jackson)
March 28: Mountain snow, cold, broken squalls in Valley
March 29: Snow with bits of clearing; heavy snow in p.m.
March 30: Clear in morning, snow squalls pm.
March 31: Clear and still in a.m. Warm sunny rest of day
April 1st: Warm, sunny
April 2nd: Warmer, sunnier
April 3rd: Warm sunny; high clouds and windy in afternoon

Oct 26

To a remote snake R. overlook — terrace above, abandoned channels again, crescent shaped...

Watery, empty fields, deep dun grass.

The north country loneliness, abandonment.

A handful of quiet geese, small ducks in a backwater, one gull.

Rocks sliding occasionally from the cliff across the river.

FOAM-CLOUD PHENOMENON

8:25

If Henry were here, he'd speculate that these foam bodies really do behave like clouds, guessing that rows of clouds can pile up on one another, and that they can stretch and break apart. And that the bubbles may be seen as analogs to the water droplets that seem to adhere to form clouds.

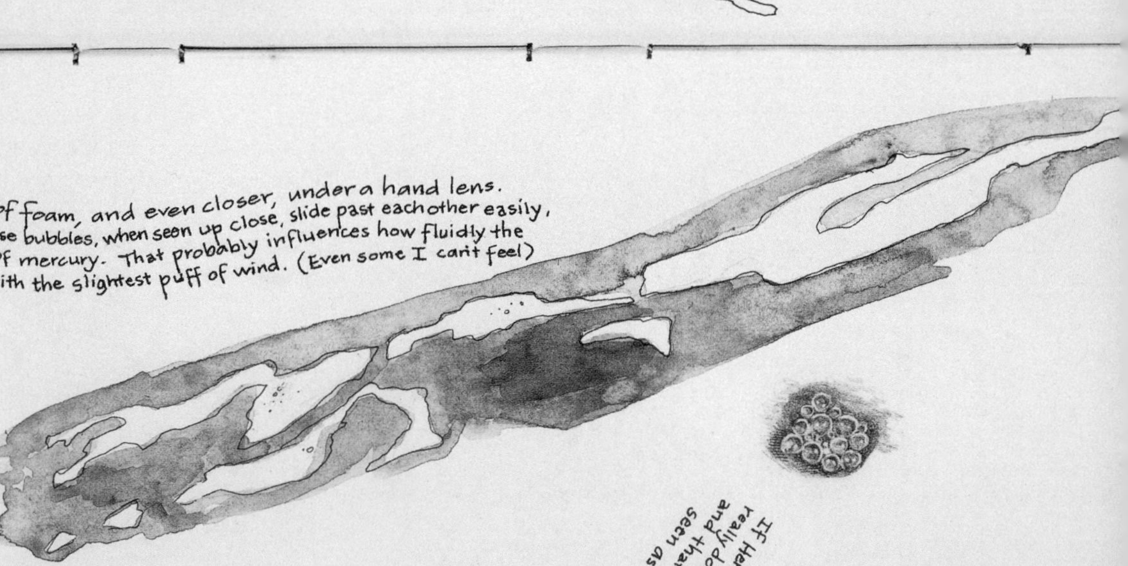

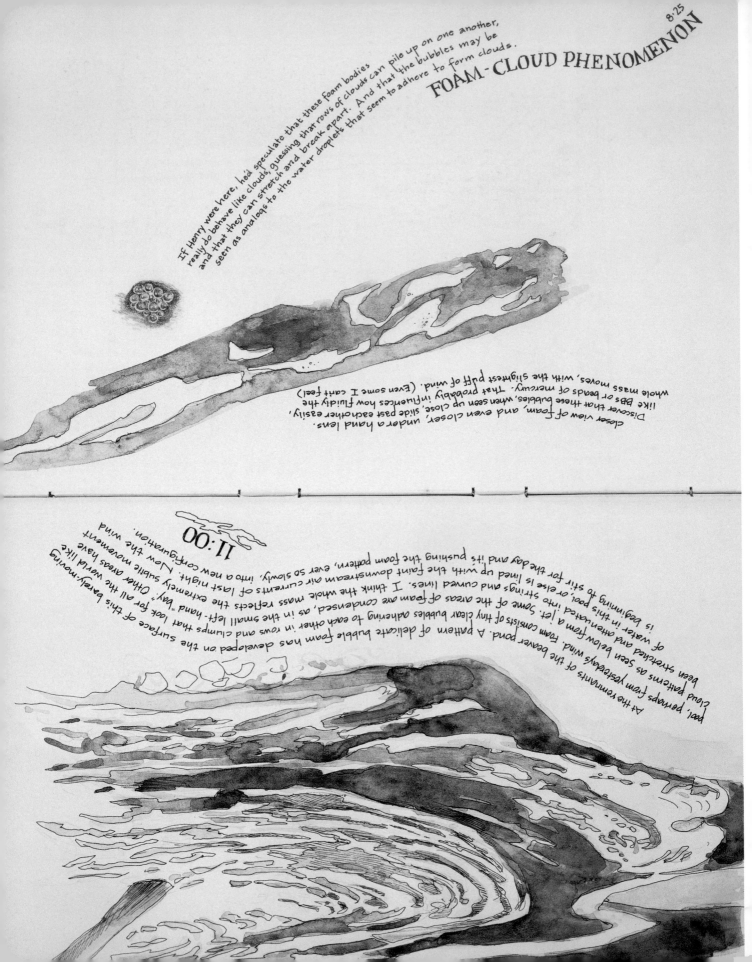

closer view of foam, and even closer, under a hand lens. Discover that these bubbles, when seen up close, slide past eachother easily, like BBs or beads of mercury. That probably influences how fluidly the whole mass moves, with the slightest puff of wind. (Even some I can't feel)

11:00

At the remnants of the beaver pond. A pattern of delicate bubble foam has developed on the surface of this barely-moving pool, perhaps from yesterday's wind. Foam consists of tiny clear bubbles adhering to each other in rows and clumps that look for all the world like cloud patterns as seen below from a jet. Some of the areas of foam are condensed, as in the small left-hand "bay." Other areas have been stretched and attenuated into strings and curved lines. I think the whole mass reflects the extremely subtle movement of water in this pool, or else is lined up with the faint downstream air currents of last night. Now the wind is beginning to stir for the day and it's pushing the foam pattern, ever so slowly, into a new configuration.

/ MARTIN WILNER

The dream was short, but its effects have been long. Martin Wilner, a psychiatrist in New York City, awoke with a jolt. He had dreamt that he was late submitting an article to an academic publication, the *Journal of Evidence Weekly*. Coming to consciousness, he realized with relief that no such journal exists, yet he could not let go of the title. After turning it over in his mind, he saw the embedded acronym: *JEW*.

As the child of Holocaust survivors, Wilner believes the dream's essence was a reminder. "Growing up for me had much to do with making constructive use of my time and appreciating the value of one's life and that of every life," he explained. The dream was an echo of George Santayana's axiom, "Those who cannot learn from history are doomed to repeat it."

Wilner also found a connection between the dream and his dual interests in psychiatry and art. Having drawn since childhood, Wilner initially felt pressed to give up art during medical school. In doing so, his grades plummeted so severely that he nearly failed anatomy. Once he began drawing again, he excelled academically. By the time of the dream, in 1998, he was busy with his psychiatric practice and the question arose again: How could he make art despite his harried schedule? The answer came in the form of a series of small notebooks, all of which Wilner titles the *Journal of Evidence Weekly*.

Wilner draws in the books during his daily subway trips from his home in SoHo to his office on the Upper East Side. He will not take the subway unless he has a journal in hand. Upon entering a car, he begins to draw and works constantly throughout the ride, his fine-point pen never minding the bumps and jostles. No matter how complete a visage, he finishes drawing once he comes to his stop, noting the date and the subway stations in a miniscule hand. Every fifth journal in the series is an accordion-style book, "to allow for variations on themes that develop in the interim volumes." In these the serpentine pen line never ends, continuing from entry to entry throughout the book's pages, with only the tiny notations providing a sense of individual sessions.

One of Wilner's favorite aspects of the subway series is the overlap of conscious and unconscious decisions. Who will be on the train is not up to him, but whom he will draw is. How long a ride will last is not up to him, but what aspect of a person to emphasize is. "The journal plays upon the tension between predestination and free will, order and chaos," he notes. And although they represent the diversity of New York, Wilner believes the portraits are ultimately about him. "It is my eye that chooses subjects preconsciously, my mind that processes the visual data, and my hand that renders the image. That is why, to a certain degree, all artists produce works that in one way or another are self-revelations."

Wilner's people may seem homely at first glance. But the simplicity of the books, with their clean surfaces (they show little to no sign of wear despite their daily workout) and neatly drawn covers bow to life's sanctity. They also acknowledge its absurdity. A fan of the cartoonist Robert Crumb, Wilner sometimes exaggerates a feature—an oversized schnoz, a too-high Afro—and notes amusing and coincidental intersections, such as a lost-looking man sitting under an advertisement, "Could you have a head injury?"

Wilner maintains several other daily projects, including *Making History*, for which he draws onto a monthly calendar something that strikes him from his daily reading of *The New York Times*. Compelled to start the project by the events of September 11th, he says, "[It] underscored for me the need to create some kind of ongoing historical visual account of the troubled world around me." Like the JEW, as he sometimes refers to the subway series, the calendars are a way to mark time while also making something of it. Even at their grimmest, the drawings are underpinned with a deep appreciation for the value of life. And for time well spent.

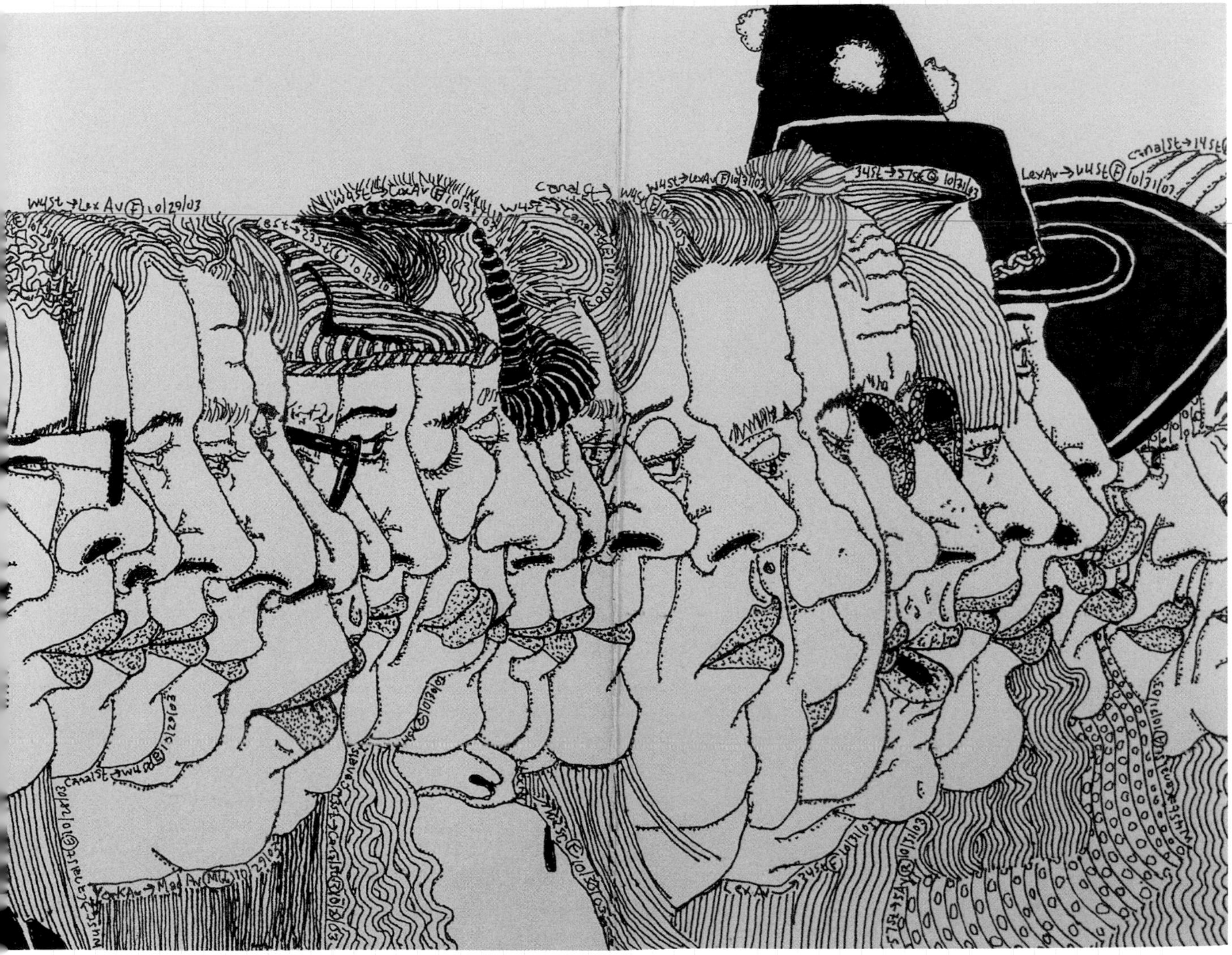
W4St → Lex Av (F) 10/29/03
LexAv → W4St (F) 10/31/03
34St → 57St (Q) 10/31/03

JUNE
2003
S
M
T
T
F
S
1
2
3
4
5
6
7
8
9
A psychiatrist who examined the truth of children's stories in parents' divorces.
10
11
12
13
14
15
16
17
18
19
20
21
22
23
24
25
26
27
28
30

MARTIN WILNER

/ RENATO UMALI

It started with showers. At fourteen, Renato Umali so disliked bathing that he began tracking how much time he spent at it. As a competitive cyclist in high school, he kept charts to document his progress. In college, concerned by his growing Burger King consumption, he logged his visits and what he ate, along with his sleeping patterns, car-related statistics, and a rating of his day on a one-to-five scale. When a girlfriend complained that they were not spending enough quality time together, Umali tracked how they spent their time and rated that, too.

Umali, now thirty-two, continues to track many elements of his life. He can tell you how many eggs he ate last year and how they were prepared (forty-six eggs eaten scrambled versus forty-four in fried rice), which restaurants he frequented most often ($215.45 spent at Beans and Barley), whom he talked to (his neighbor and friend Sarah led the list for the second straight year), and where he slept. The practice culminates in the Umalis, a tongue-in-cheek awards ceremony.

Although Umali's tracking can seem like eccentric navel-gazing, the filmmaker/musician is earnestly intrigued by the projects and insists they do not interfere with his life. "In fact," he says, "it enriches it." The quantitative part is easy, just some quick entering on an Excel spreadsheet. But the qualitative entries are more meditative and enjoyable: "They force me to think about the day and really remember what happened."

Every year he tries to add one new element to his tracking journal. This year it was shoes. At the end of 1999 it was a project called "I Learn Something New Every Single Day," for which he takes a daily digital self-portrait and combines it with one sentence about the most important thing he learned that day. Whether looking disheveled in his apartment or blinking into the sun outside a coffee shop, Umali stares unemotionally into the lens. In addition to showing his physical growth, he also hopes to pinpoint moments of emotional growth. "I've sometimes wondered, *When did I get the values I have?* That is, when did I know that racism was bad; when did I become anti–capital punishment? I hoped, and still do, to try to capture such major changes or discoveries within myself."

A music major in college, Umali cites seemingly unrelated influences, including John Cage, Scrabble, and baseball. "I loved baseball cards as a kid. You can look at a fourteen-year career and tell so much about how a life was lived just by the numbers," he notes. Like baseball, Scrabble is also about elegance played on a grid of order. Umali competes in Scrabble tournaments and says his journal keeping has influenced his wordsmithing: "It has refined my mind to think about letters and words and helps my brain store stuff in a particular way." And it's beautiful, he adds, intoning vowel dumps like poetry: "Eulogia, aioli, oidia, zoeae."

The beauty behind the information he collects is part of what compels Umali. He finds it reassuring to so clearly be able to watch life's ebb and flow. And though he's pretty certain he will not find it, he still enjoys trying to pinpoint happiness. "If I track consumption, such as going out to eat, social events, and then correlate that with my mood, ostensibly it should indicate what makes me happy." But he laughs as he says this, and the sound of it admits both the futility and the charm of his undertaking.

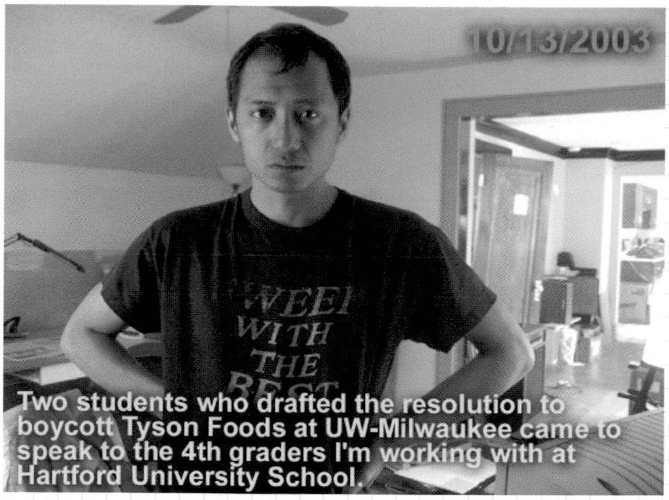
10/13/2003
Two students who drafted the resolution to boycott Tyson Foods at UW-Milwaukee came to speak to the 4th graders I'm working with at Hartford University School.

10/14/2003
The actor, Martin Sheen, is a radical, activist Catholic who believes in going to church.

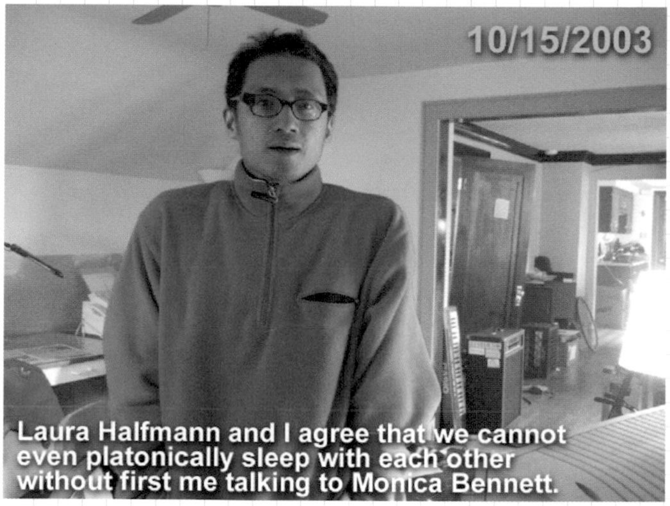
10/15/2003
Laura Halfmann and I agree that we cannot even platonically sleep with each other without first me talking to Monica Bennett.

10/16/2003
Elizabeth Coggin is "hiding out" at her parents' house in Madison, Wisconsin.

10/17/2003
Monica Bennett is fine with all the intimate revelations about her in this project.

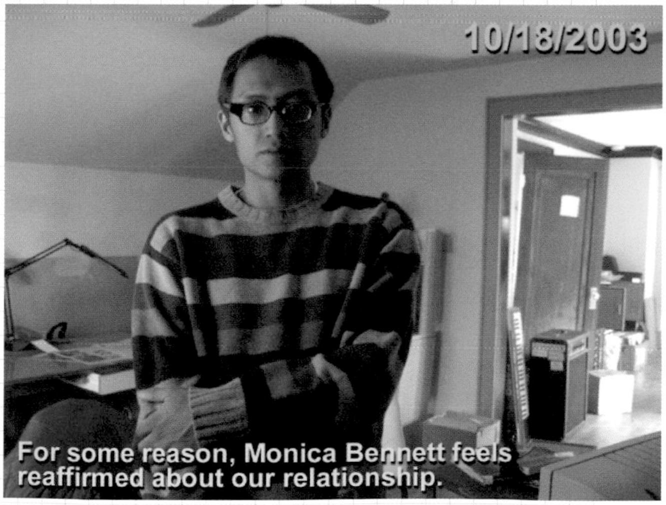
10/18/2003
For some reason, Monica Bennett feels reaffirmed about our relationship.

/ MASAYOSHI NAKANO

Masayoshi Nakano, an engineer for Hitachi in Tokyo, began taking daily walks after retiring at age seventy. Mornings were devoted to the diverse tours through the Musashino, a wide, historically rich region that is dotted with towns stretching from western Tokyo to the mountains. Afternoons were spent creating intricate maps depicting the walk. In the bound pages of the journals in which he drew, he also noted shrines, temples, rivers, and other significant sites. Like Bonsai gardens, the books were miniature re-creations of real landscapes.

The practice was a way for Nakano to more deeply understand his roots, says his daughter-in-law, Emiko Nakano. "He thought he was bred by the nature of the Musashino area, and so he wanted to know about it," she says, adding that "this is a very Japanese way of thinking," referring to the belief that a place can have a direct impact on a person.

Nakano based his walking routes on a two-hundred-year-old map, preferring to visit streets and sites laden with the past. He spent time at the library and in the offices of shrines, furthering his understanding of the landmarks he visited. He only returned to the same place when he had questions about it.

Nakano continued his practice for almost a quarter century, finally abandoning it at age ninety-three, when his eyesight began to fail. He filled about forty books with his meticulous notations and the small black-and-white photographs he glued in. Although they were not intimate by many standards, they provided distances and facts not very different from what we might find in a guidebook. But to the elderly engineer they were personal, because they were based on his subjective perceptions. And that was their undoing.

Finding little value in them beyond their making, he burned all of them except for one completed book. It is hard to imagine the destruction of the intricate maps, the years of work, the complex memories and knowledge he surely built up during that time. But Emiko says her father-in-law never made any pretense of being an artist. "His curiosity was strong," she says, "but he did not fixate on things."

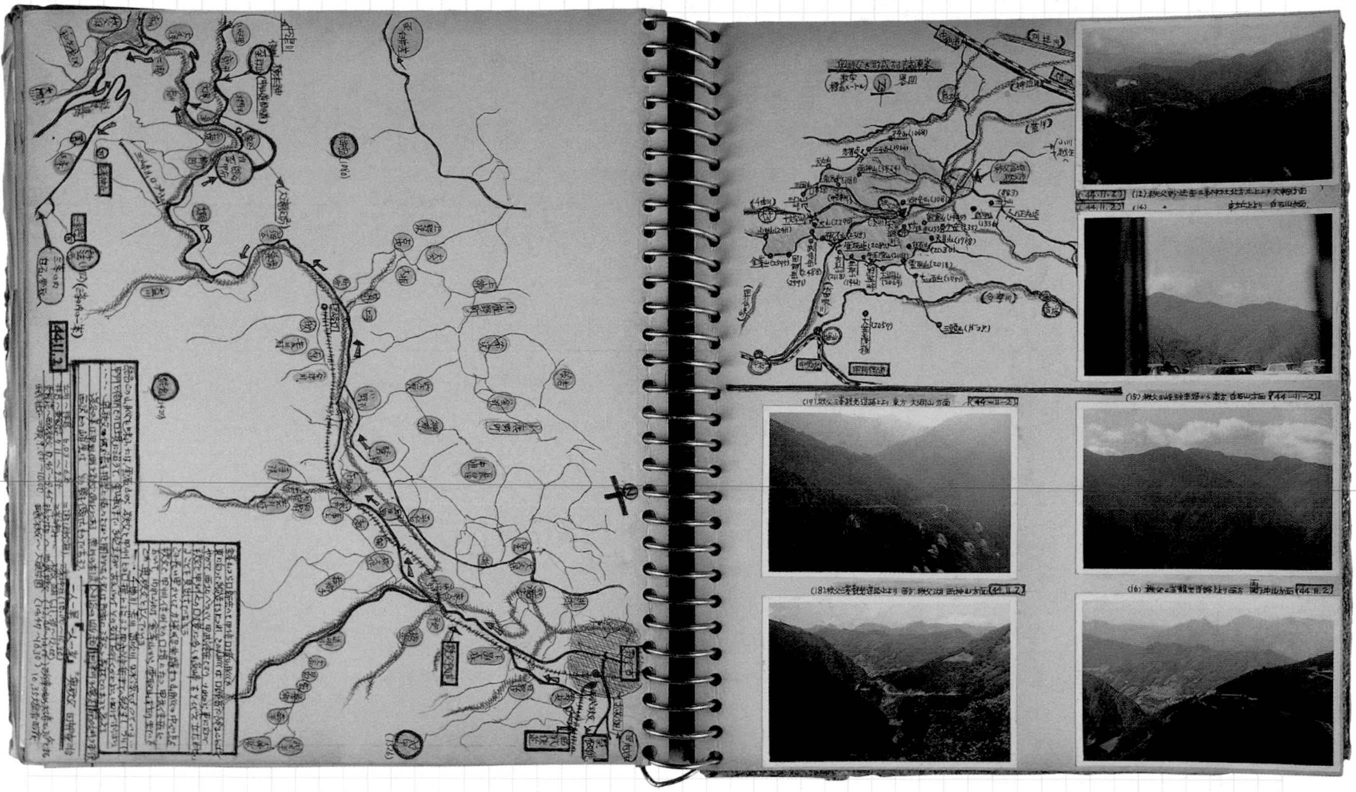

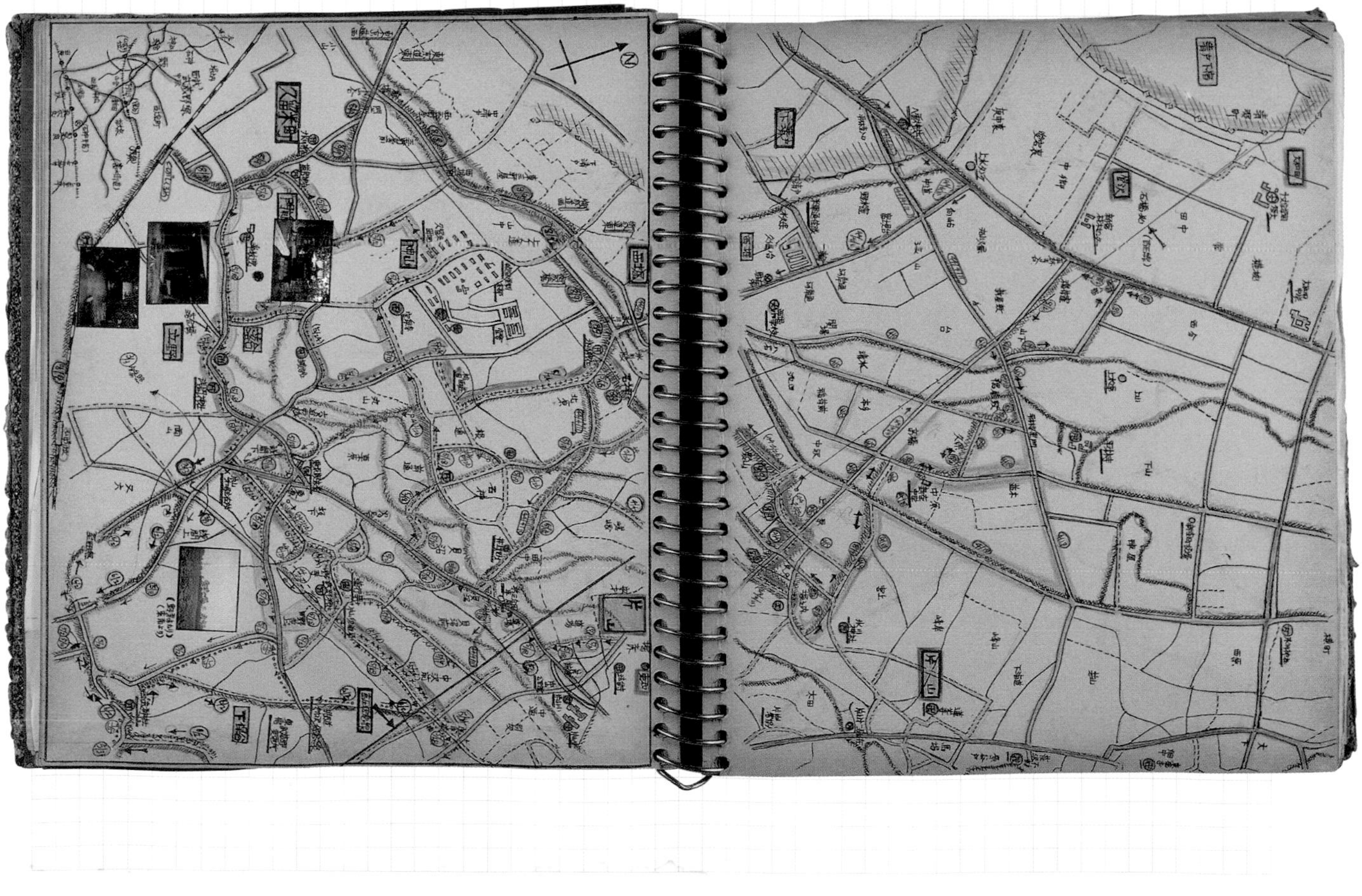

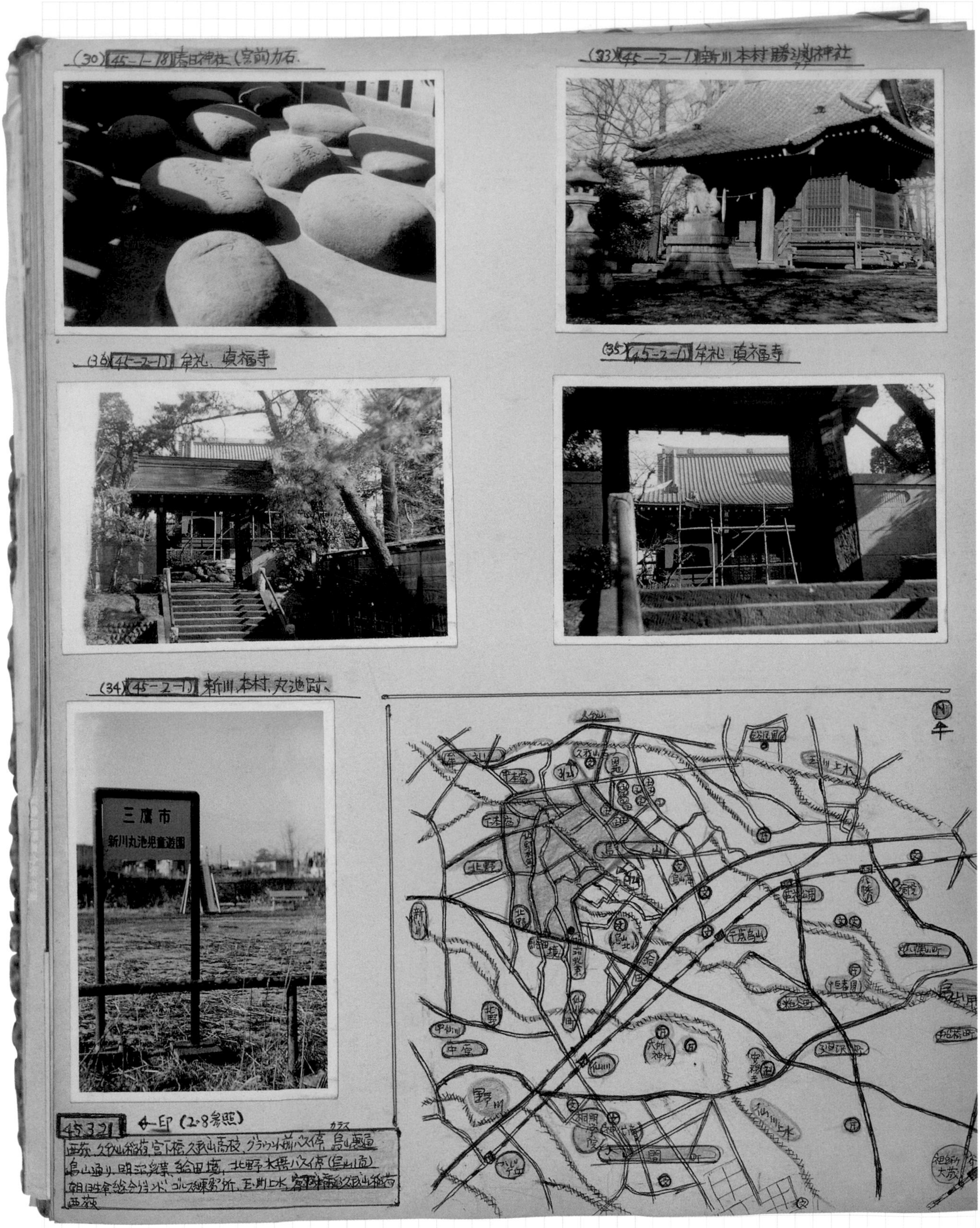
(30) 45-1-18 春日神社(宮前)力石、
(33) 45-2-1 新川本村 勝淵神社
(36) 45-2-1 牟礼、真福寺
(35) 45-2-1 牟礼 真福寺
(34) 45-2-1 新川、本村、丸池跡、
三鷹市
新川丸池児童遊園
45.3.21

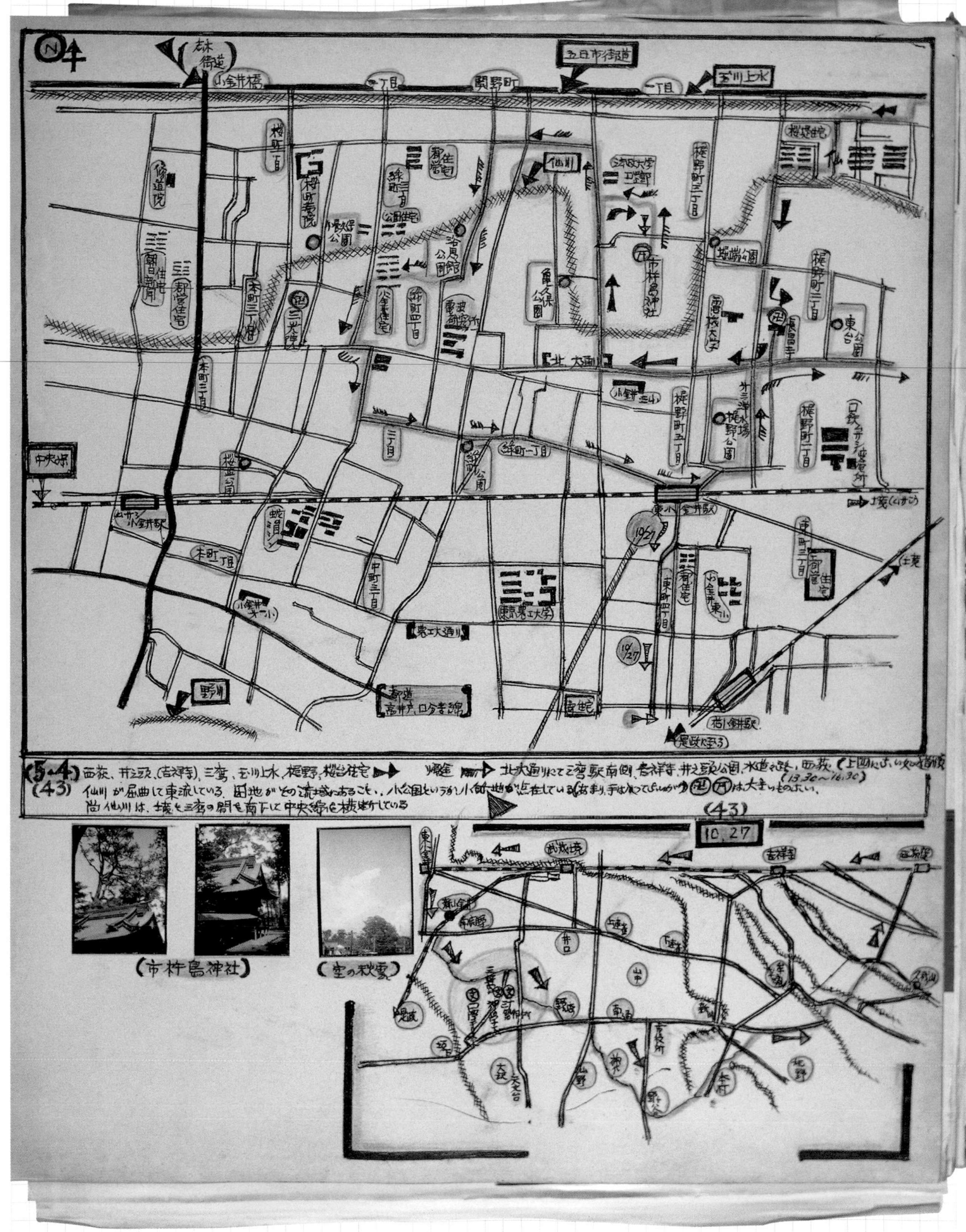
玉川上水
関野町
五日市街道
小金井橋
桜町一丁目
市杵島神社
北大通り
東小金井駅
東京農工大学
中央線
梶野町五丁目
10.27
(43)
(市杵島神社)
(空の秋雲)
吉祥寺
武蔵境

02 / REFLECTION

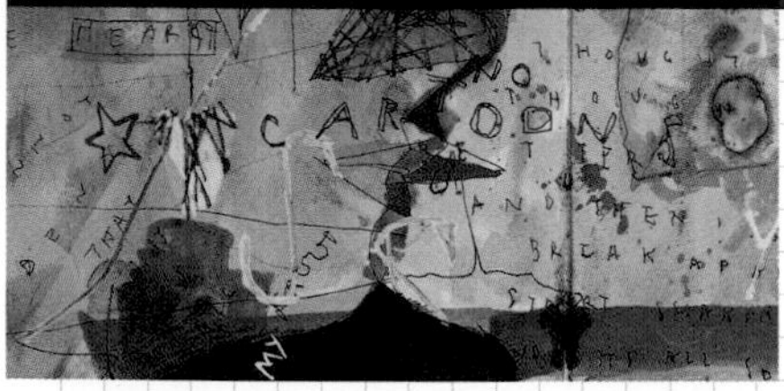

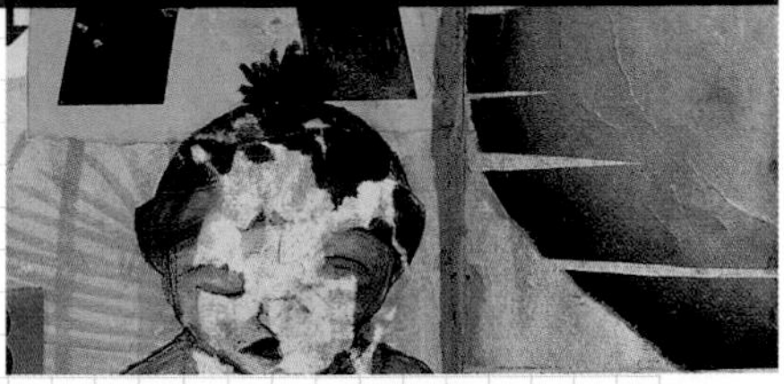

/ REFLECTION

In her book *Peripheral Visions*, anthropologist Mary Catherine Bateson writes of attending daily mass in Manila. For months, the old priests mumbled the same Latin mass until a younger priest took over the services, enlivening them with guitars, English, and other touches. One day Bateson realized with surprise that she was bored. The novelties actually highlighted the mass's repetitiveness rather than celebrating its simplicity. This phenomenon, Bateson argues, has inflicted modern culture: "Getting up in the morning, taking a shower, brushing one's teeth, eating a bowl of cereal, hundreds of such peaceful activities have been tarted up with flavorings and music and gadgetry, so that after a brief period of novelty they become not bland and comfortingly familiar but irritatingly boring."

Reflection is one antidote to the numbness caused by this cultural overload: patient, ongoing consideration of the significance of the world to oneself. Our society makes little room for reflection; we are so focused on the future that thoughtful examination of the past and present are rarely encouraged. Yet to be fruitful, reflection must be honed through practice, it must become ritualistic. As Bateson continued, "Rituals use repetition to create the experience of walking the same path again and again with the possibility of discovering new meaning that would otherwise be invisible."

Artists, of course, are steeped in ritual. Stretching a canvas, cleaning a studio, painting a watercolor at dawn—are all forms of ritual, as is the journal entry a daily practice for these visual thinkers.

It is no mistake that all of the contributors to this section are artists. In our word-laden culture, they are a rare group for whom symbols, color, and composition are a more comfortable language than that of verbs and nouns. More than one contributor commented, "I'm not much of a writer," almost embarrassed that a book so personal in nature should be largely visual rather than construed in fully formed paragraphs. But even the accomplished writers in this group know that images take them down unexpected roads, helping them to unravel different aspects of memory and experience.

Painter John Copeland's pages range from dark to joyful and frequently mull a personal event from different angles. He talks of how his daily entries reach a momentum that becomes "addicting." Tucker Shaw began his photographic project, "Everything I Ate," out of whimsy, but has discovered reverence for even the most prosaic of meals. Through her collage-style journals, art student Marcy Kentz records patterns in her world that might otherwise have been lost to her. As a more seasoned artist, Idelle Weber knows the value of daily drawing. Her monthly calendars, on which she sketches tiny portraits, ground her as solidly as any written record. Architect Anderson Kenny's journals are more provocative. In them he painstakingly questions his identity, its roots, and his individuality. Identity is at the base of all these journals. Who am I? Where am I going? Why? The questions are usually the same. The answers are always different. In responding to them repeatedly, these artists find their way.

/ JOHN COPELAND

In his journals, John Copeland broods about his paycheck-to-paycheck existence, laments about late-night indulgences, and negotiates with the creative force that seems to both buoy and tear at him. Though you would not know it from the darkness of these pages, Copeland is quite successful for his age. He has been a regular contributor of editorial illustrations to such publications as *The New York Times* and *The Nation* since the age of twenty, and now also teaches part-time at Pratt Institute. He's quick to dismiss the illustrations, however, ("It pays the bills"), and makes clear that painting and drawing are his real loves, both of which derive from the journals.

Thick with gesso, ink, watercolor, glue—you name it, he's used it—the smallish books are a sort of diary-cum-laboratory. Although one senses the tenacity with which Copeland attacks their pages, the same energy that he takes out on the Everlast punching bag appearing throughout his journals, there is also a distinct discipline to them. He carefully starts with a neat, white, narrow border, a safety zone between mayhem and the centuries-old practice that is the artist's sketchbook. The pages are numbered in pencil and usually titled.

Copeland started keeping the books as a student at the California College of the Arts in the mid-1990s. Though their ostensible purpose is to explore mediums and styles, they've also become a therapeutic outlet, a quality Copeland readily acknowledges. He sometimes looks through old books and thinks, "Jesus, what the hell was wrong with me?" Coding, layering, and omitting names all make the images more ambiguous than they initially seem, allowing him to feel comfortable sharing them with anyone interested, including would-be clients. "People respond to their honesty," he observes. "I've gotten more jobs through them than via my regular portfolio; people sense commitment and vigor in the journals."

Copeland has learned discipline from the books and works in them every day. "They are somewhere I can concentrate my efforts and see things evolve and develop," he says of their effect on the rest of his art. "They build a very palpable momentum. When you get a series going well it encourages keeping each page up to a certain level and can become addicting."

13 → NOPE
IF FOUND PLEASE RETURN TO:
JOHN COPELAND
369 JOHNSON AVE. 3RD FL.
BROOKLYN, N.Y. 11206
718-418-7904
"CHARLIE, THIS IS WHAT I THINK:
LOVE, THE DIFFICULTIES OF REAL COMMUNICA-
TION, THE REASON FOR WANTING TO
HAVE A REASON FOR STAYING
ALIVE, THESE HAVE CON-
CERNED ME TOO EVER
SINCE
I
CAN
REMEMBER." – NAT
FROM LETTER TO
CHARLES MINGUS
CANCELLED

tending wounds
up Knots
BACK TO THE SEA : BYE BYE

ARMAGEDDON
IN THE HOUSE OF CARDS.

impatient
ALWAYS ON MY SLEEVES
MAY27

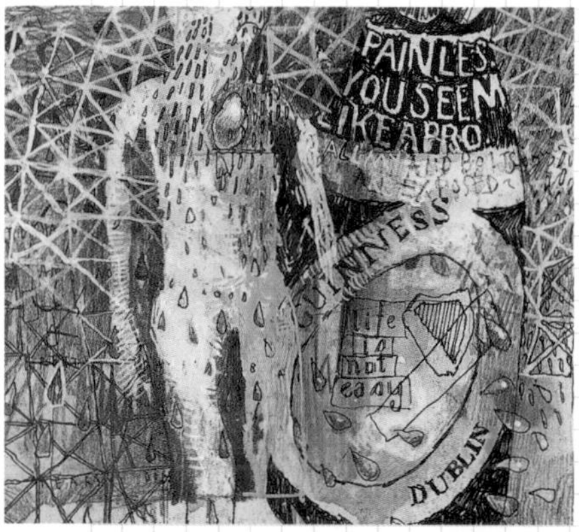
PAINLESS YOU SEEM LIKE A PRO
DUBLIN

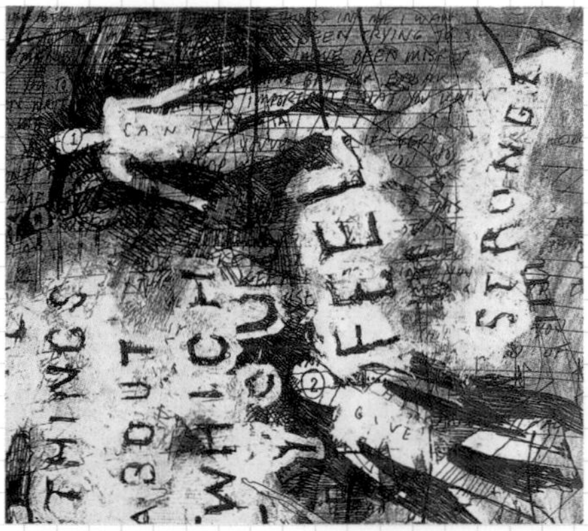
STRONG

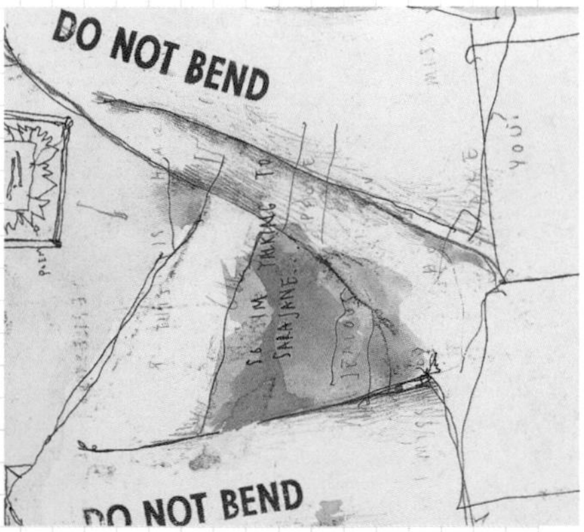
DO NOT BEND
DO NOT BEND

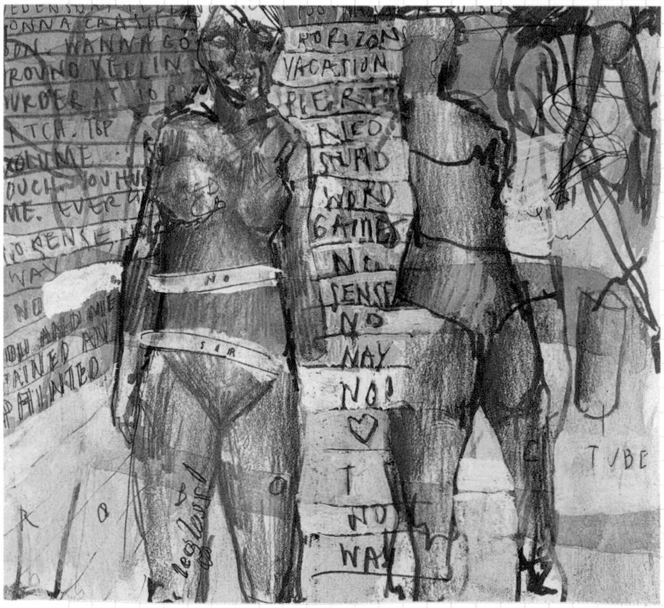
TUBE

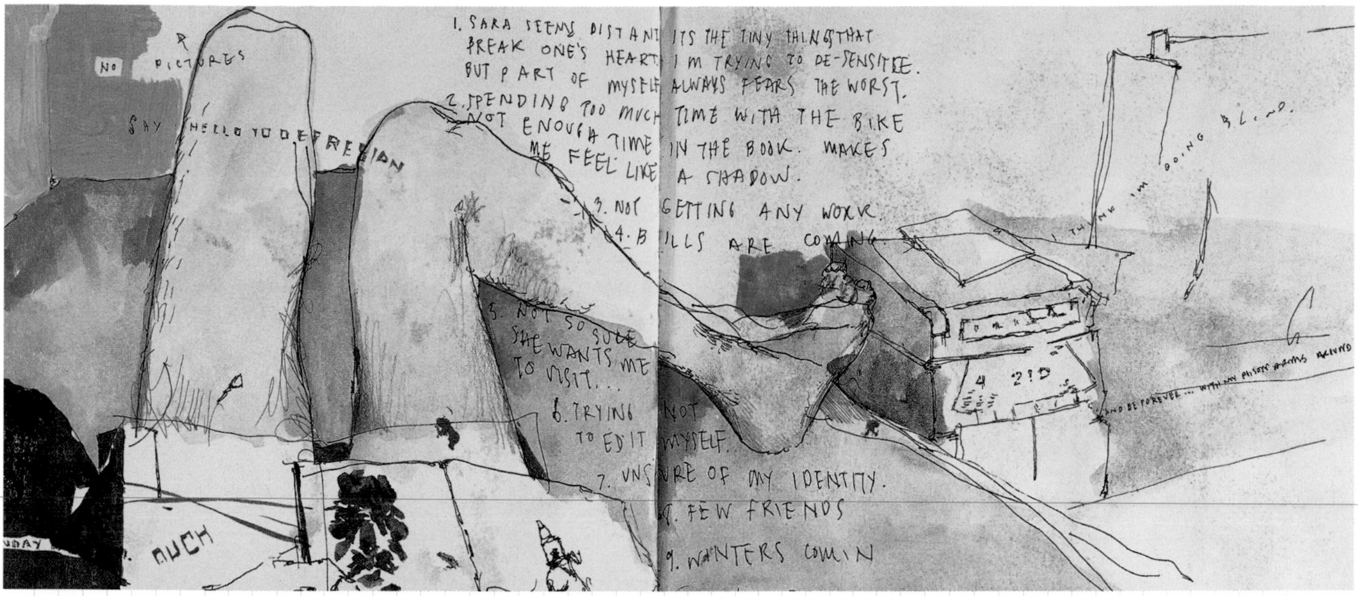
NO PICTURES
SAY HELLO TO DEPRESSION
1. SARA SEEMS DISTANT ITS THE TINY THINGS THAT BREAK ONE'S HEART. I'M TRYING TO DE-SENSITIZE. BUT PART OF MYSELF ALWAYS FEARS THE WORST.
2. SPENDING TOO MUCH TIME WITH THE BIKE NOT ENOUGH TIME IN THE BOOK. MAKES ME FEEL LIKE A SHADOW.
3. NOT GETTING ANY WORK
4. BILLS ARE COMING
5. NOT SO SURE SHE WANTS ME TO VISIT...
6. TRYING NOT TO EDIT MYSELF.
7. UNSURE OF MY IDENTITY.
8. FEW FRIENDS
9. WINTERS COMIN
I THINK I'M GOING BLIND.
MUCH

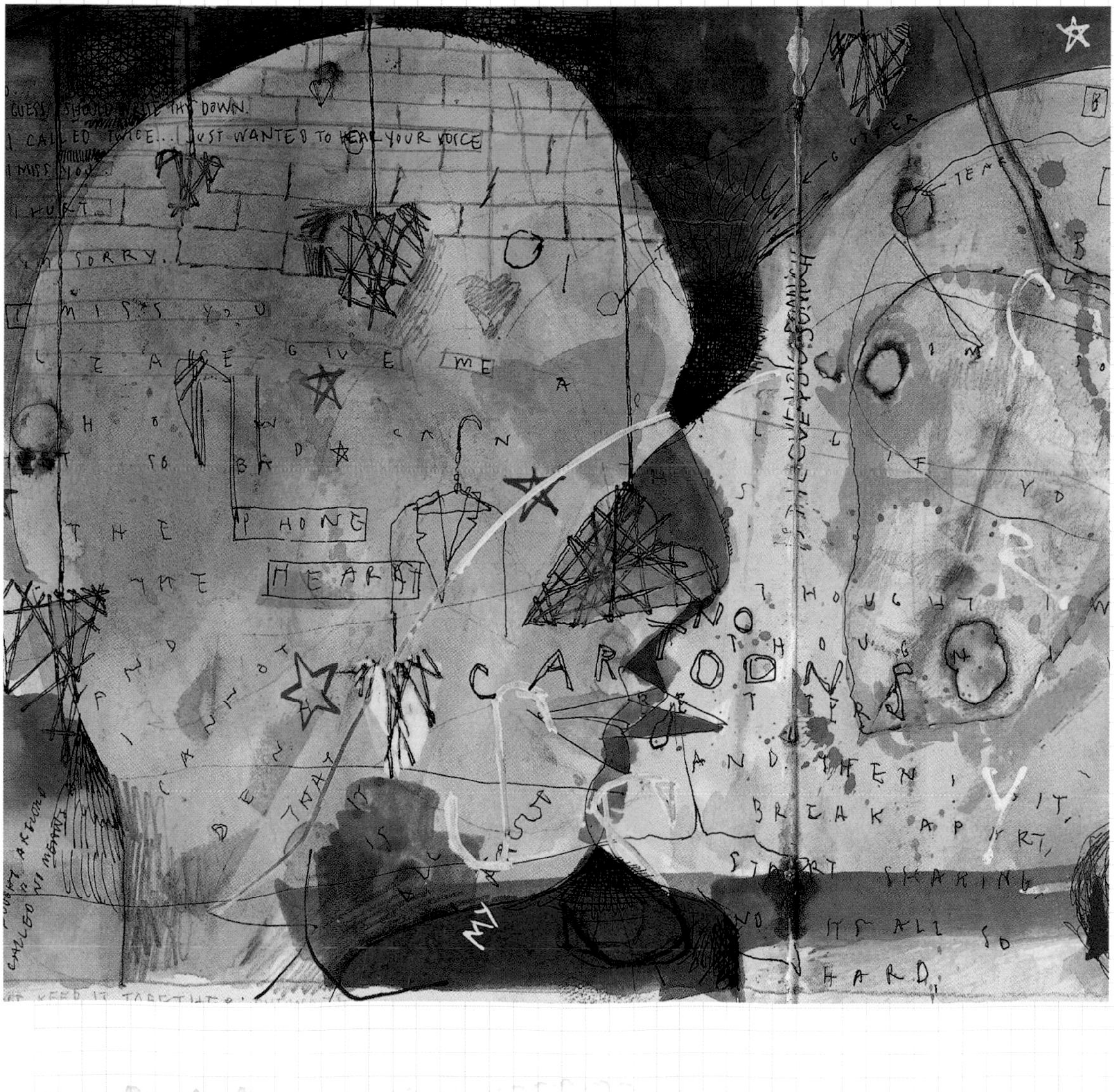
GUESS I SHOULD WRITE THIS DOWN.
I CALLED TWICE... JUST WANTED TO HEAR YOUR VOICE
I MISS YOU
I HURT
I'M SORRY.
I MISS YOU
PHONE
HEART
CARTOONS
AND THEN I
BREAK APART
START SHARING
NO ITS ALL SO HARD.

/ TUCKER SHAW

More than midway through a project to photograph everything he eats for a year, Tucker Shaw says he can now "see a story in a bagel." What began as pure documentation has taken on a deeper meaning for Shaw, who carries a digital camera with him at all times so he can snap a snack or a four-course meal before indulging.

"The process has become more important than the product," he says of the photographs he began taking in January 2004. "I never expected to find so much to consider in my food, such as the meaning of the same bowl of oatmeal every morning."

Though he had never kept any sort of journal, Shaw was drawn to the project because of his love for food. "A good eater," he says he loves everything about food—cooking, shopping, restaurants—and all variety of fare from haute cuisine to junk food. Shaw noticed that when he went on vacation he often photographed things he ate and those images turned out to be his favorites. "They were the most evocative," he notes. "A picture of a meal helped me to remember who I was with, where I was, and what sort of mood I was in."

Although Shaw believes part of the beauty of his project is that food is universal—"Everybody eats"—and thus crosses cultural lines. His food diary is no doubt affected by the fact that he is single and living in New York, providing him with a greater selection of food than he could have almost anywhere in the world and no personal strings attached to meal time or menu.

The project has heightened his awareness of what and when he eats. Awake in the middle of the night, he'll sometimes pause before photographing a bowl of cereal (the most frequently occurring item); "Do I want people to know that I'm eating *now?*" he'll wonder. Besides this self-consciousness, he's also become more curious about food, never turning down the opportunity to eat at someone's house or try a new dish. On a recent trip to Montana, he became bent on catching a fish so he could photograph it before preparing and cooking it.

Friends with whom he regularly eats have become accustomed to Shaw's ritual. When the food arrives at a restaurant and they want to dig in, he makes them wait while he moves glasses out of the way and adjusts a shot. The pause, he believes, forces them to think about the food in a way most of us rarely do these days. "I feel like my grandmother making people say grace," Shaw half laughs. "It's as though I'm saying there's something here. Let's all just notice it for a moment."

The New York Times
States' End Run Dilutes Burden For Special Ed
Her Home Silent, Nancy Reagan Fou
THE 40TH PRESIDENT

12 BROWN EGGS

/ MARCY KENTZ

Marcy Kentz says her sophomore and junior years of high school were rocky. She got kicked out of school and ended up in an alternative program. Realizing that her education had come to a halt, she managed to re-enter the first school, despite her discomfort there. Through it all, she retreated to her journal: "I drew and wrote horrible things, like a broken open skull with the words, 'I have planted a karmic virus in my soul and it's destined to go off.'" Now attending an art college in California, she laughs at her theatricality. "My journal was a complete savior for me, because otherwise I'd have been breaking down and crying. But instead, I just opened it up."

The daughter of two artists, Kentz has kept journals since she was eleven, first traditional diaries and then sketchbooks. An art teacher's collage-style journals gave her "permission" to marry the two forms. "The new style has made my journals more personal," she observes. "Now, everything means something to me." Combining collage with her meditative writing and personal musing has also turned her into a hoarder, storing bus tickets, movie stubs, snapshots of friends, and receipts in the back pocket of her Moleskin journal. She works the detritus into pages during marathon journal sessions that sometimes do not end until twilight.

Themes reappear in Kentz's work—the compulsions of a young woman trying to make sense of her world. She collects images of clocks and any kind of paper with a digital read-out on it as a way to account for her life. "All of it is evidence of what I've done that day," she comments, echoing the sensibility of Martin Wilner's *Journal of Evidence Weekly*. Numbers in general attract Kentz because "they are so odd. We made them up and yet we've given them all this meaning." She also uses a lot of arrows, because her life feels directionless right now.

Kentz loves the way the journals clearly delineate moments in her life, and she takes almost as much pleasure in reviewing the finished pages as she does in making new ones. Omnipresent now, she says of them: "They live life with me."

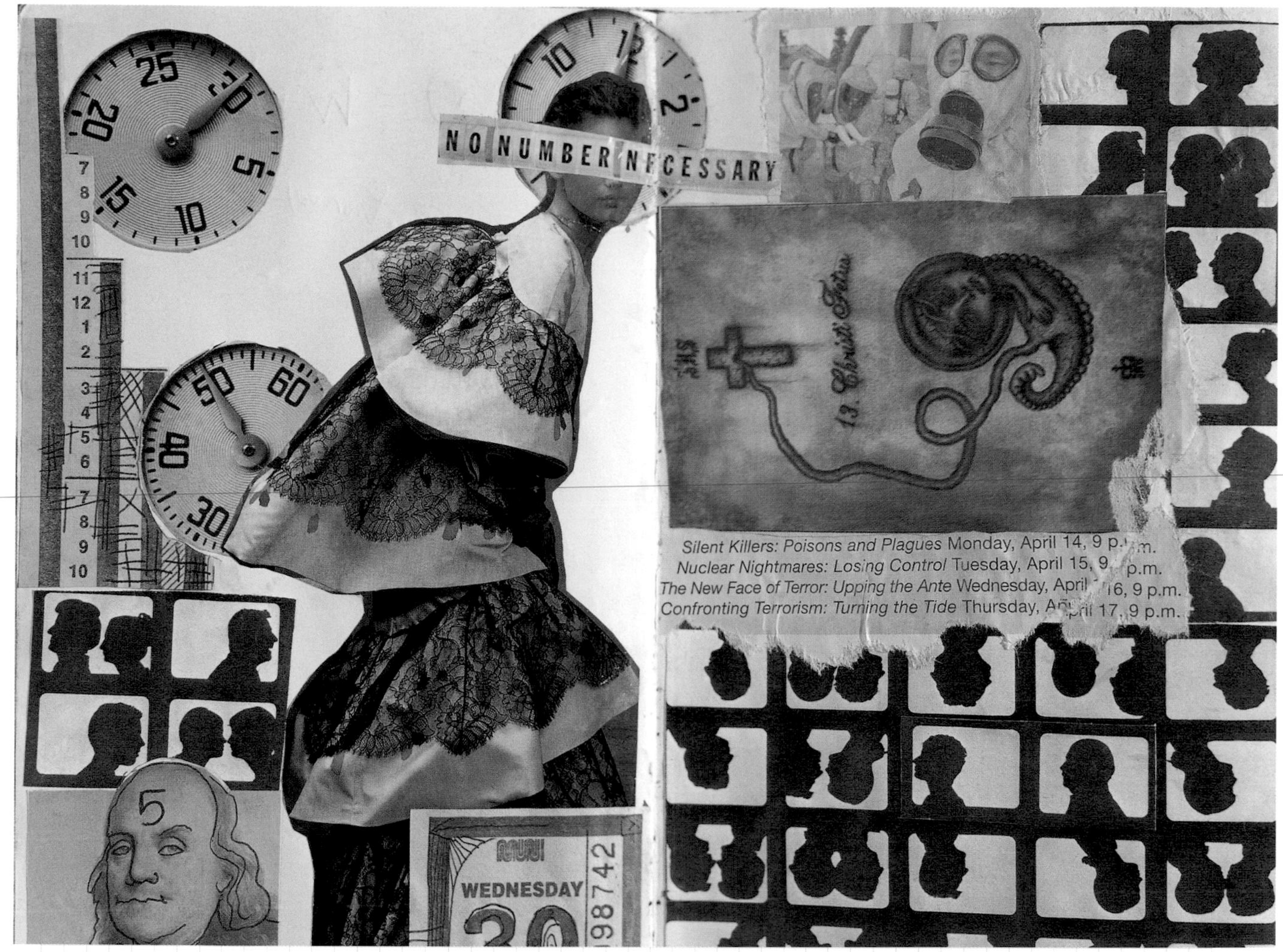
NO NUMBER NECESSARY
Silent Killers: Poisons and Plagues Monday, April 14, 9 p.m.
Nuclear Nightmares: Losing Control Tuesday, April 15, 9 p.m.
The New Face of Terror: Upping the Ante Wednesday, April 16, 9 p.m.
Confronting Terrorism: Turning the Tide Thursday, April 17, 9 p.m.
WEDNESDAY
98742

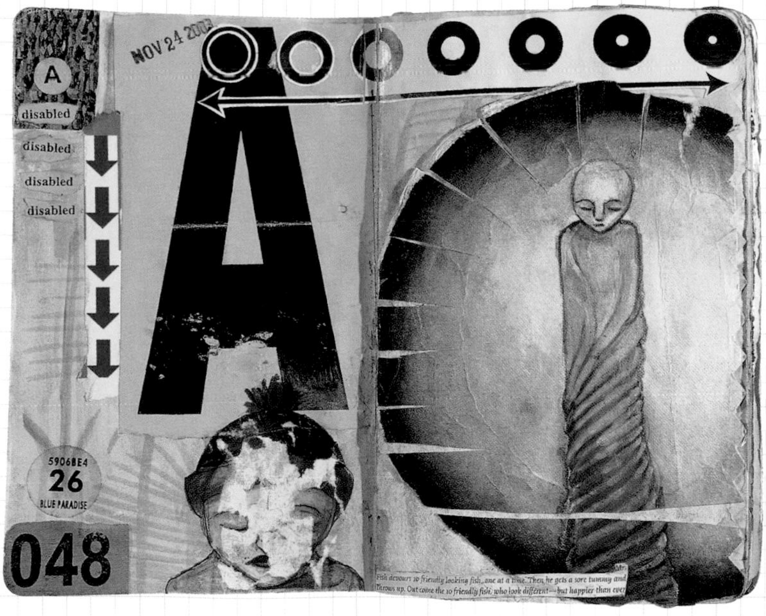
NOV 24 2003
A
disabled
disabled
disabled
disabled
A
26
BLUE PARADISE
048
Fish devours so friendly looking fish, one at a time. Then he gets a sore tummy and throws up. Out come the so friendly fish, who look different—but happier than ever.

CAMEL
M
ONLY
Summer
2003
LiveWire
89¢
+tax
+CRV
X INDICATES P

12
3
6
2 06/11 12:39P P
3 06/12 08:30P O
4 06/12 09:05P O
5 06/12 09:23P O
51 06/14 09:34P
58 06/14 10:25P
76 06/27 01:33P
77 06/27 01:56P
78 06/27 03:12P
79 06/27 04:08P
81 06/27 04:16P
82 06/27 05:08P
83 06/27 06:32P
84 06/27 08:03P
92 06/29 12:56P
93 06/29 12:58P
94 06/29 01:00P
97 06/29 01:39P
104 06/29
105 06/29
127 07/01
128 07/01
129 07/01
130 07/01
131 07/01
132 07/01
133 07/01
134 07/01
135 07/01
136 07/01
137 07/01
138 07/01 06:00
139 07/01 07:32
140 07/01 07:34
156 07/04
157 07/04 06:35P
158 07/04 06:36P
159 07/04 06:44P
160 07/04 09:05P
161 07/05 11:25A
162 07/06 12:22A
163 07/06 12:38P
164 07/06 03:28P
165 07/06 04:07P
166 07/06 06:00P

27 06/22 09:21P
28 06/22 09:37P
181 07/07 07:27P
182 07/07 07:28P
183 07/07 07:28P
184 07/07 07:32P
185 07/07 07:39P
100 06/17
North Holl
34 06/23 03:00P
35 06/23 04:57P
107 06/18 12:35P
108 06/18 03:15P
109 06/18 03:16P
36 06/23 08:38P
37 06/23 08:39P
38 06/23 09:23P
39 06/23 10:58P
40 06/23 10:59P
San Franci
Corte Made
Sonoma
Glen Ellen
193
194
195
196
197
198
199
200
Sherman Oa
Valley Vil
48 06/24 12:49
49 06/24 04:48P
50 06/24 04:56P
51 06/24 05:04P
52 06/24 05:09P
53 06/24 05:13P
54 06/24 05:38P
55 06/24 06:11P
West Holly
56 06/24 06:12P
57 06/24 06:14P
58 06/24 06:16P
59 06/24 06:19P
60 06/24 06:20P
208 07/09 01:25P
209 07/09 01:28P
210 07/09 02:00P
211 07/09 02:38P
212 07/09 02:45P
213 07/10 12:07A
214 07/10 08:24A
215 07/10 01:37P
216 07/10 01:37P
217 07/10 02:21P
218 07/10 02:48P
219 07/10 02:49P
Redwood Ci
Berkeley
Los Angele
Burbank
61 06/25 01:10P
62 06/25 06:36P
63 06/25 06:37P
64 06/25 09:13P
65 06/25 09:14P
66 06/25 09:16P
06/26 10:03A

/ IDELLE WEBER

"My belief is that it's better to work than not work," Idelle Weber said while standing in her studio, a large, modern box of a room that resembles a museum gallery. Pinned to the walls behind her were hundreds of drawings of human heads. There was a woman in sunglasses on a pink postage stamp-size Post-It note; two young men stuck their tongues out toward each other on the back of an envelope; a pastel toddler, Weber's grandchild, slept on a piece of Kraft paper. All of them were the work she'd done when it was best to keep working, when it might have been easier not to.

She's hardly been idle. Weber's career spans a half-century and includes an impressive array of styles and professional successes. But every creative career has periods when the work does not flow or other obligations take precedence, and this is when the heads have helped. Once she got sick from printmaking solvents and remembers drawing on "a lot of envelopes" during her recovery. When her children were young there were many times when she could not paint as much as she wanted. And most recently she has spent hours in the hospital while her husband was recovering from an illness. Always, she's continued to do whatever work she could, using any scrap of paper available.

In the past five years, Weber has come to rely on Post-It notes for her incessant drawing. "It started when I got a PalmPilot," she recalls. "I needed to see the whole picture, so I'd print out the monthly calendar and carry it with me." She covered the eight-and-a-half-by-eleven-inch sheets with drawings and notes to the point that she sometimes needed to print out another copy of the month before it ended. She began using the Post-Its, drawing on them and sticking favorites onto the page, because they were a way to sketch while still being able to look at the writing underneath.

She usually uses the same color sticky note and the same medium (e.g., charcoal, ballpoint) throughout a page. Throwing the small pads into her purse before she goes out, she sometimes draws people from life, like when she rides the subway. More often, she works from memory or imagination. Despite their diminutive size and prosaic subject matter, she carefully thinks through each one.

Visual by nature, the calendars feel like journals to her, serving a similar purpose to that of a written account. "Whether it's a release or a feeling of days passing or whatever I did in that period of time," she notes, trying to pinpoint their function. "I can look back at them and remember what I'm doing."

September
2001
Wednesday
CHANGE AT THE CENTER
workout
John Lavelle
picks up cabinet
9/11

July
August
2003
ALTACE 2.5 mg
Lipitor
20 mg
MRI MRA
East Side
Imaging
Tuesday 4 Wednesda
Jan 6

/ ANDERSON KENNY

"I can often be seen lurking about the house in week-old pj's, drinking juice, and using Rachael's good white napkins to clean my hands and brushes. There is no ritual. There is no special place. I do not have to be facing east. I do not have to be kneeling beside my bed. When I open those books, the margins of my world and the cone of my vision is limited to the edge of the page no matter where my body may be."

Anderson Kenny's description of his journal practice was surprising because his journals suggest a very tidy author. With their clearly defined borders and small, tight drawings, they do not have the same frenetic energy as some journals, nor a sense of spontaneity. In fact, when Kenny and I began our correspondence and I indicated that I was looking for the raw messiness of working books, he immediately defended his pristine volumes as hard-working, well-traveled, and very much the stuff of creative processing.

Kenny turned to a career in architecture after having trained both in art and science. Some of his entries belie his professional interests, including a droll rendering of a "Dog Haus" on stilts with a Gehry-esque sloped roofline, and another of a lodge imagined as a place where his brother's passion for hunting and Kenny's love of design might peacefully coexist. More important, as this last entry suggests, the journals are a therapeutic reckoning of his privileged upbringing in Southern society.

Describing his sheltered childhood, Kenny is unflinching: "I was an adult before I discovered some basic things, like how flawed it is to reduce a whole group of people into one stereotype. Not everyone viewed the rebel battle flag as a symbol of heritage. Not everyone had a 'nigra' named Sam who mowed the grass or a 'colored lady' named Lilian who cleaned the house." Kenny has an ear for Southern speech and sprinkles it freely and impishly in conversation, with more than a hint of self-deprecation.

In his twenties, Kenny woke up to his family's homogeneity, and the journals were his private place to channel his rebellious energy: "I was free between the pages." He believes they've helped him to grow more in ten years than in the previous twenty.

A painter who regularly shows his work, Kenny uses a variety of materials in the journals, including overlays with tissue, gesso, and pencil sketches. The results are coded images whose meaning is not apparent to anyone but their author. He works on journal pages over long periods of time, giving them a date and time when they finally feel completed. The extended process is part of the journals' curative nature and probably also accounts for their orderliness. "I'm not big enough or smart enough to understand all that I 'see' when I start a page. I have to work it out over time," he says.

Describing an entry about Sam, the ancient man with skin so black it was almost blue who mowed his family's lawn, Kenny writes, "It is indicative of how I feel about Sam, or at least my confusion about Sam. On the one hand, I was curious about him. Why he was so dark. Why he only ate in the kitchen. Why he spoke to my grandmother and grandfather differently than to Lilian. So what you see in the journal entry is a lot of conflicted feeling represented with faint words and shadowy marks, but there is no obvious correlation back to Sam."

Kenny recently moved to Connecticut, leaving Tennessee behind. He is busy being a voyeur in a new place and is unsure where his journals will take him now that he's not dealing so directly with childhood ghosts.

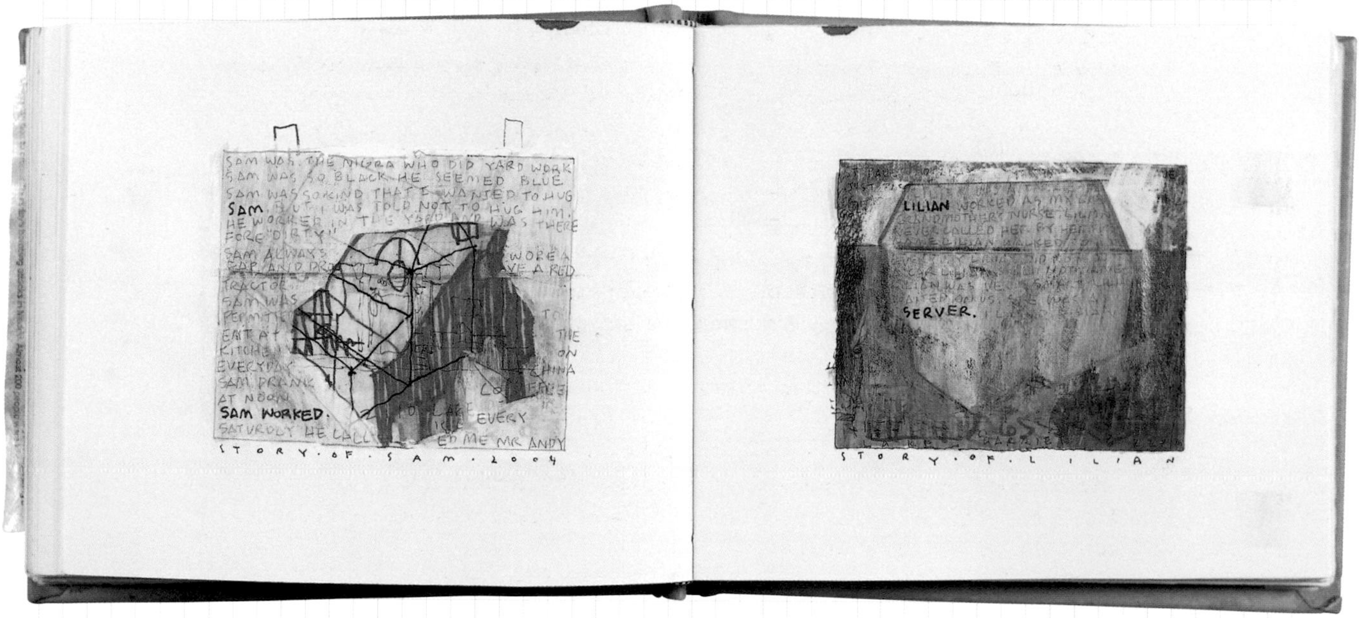

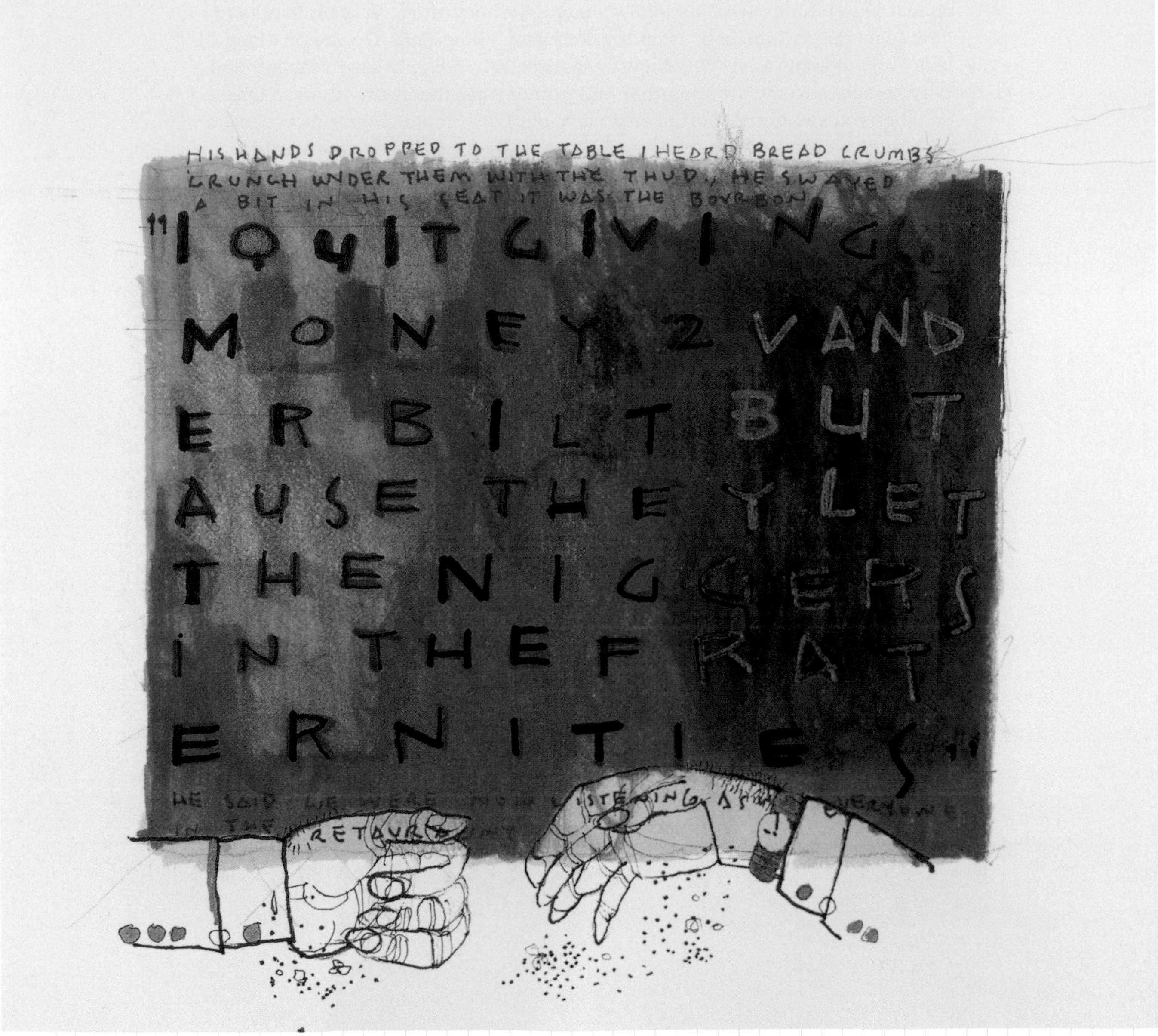
HIS HANDS DROPPED TO THE TABLE I HEARD BREAD CRUMBS
CRUNCH UNDER THEM WITH THE THUD, HE SWAYED
A BIT IN HIS SEAT IT WAS THE BOURBON
"I QUIT GIVING
MONEY 2 VAND
ERBILT BUT
AUSE THEY LET
THE NIGGERS
IN THE FRAT
ERNITIES"

A · JOURNAL · BY · ANDERSON · KENNY · JUNE · 06 · 2003
2003 MIDDLE PASSAGE

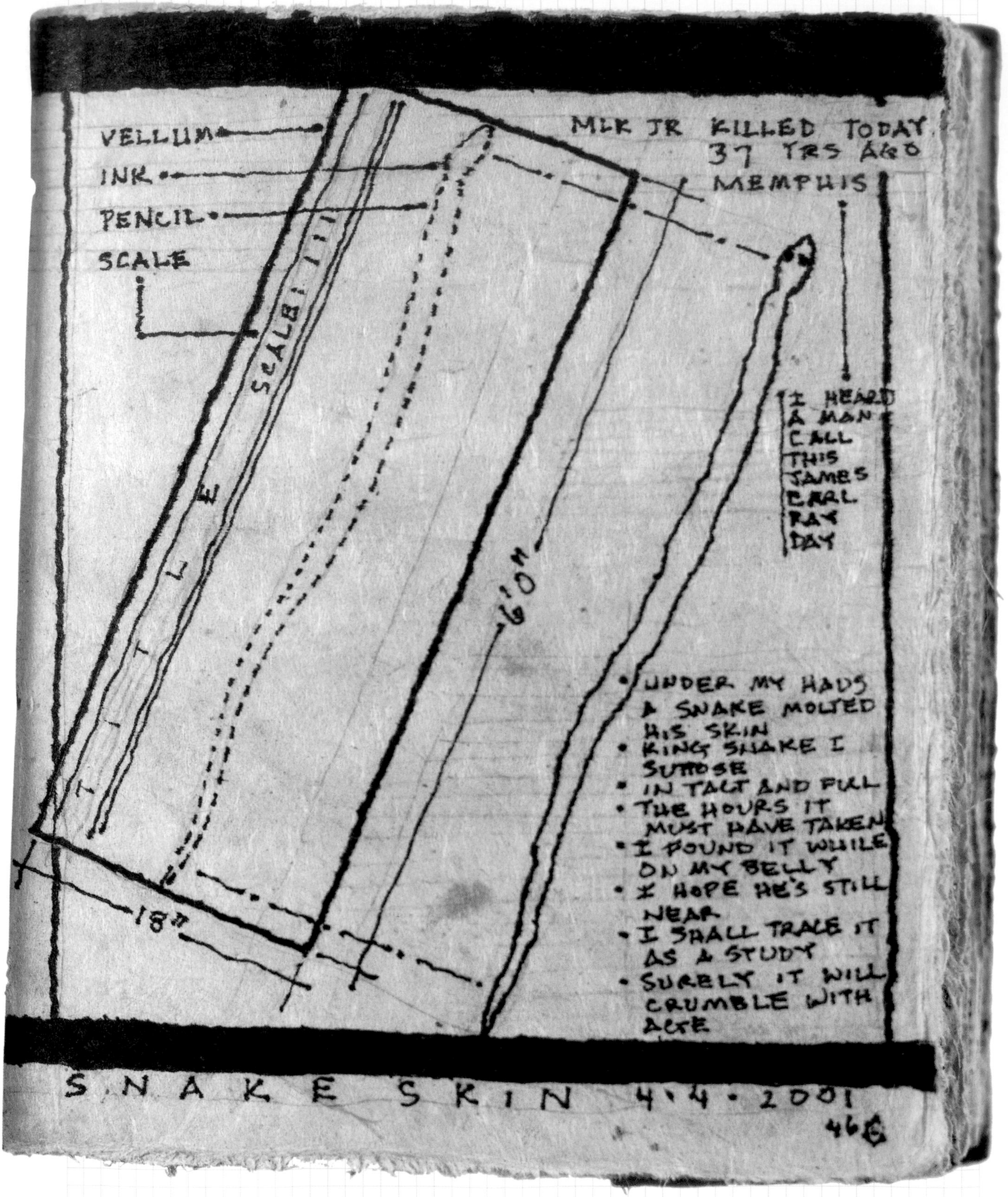
VELLUM
INK
PENCIL
SCALE
SCALE: 1:1
TITLE
MLK JR KILLED TODAY
37 YRS AGO
MEMPHIS
I HEARD A MAN CALL THIS JAMES EARL RAY DAY
6'0"
18"
• UNDER MY HAUS A SNAKE MOLTED HIS SKIN
• KING SNAKE I SUPOSE
• IN TACT AND FULL
• THE HOURS IT MUST HAVE TAKEN
• I FOUND IT WHILE ON MY BELLY
• I HOPE HE'S STILL NEAR
• I SHALL TRACE IT AS A STUDY
• SURELY IT WILL CRUMBLE WITH AGE
SNAKE SKIN 4·4·2001
46

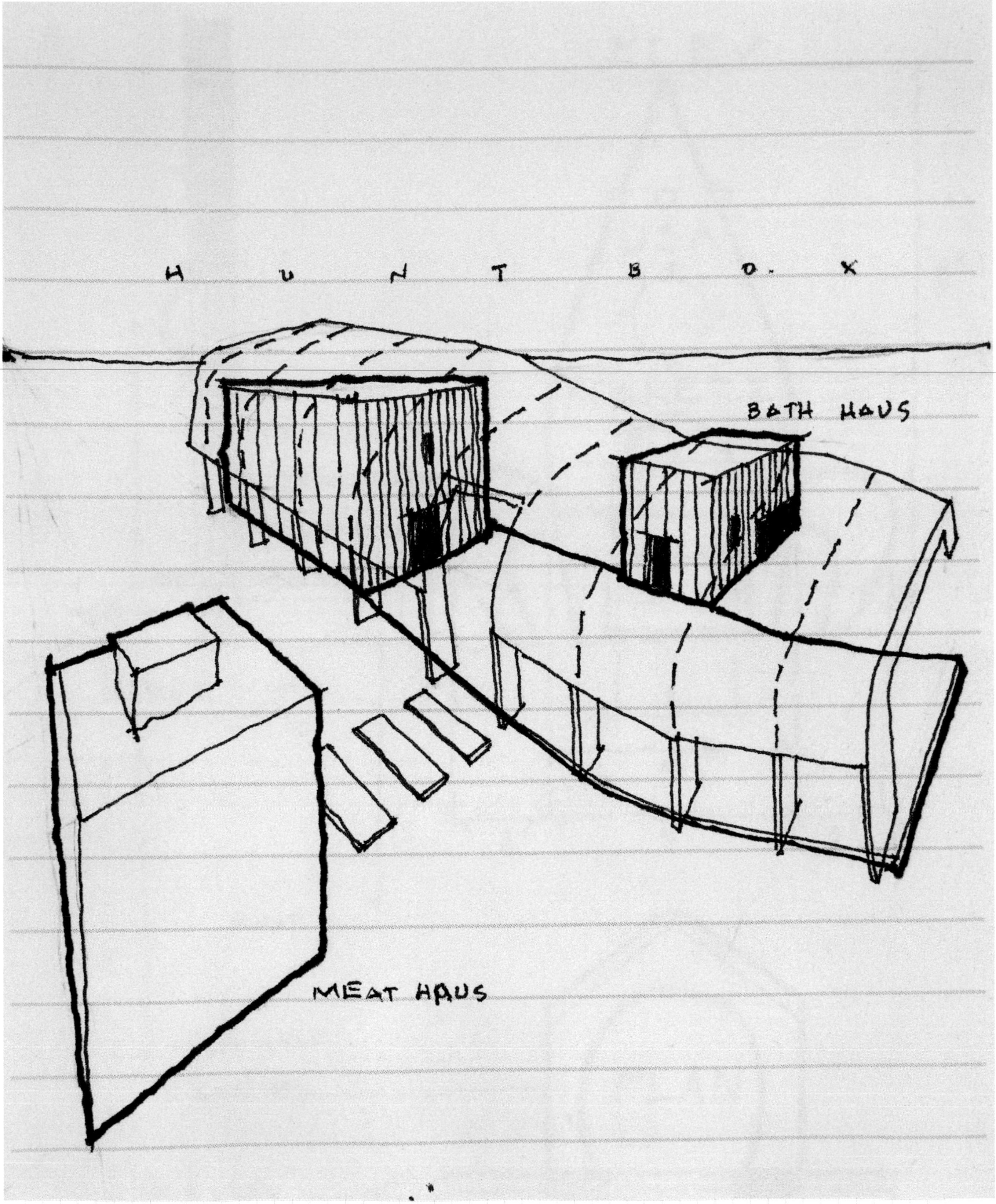
H U N T B O X
BATH HAUS
MEAT HAUS

03 / EXPLORATION

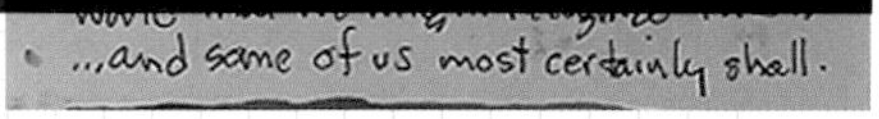

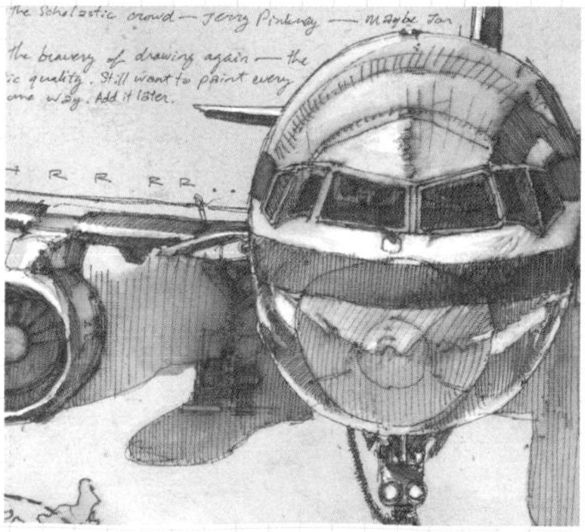

/ EXPLORATION

Travel revitalizes. Even the most conventional tourist knows this. Transported away from schedules and familiar sights, our senses are reawakened. It is easier to see when the sights are uncommon, easier to smell when the scents are unfamiliar. The trick, then, is to carry this heightened awareness with us when we return home.

To achieve this state without ever leaving home is more difficult still. It takes great discipline, resembling the Zen practice of *shoshin*, or beginner's mind, in which a childlike sense of anticipation and awe is brought to all of life's experiences. But the payoffs for artists, who barter in a sensory economy, are great. By accessing a travel-like state, an artist can capture emotions, colors, and the other raw materials that make their work ring true. As Zen master Shunryu Suzuki writes, "In the beginner's mind there are many possibilities, but in the expert's there are few."

If there are experts among travelers, Pico Iyer would qualify. An inveterate travel writer whose explorations of places as far flung as Damascus and LAX verge on sociological studies, he has said that he was initially drawn to travel as an escape from his "rectilinear" California existence. Having walked on much of the globe, what now propels his wandering is internal exploration: "The physical aspect of travel is, for me, the least interesting; what really draws me is the prospect of stepping out of the daylight of everything I know, into the shadows of what I don't know, and may never know…a trip has been really successful if I come back sounding strange even to myself; if, in some sense, I never come back at all, but remain up at night unsettled by what I've seen."

Many of the journals in this chapter recount amazing journeys, all of which have taught their authors "beginner's mind." There is Sophie Binder's year-and-a-half-long bicycle trip around the world and Carol Beckwith's intrepid explorations of Africa. Gary Brown started his journals during a trip to Italy in the early 1960s, while Lyle Owerko's journals erupted after a lengthy travel sabbatical.

The other journals here are examples of the creative mind's ability to "slip through the curtain of the ordinary," as Iyer has put it. Lynda Barry works on her pages every day, wondering where her brush will take her but always entering the flow without expectation. Erica Bohanon is equally devoted to her daily furniture sketches, finding unanticipated ideas in them that would not occur in her usual practice. Scientist Erwin Boer scrutinizes conundrums and curiosities in his notebooks, which are the place where his imagination runs wild. David Byrne's journals reflect his diverse interests and resemble a bulletin board of seemingly disconnected ideas. The 1,000 Journals Project was started to encourage nonartists to reconnect with visual play, something to which Andrew Swift and John Clapp (who are both illustrators and professors) have devoted their professional lives. Each of them uses the journal as his personal playground.

/ SOPHIE BINDER

Sophie Binder describes the combination of drawing and biking as the perfect marriage: "I'm traveling ten to twenty miles per hour and I see things that I wouldn't see in a car. I see. I stop. I draw. You don't have to find a parking spot. You just stop." The thirty-seven-year-old Frenchwoman should know. From April 2001 to June 2002 she rode her bike around the world, filling seven journals with sketches and watercolors of her solo adventure. She dubbed the trip: *The World, Two Wheels, and a Sketchbook.*

Binder says that both biking and drawing hone her skills of observation. This is true even in the most visually spare environments. "In the desert you're crossing a basin for twenty-five miles and nothing seems to change. So you start to focus your horizon on things closer to you, and suddenly there is all kinds of life along the road."

Sounding a similar chord, she describes her experience of drawing while traveling: "There's a story in every sketch I do. I remember so clearly every place where I was when I made it, unlike photography, where you snap a shot and move on. There's not one photo [from the trip] that holds the meaning of the drawings."

Binder's goal to "draw her way around the world" established her itinerary. Rather than touch quickly on tourist sites, she visited a few places for longer periods. "I was in Hanoi for eight days," she says by example, "but only visited two places. I was determined to use my time to draw." Weather conditions sometimes affected her drawing habits, as well. Too much wind or rain might mean that she'd end up drawing by memory at a guesthouse at night rather than during the day, producing more abstract images. Her style was often dictated by location. In Asia she was determined not to use black and white because the colors were so overwhelming. And in Italy, bewitched by the architecture, her drawings were more detailed and focused on buildings rather than people.

In the immense Jordanian desert of Wadi Rum, Binder was struck by the acute solitude of the place: "A towering *jebel* is providing me with much needed shade and facing me is a wall of even taller sheer vertical rock, an ever changing palette on which the sun is painting while following its path toward the west.... I am absolutely alone. I do not know where I am."

Her most memorable interactions were with children who were intrigued by the rare sight of a lone Western woman with beautiful books and art supplies. In the Syrian desert, on the border of Iraq, Binder spent September 12, 2001, painting watercolors at an ancient stone ruin. The finished images, iridescent with streaks of amber light, are reminiscent of Stonehenge. Strong gusts made the painting difficult. A boy with a stone approached her. "There. That will help," she recalls him saying, as he weighted down a page that had been blowing closed. And though she does not have a drawing of him, the boy is clearly perched there in the watercolor in her vision.

Café
Grand Bazaar
Sandal Bedesteni Sk.
8.6.01
(A carpet Seller offers me coffee).
own is earning me all kinds of propositions, honest or dishonest!
They are pretty easy to push back even if some men can be rather
pushy and obvious about what they want! I had to deal with a few
Grand Bazaar
8.6.01

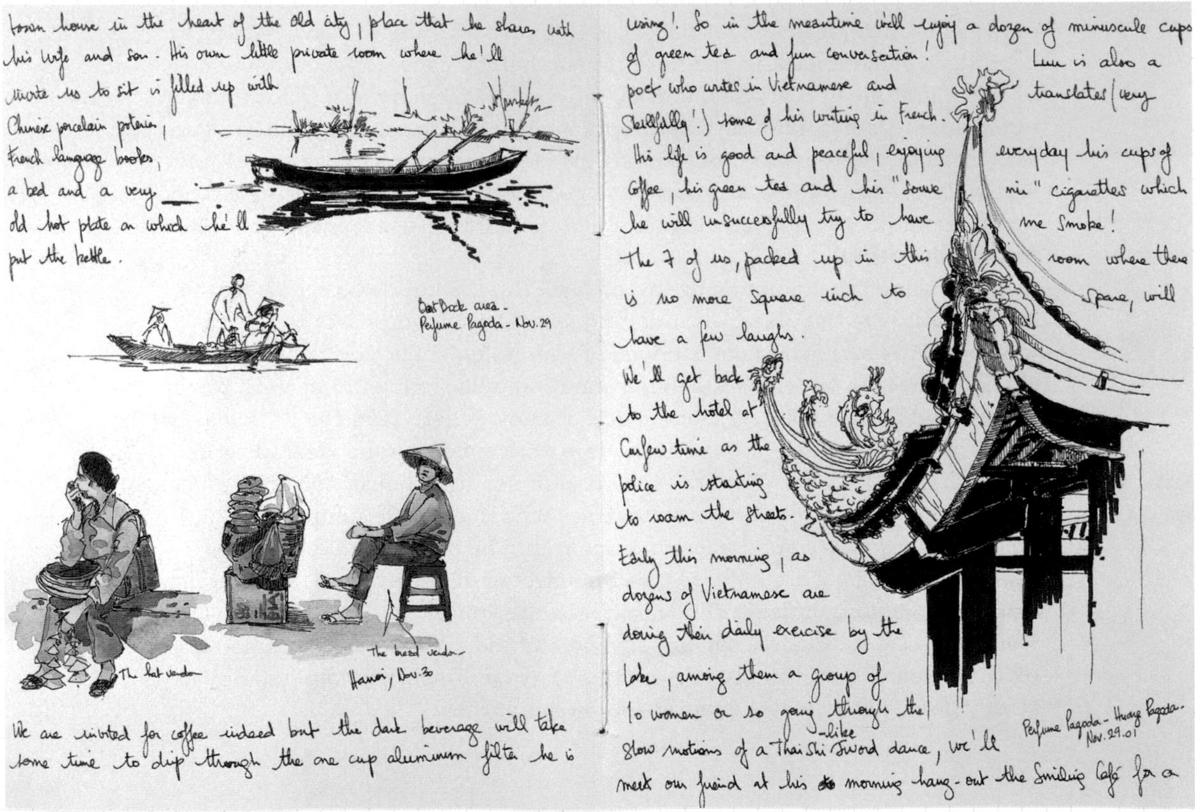
town house in the heart of the old city, place that he shares with
his wife and son. His own little private room where he'll
invite us to sit is filled up with
Chinese porcelain poteries,
French language books,
a bed and a very
old hot plate on which he'll
put the kettle.
Boat Dock area.
Perfume Pagoda - Nov. 29
The hat vendor
The bread vendor
Hanoi, Nov. 30
We are invited for coffee indeed but the dark beverage will take
some time to drip through the one cup aluminum filter he is
using! So in the meantime will enjoy a dozen of minuscule cups
of green tea and fun conversation!
Luu is also a
poet who writes in Vietnamese and
translates (very
Skillfully!) some of his writing in French.
His life is good and peaceful, enjoying
everyday his cups of
coffee, his green tea and his "Souvenir" cigarettes which
he will unsuccessfully try to have
me Smoke!
The 7 of us, packed up in this
room where there
is no more Square inch to
spare, will
have a few laughs.
We'll get back
to the hotel at
Curfew time as the
police is starting
to roam the streets.
Early this morning, as
dozens of Vietnamese are
doing their daily exercise by the
lake, among them a group of
10 women or so going through the
-like
slow motions of a Thai Shi Sword dance, we'll
meet our friend at his morning hang-out the Smiling Café for a
Perfume Pagoda - Huong Pagoda.
Nov. 29.01

where I found closed doors. It only opens at 6:00 AM!
Waiting in line I'll deal one last time with the "
do you change french coins" touts and other carta kids

The Dilwara temples stand in an enclosed compound that holds 4 of them - Each one is a masterpiece of lace work carved and sculpted out of marble - It is absolutely impossible to imagine how the sculptors achieved such work - It's intricate to the highest degree - What makes it even more stunning is the fact it is not painted, it is pure marble that let the light play with the carving surfaces - It is a totally overwhelming place & of total beauty - Elephants are marching holding each others trumps in overhead frieze crowning an alcove - Buddha-like figures dance on the columns in positions that would make me see a chiropracta in a hurry!

Dilwara temple - Accross Vimal Vasahi: House of Elephants 10.14

Arches of lacework span areas between columns which do not offer one square inche of non-Sculpted surface -

Detail Dilwara temple 10.14 Vimal Vasahi

Detail - Vimal Vasahi Temple 10.14

It is an over dose of detai that will make my pen and sketch book very bus

I'll spend 5 hours in the Dilwara temples and village -

Drawing in the temples will owe me quite a "few" visits from Indians curious to see what I am doing, knowing where I come from, my name.... At time I will be totally surrounded! People will come and seat right next to me.

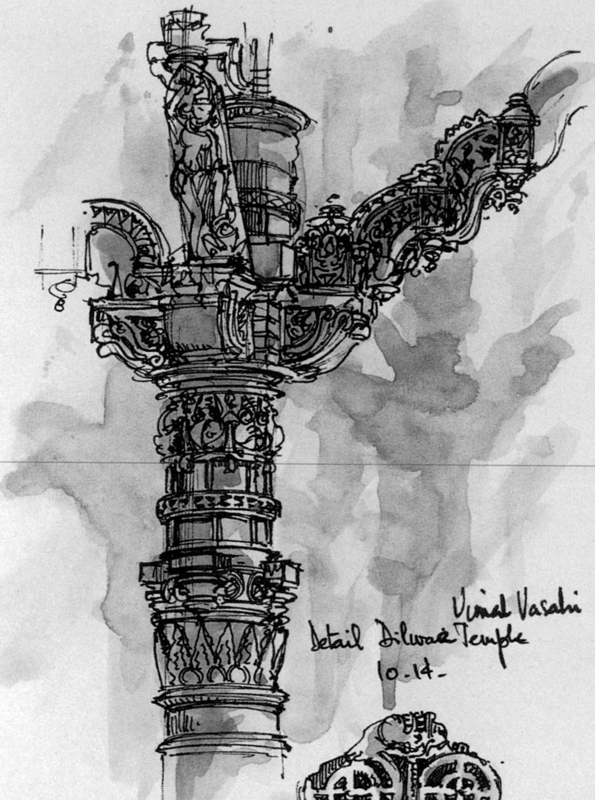

Vimal Vasahi
Detail Dilwara Temple
10.14.

Column Detail
Vimal Vasahi Temple.
10.14

Detail Tejpal Temple. 10.14

At some point, two groups will form on each side of my sightline, so nobody gets in the way of my drawing. A kid will ask me for an autograph, then another one! Many will talk to me for a while. An afternoon when my personal space will reduced to nothing but when my contact with the Indian people will be unforgettable.

mnoen Saduak
Market

/ CAROL BECKWITH

As a child in Boston, Carol Beckwith kept an intricate journal inspired by her French lessons. She made collages of an imagined life in Paris and created three-dimensional houses that opened up like a pop-up book into multiple rooms. Her adult journals are no less enchanting, though the magic springs from real adventures.

Arriving in Kenya as a twenty-three-year-old art student, Beckwith was immediately captivated. "Africa took my heart," she says simply. "It's my spirit home." In the past thirty years, she's traveled to thirty-six African countries, visiting more than 150 cultures and covering over 270,000 miles.

Art is central to her visceral connection to the continent. As a young painter, she was delighted to discover an African aesthetic tradition that focused on survival rather than gallery walls. Tools for cooking or farming were beautiful, as were masks and amulets related to fertility or weather patterns, but they all served practical, indeed vital, purposes. In order to best document such objects and to tell the stoies of the people who use and make them, Beckwith's own art became more practical; she switched from painting to photography, its linear nature better suited to narrative.

In the 1980s, Beckwith began working with Angela Fisher, an Australian with a background in sociology and jewelry making. For their unparalleled tome, *African Ceremonies*, a two-volume book spanning eight hundred pages, the two women spent ten years in the field, traveling, photographing, and earning the trust of the people they documented. Realizing how little, if any, research exists about the people and places they were photographing, they committed themselves to spending evenings during their journeys to writing down what they saw and learned during the day. Months later, when their photographs were developed in London, the journal notes helped them decipher the images. The notes were even more valuable when it came time to write, which was sometimes years after a research trip.

Describing the process of one of their trips (the pair have since written seven books together), Beckwith says they do as much preparation as possible from their base in London. "Say you're going to the mountainous southwest corner of Ethiopia near the border of Sudan," she provides as an example. "You research the area, try to get permits, arrange what you can. Then you get to Africa and organize a mule train to take you over the 10,000-foot mountains. Once you arrive, you find the village chief and begin at square one because he has no idea you've been planning to come here for months; he doesn't know who you are. So you start the process of gaining his trust, which might take days or weeks, during which time you never take out your camera."

"The journals start with the first step off the plane," she comments. "They reflect a life lived in Africa on a daily basis." Except for the to-do lists she makes in books prior to a trip, Beckwith rarely keeps a journal in London. She believes this stems from the relatively safe, predictable existence she leads in the west as opposed to Africa, where her assumptions and habits of mind are challenged daily. These journals, she says, are about "intuition, storytelling, and joy."

Although she considers the journals to be very personal—Beckwith and Fisher are the only ones allowed to dip into them—she's also aware of their role as source material. Once, she glued together a group of pages about a romance with a desert nomad chief, unsure of how she'd feel about them when it came time to use the journal to write a book. As she approaches her tenth book on Africa, Beckwith is interested in returning the journals to their painterly roots and has started taking more art materials with her on recent trips. Pondering an upcoming trip to Mozambique, she says, "They're living things, they need to grow."

Swahili hand and foot designs painted with Henna (inspired by Swabaha Athman Omar Khatib in "HENNA DRAWINGS" of LAMU)
A Swahili girl, just before marriage, undergoes a series of beauty treatments to mark her transition into womanhood.
She is isolated in her room behind a curtain for two to three days while the Henna is applied to her hands, arms and feet.
The dye is made of powdered henna, water, and the juice of unripe lemons, which darkens the color.
Five to six applications are made to ensure that the henna will not fade too soon. Each application takes two hours to dry.
The process, from be-ginning to end, may take up to twelve hours.
LAMU ISLAND, KENYA
DEC. 31, 1995.
Decorated with henna and veiled from head to toe, the bride sits on her wedding bed awaiting the first visit from her husband. He may not see her unveiled until their wedding night.
The groom enters her bedroom carrying a small necklace made of gold or coral. He lifts the curtain surrounding her bed, which is strewn with fragrant jasmin flowers, and places the necklace in the bride's hand.
A playful hand tussle then occurs, and whoever ends up holding the neck-lace is believed to have the upper hand in the marriage.
In olden days, the bride would be accomp-anied by her "Somo" who hid under her bed to assist the husband if the virgin-bride re-sisted consummating the marriage.

SURMA clay & wooden lipplates from southwest Ethiopia:

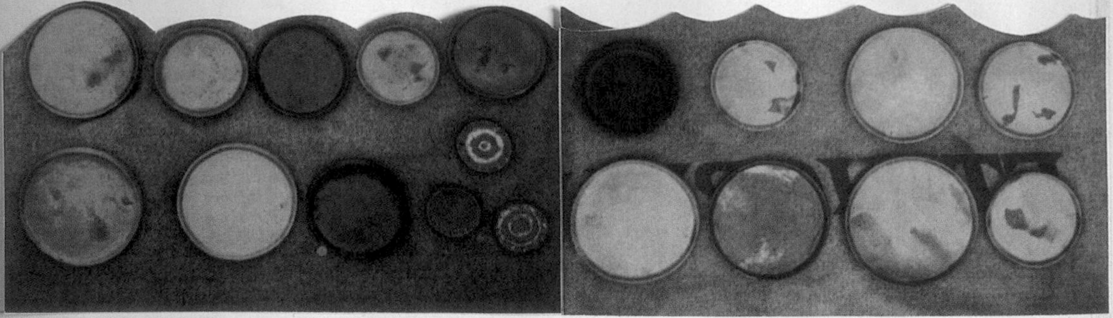

Lipplates must be worn by married women in the presence of men

The earliest lipplates were made of a light balsa wood.

Recipe for Fashioning lipplates: 1) Grind clay into powder 2) make it into a mound + pour water into center. 3) Roll in hands into a ball 4) Flatten it into a disk 5) Knead edge with fingers to form rim. 6) Crush seeds + rub powder onto rim 7) Color plate with red + black powder 8) Leave plate for 2 days to dry + harden. 8) Build fire with corncobs + grasses 9) Put plates on heated grasses 10) Bake for twenty minutes 11) Remove from fire and cool.

OUTDOORING OF SHAI DIPO GIRLS
APRIL 17. · SATURDAY
100
DIPO-YO = Dipo girl. (s)
We arrive in heavy rain and acc. to plan go to the home of GLADYS · our friend & guide & her children: Antoinette & Sackitey
Gladys makes us breakfast while we wait for the rain to stop.
OUTDOORING OF DIPO-YO APRIL 17.
DIPO-YI = plural
umbrella
mothers of DIPO GIRLS
Dipo Judges
Chief Chartey AWAH & his linguist
DIPO GIRLS
KLAMA MUSICIANS
DANCE AREA
DIPO GIRLS
MOTHERS
VILLAGE CROWD
GUESTS · INT'L WOMENS CLUB
Village
Each Dipo girls sits on a tiny stool whitened with chalk ~ There are no benches or chairs like in Somanya
Girls from 3 stages of Dipo are represented:
1) 1st STAGE: Girls wear tall straw DIPO-PE HATS. and Red-loin cloths looped over several strands of waiste beads
2) 2nd STAGE: Girls wear elaborate basket like hair/head helmuts + pounds of beads around hips & neck with colourful loin cloths draped through beads - plus armlets, kneelets, anklets etc.
3) 3rd stage: Girls wear head scarves over shaved heads, elaborately patterned & colourful cloths from waiste beads & again, necklaces, anklets + armlets. Their bodies are patterned w white painted designs
· DIPO-YI ·
NARKI DEMUE BIANKI
The Int'l Womens Club have created a dipo dance competition amongst the various "houses" of Dipo girls with presents wrapped in silver paper w ribbons for the best dancers.
The dancing is organized beautifully & carefully. Girls with exceptional skill are given cedi-bills, tucked into their breast beads by admirers
Several little girls steal the hearts of the crowd with their stylish klama dancing.
Two dances:
1) The klama w mini foot shuffles, faces looking downwards, hands extended forward + moving from side-to-side - then turning around w back to audience - and finally full cycle back to the front.
2) Circle Dance: girls waving flywhisks run in a circle & end in an embrace with their dance neighbor.
The Shai Dipo Custom is 400yrs old
Winner MARKU "NO. 1"
AYONGO
YOMLE
LEFT TO RIGHT: NARKI, DEMUE, AYONGO

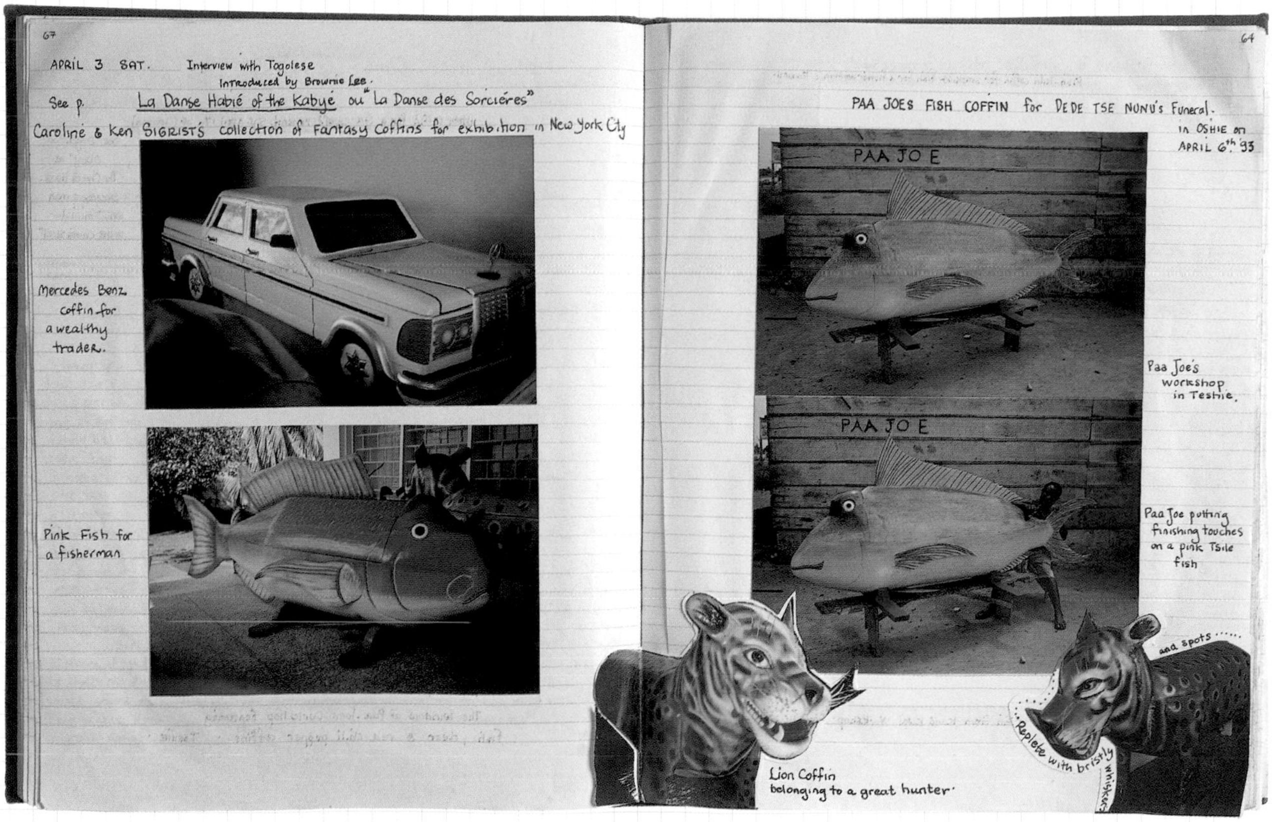

67
APRIL 3 SAT. Interview with Togolese introduced by Brownie Lee.
See p. La Danse Habié of the Kabyé ou "La Danse des Sorcières"
Caroline & Ken SIGRIST'S collection of Fantasy Coffins for exhibition in New York City
Mercedes Benz coffin for a wealthy trader.
Pink Fish for a fisherman
64
PAA JOES FISH COFFIN for DEDE TSE NUNU's Funeral.
in OSHIE on APRIL 6th 93
PAA JOE
Paa Joe's workshop in Teshie.
PAA JOE
Paa Joe putting finishing touches on a pink Tsile fish
Lion Coffin belonging to a great hunter.
Replete with bristly whiskers
and spots......

CAROL BECKWITH

(B)

JANUARY · 1990 · SURMA —

MON.	TUES.	WED.	THURS.	FRI	SAT	SUN.
1 GAM Arrive in Addis NEW YEARS DAY Dinner at WORKUS	2 official preparations w MEKURIA and SARI	3 DEP>TUM CAMP on TUM AIRSTRIP	4 TUM TO MAGI "peace w Love" HOTEL	5 MAGI TO ADICAS MALARIA PILL DAY	6 Adicas To KORMU	Genna Day 7 SURMA Wedding nr. Bikaden
8 KORMU camp site activities "dula" fight on hillside Administrator arrives.	9 #1 CATTLE CAMP (Kola + Barchini) JEWELRY Administrator's village meeting + speech Tape dance music	10 CATTLE CAMP #1 Admin. leaves Kormu	11 FULL MOON Gold panning Village visit w out cameras to meet women FULL MOON	12 Body painting Cattle Camp PM #2 NIGHT DANCING	13 Birds. "DAY OFF" Hut building in camp children's snake + frog dance	14 DONGA by Kibbish River
15 CAMP Chinoi interview Olinya Interview Children's Dance	16 AM DONGA at Goudel River scenes	17 1st RAIN Interview w Naterro Reggé Wild married womens dance	18 VISIT TO CHIEF DOLETI + INTERVIEW NADWAYBU MARLÉ INTERVIEW	19 CB MUSIC Taping Chinoi, Kolaholi & Muradit & Bikaden CLAY POT MAKING	20 FUNERAL BURIAL at ZABANYAS	21 MAKING BRE FUNERAL w cows circling grave. WEDDING at Chief Doletis
22 MUSIC TAPING FUNERAL CATTLE arrive at grave w gun shots	23 INTERVIEW w Ole Regé LAST DAY OF FUNERAL	24 DOMESTIC village scenes with OLINYA DOLETI'S (GROOM) in hut FINAL FIRING OF POTS	MISSED: Funeral Donga 25 DOMESTIC SCENES at Ole Beyene's RIVER BATHE Bombay's argument Natunya's village.	26 DOMESTIC INDOOR-FLASH at BAMBOO's Translation of Bamboos Fight. DOMESTIC SCENES in 2 villages	27 Kolaholi's village Translation of Funeral Song · Ole Koro GOAT stomach PREDICTIONS Kolaholi's Fathers village	28. Olinya's HUT (FLASH) DAVID STARTS RECORDING MUSIC RIVER DIP

CONT. page 75

LAND & FEBRUARY 75

MON.	TUES.	WED.	THURS.	FRI	SAT	SUN
29 (A+C) PAINTED-BODY +face competition	30 CATTLE CAMP Kolaholi John films GROUP BODY-PTNG. by RIVER	31 * INTERVIEW with GERSI BALONI PAINTED GIRLS PORTRAITS	1 KORMU DONGA w DOLETI TRANSLATION OF DOLETI RIVER BODY PTNG.	2 Local Village photos (A+C) BURNING OF FIELDS	3 Village (A.) Birds (J.) Children's Portraits	4 Village views (A+C) BORDÉ (J.) Children's portraits + swim
5 Male BODY Painting MUSIC STUDIO CHILDREN'S PORTRAITS	6. VILLAGE VIEWS Portraits CATTLE CAMP	7 DONGA nr. Kibbish GIRLS PTNG. by river HEAVY RAIN	8 RAIN ALL DAY	9 FULL MOON DAVID PTED by river SURMA MALE PTED. FACES	10 MALE FACE PTNG. by River MUSIC HUT PACKING	11 KORMU to ADICAS (2½ hrs)
12 MAGI 3½ hrs. SHOPPING FOR SURMA	13 MAJI MARKET DAY TUM 4 hrs.	14 TUM ~~To ADDIS~~ AIRPLANE NEVER COMES	15 TUM Haddis' Hotel	16 12:45 plane arrives. TUM TO ADDIS	17	18
19	20	21		23	24	25

Kolaholi Chinoi (TOP) Me MURADIT

CALABASH

GOURDS

INCISED

CONTAINERS

/ GARY BROWN

Spending a semester in Venice, art professor Gary Brown loved to explore the city's hidden corners. "Everyone goes to the Piazza and the Bridge of Sighs," Brown says, "but if you really look, you find these wonderful, small places off the beaten track." One day he happened into a small courtyard with a well, the kind of intimate place that was the focal point of European neighborhood life in an earlier era. He took out his journal and began to sketch.

A few people, all locals, stopped to watch Brown work. "Being an observer makes people gravitate toward you," he says, noting that the Italians in particular have a love of drawing. "Even their graffiti is better!" he laughs. As he whiled away a morning in that glorious courtyard—as he refers to it now—he was aware of others entering, snapping a picture, and then darting off. "How many shutters I heard click," he recalls, "and yet no one stayed for more than a few seconds."

He began fine-tuning his artistic sensibilities when he won a grant to study in Europe for two years as a graduate student. "I stalked da Vinci and Michelangelo and Dürer," Brown says. Though he had kept sketchbooks as an art student, they became more elaborate; he even made his own leather-bound book with rag paper. Trying to pinpoint the evolution from sketchbook to journal, Brown thinks that the sketchbooks, which he still keeps, are more utilitarian. They are stacked in his studio, as opposed to the journals, which travel with him from home to work and accompany him on trips. In the journals, he makes notes for self-improvement ("Join a gym" was a perennial entry for years), copies in calendars, jots down restaurant addresses, ponders friendship and death and spirituality, and draws. Always, always the drawings.

Brown now has more than four hundred sketchbooks and fifty journals. They have become the focus of his art, including several exhibitions of his work. Defining their role, Brown writes, "[The journal is] my secret friend, enemy, counselor, definitely my map and at times a thief. It takes memory for us, the continuous accounting. Morally straight, it doesn't lie. It sharpens you, your dreams, and your eyes stay wide as a child's."

RIJKSMUSEA
Bewijs van Toegang
Op aanvraag te tonen
224740
224741
95 cent
CONTROLE
75 ct
some Japs + only
Charters & hand-made (blue)
+ another across from Heineken brewery
American Hotel
Frans Hals assistant
Lysster
daughter of Shakespeare
17th century gossip
ambassador to Holland
Delft China 17-18th C.
Chinese
Italian / Persian
reading: Agatha Christie
Hercule Poirot & Jane Marple
13 for Lucky
read: £1.95 The Language of Pattern
Thames & Hudson / London publishers

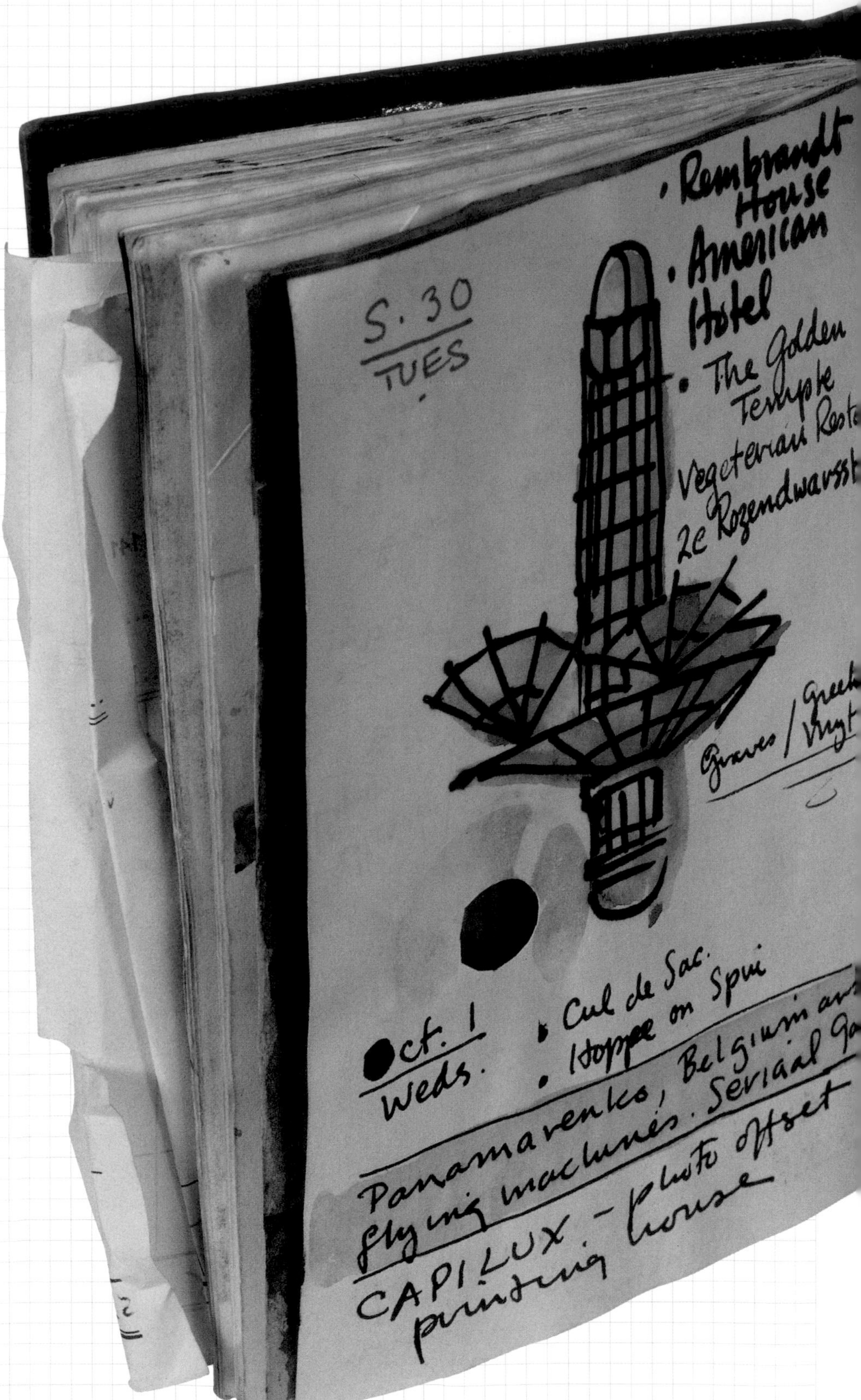
S. 30
TUES
Rembrandt House
American Hotel
The Golden Temple
Oct. 1
Weds.
Cul de Sac.
Hoppe on Spui
CAPILUX - photo offset
printing house

GARY BROWN

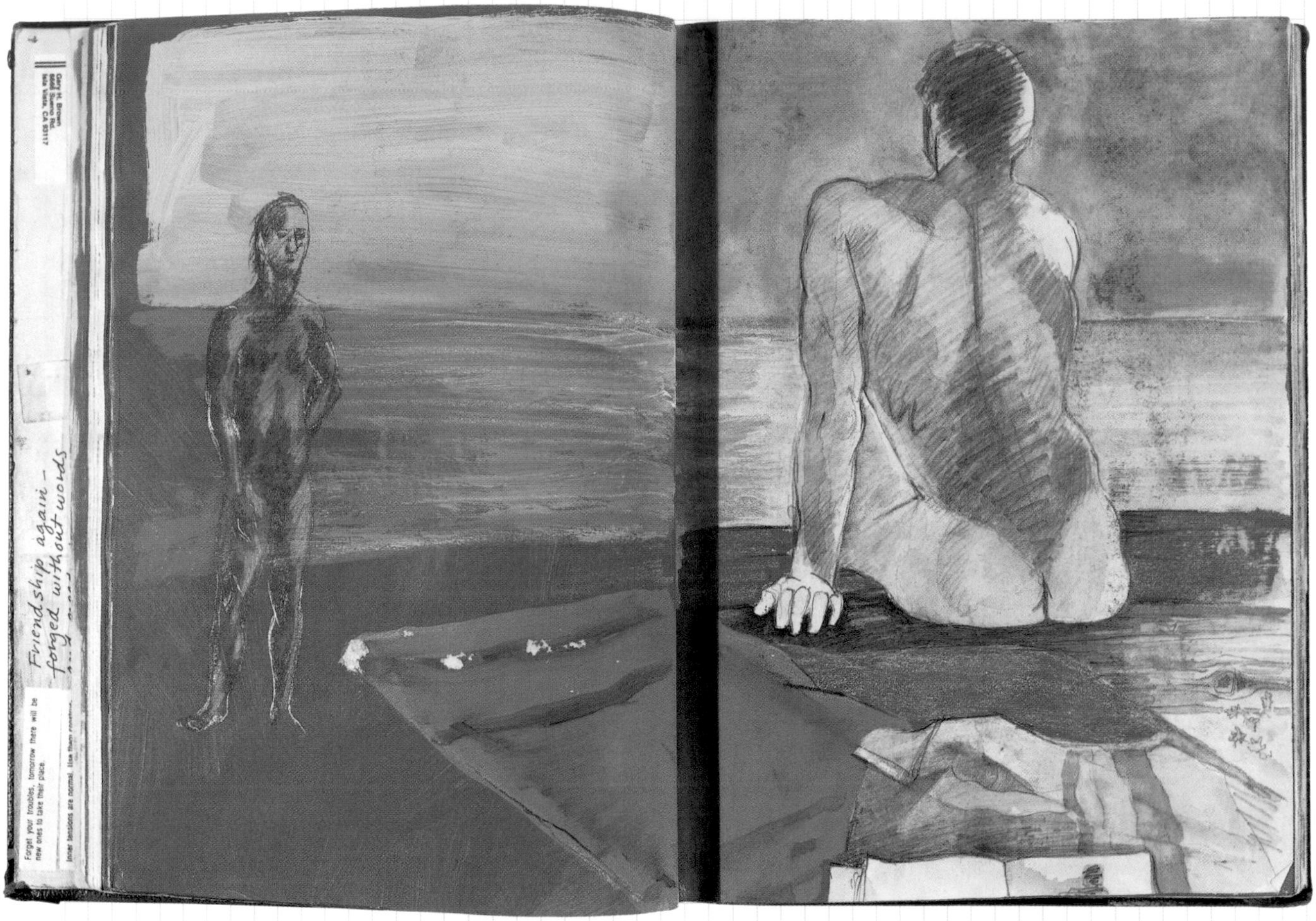
Gary M. Brown
Isla Vista, CA 93117
Friendship again –
forged without words
Forget your troubles, tomorrow there will be new ones to take their place.

= 15,00 €
AN
265-30.01.03
Canadian Bank Note
Design / Conception : Denis L'Allier
Photography / Photographie : Guy Lavigueur
IMBRES
A
450300
Lowe-Martin
Canadian Rangers
Celebrating 60 years of history
Rangers canadiens
Célébrons 60 ans d'histoire
P11111

GARY BROWN

Don't give up hope.

TWO BODIES.

Y. H. Brown
Sueno Rd.

Friendships

– If we are lucky in our friends they leave us not only memories but a kind of guidance and example.

– the golden treasure of this world .. to those who know how to preserve it is friendship.

YOUR SENSE OF HUMOR ENABLES YOU TO GLIDE THROUGH LIFE'S DIFFICULT PERIODS.

friendship is like a passport, needs to renewed periodically.

LOYAL, TRUE AND KIND, REMEMBER GOOD FRIENDS LIKE THIS ARE HARD TO FIND.

...ed without words and needing none.
XII. 19. 84

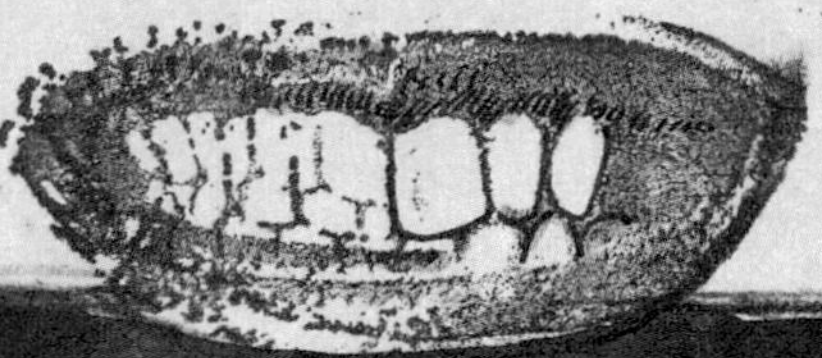

CAPTAIN BOOTH'S JOURNAL 1983/4

Your zest for life will win you many interesting friends.

...tensions are normal. Use them construc-
...y and make them work for you.

DAEDA-LOGIST

Gary H. Brown
6666 Sueño Rd.
Isla Vista, Ca.
93117

968-4371

OR → c/o ART DEPT. U.C.S.B. 93106

"I know nothing more noble than the contemplation of the world."
—Flaubert

/ LYLE OWERKO

In 1999 Lyle Owerko went on a yearlong journey to re-train his eyes. As a commercial photographer who had grown up studying with a classical artist in Ontario, he was eager for a chance to unlearn the rules on which he'd been reared. He knew his journal, already an important part of his professional life, would be central to his expedition.

Initially the journals maintained the relatively rigid, gridlike style of his work-related notebooks. Gradually, though, it dawned on him that instead of being a busy guy with an overflowing calendar, he had no more pressing goal than to visit a tea shop or to explore a particular neighborhood. One day, while sitting in a park in Tokyo, he recalls, "I was writing with a set of newly discovered acrylic markers, when one of the pens unleashed a flood of ink. Looking at the mess on the page, I dipped a finger in the large drop of fluid and swished it around." As though shedding his skin, he began to break loose from the rules that had bound him.

Africa, his next destination, opened him up more. Not only was there the sheer beauty and extremity of the conditions, but a dearth of materials also challenged him in new ways. He was forced, for example, to rely on mini-labs to process his film. The prints, developed in the back of a gas station in some village in Tanzania or Kenya, were of poor quality but were perfect for tearing up, drawing on, and working into journal pages. Madison Avenue glossy perfection became a distant memory.

He also let go of his intention to write prodigiously. Rather than force grandiose reflections, he began to enjoy the silence and respect it. He wrote with a paintbrush, sometimes repeating a single thought, the undulating words more akin to meditative practice than a diary entry.

Owerko believes the commitment he made to work in the journal every day was vital to the stylistic growth that is visible in the journals from that year. "Day after day the loosening up occurred as I freed myself from the notion of outcome and accepted chance and circumstance into each page," he comments. His eyes refocused and became sensitive to his location.

Rather than gluing images from pop culture into his everyday journal, a habit that makes him feel like "a bone collector," Owerko is trying to hang onto the freedom of the person he was when in Africa. He wants his work journals, which tend to fill up with phone numbers, notes, and images, to be more like his travel journals, and for the "different streams" of himself to run together. The nomad and the urban dweller have become one.

MY FAVORITE COLOR IS AFRICA.
– NEWARK AIRPORT FEB 21st 2002

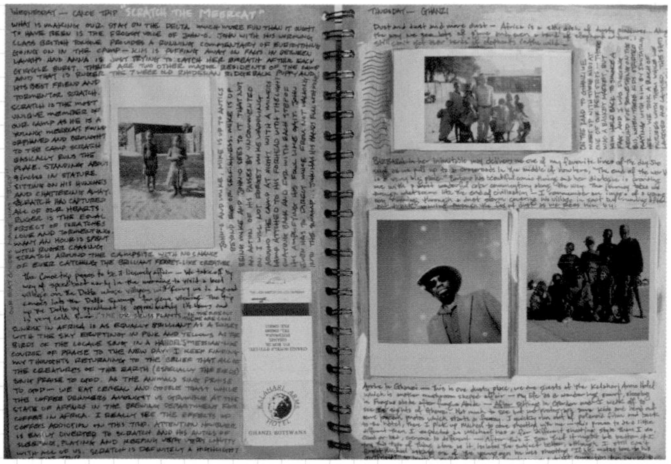
"SCRATCH THE MEERKAT"
GHANZI BOTSWANA

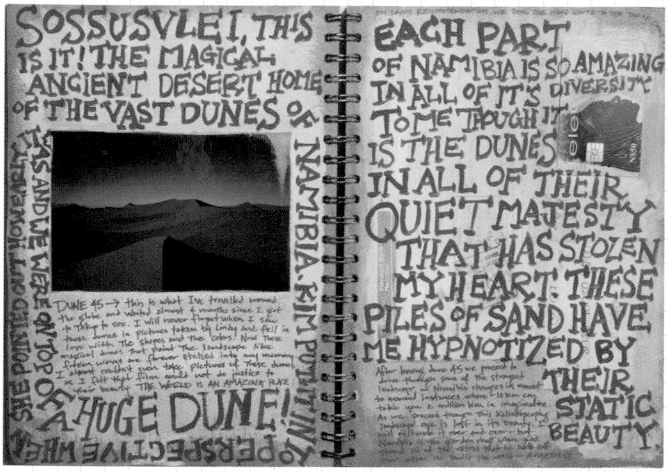
SOSSUSVLEI, THIS IS IT! THE MAGICAL ANCIENT DESERT HOME OF THE VAST DUNES OF NAMIBIA.
A HUGE DUNE!
EACH PART OF NAMIBIA IS SO AMAZING IN ALL OF IT'S DIVERSITY TO ME THOUGH IT IS THE DUNES IN ALL OF THEIR QUIET MAJESTY THAT HAS STOLEN MY HEART. THESE PILES OF SAND HAVE ME HYPNOTIZED BY THEIR STATIC BEAUTY.

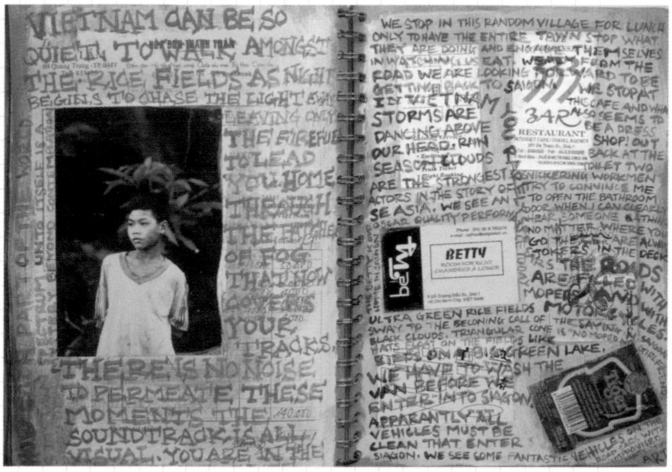
VIETNAM CAN BE SO QUIET TO WALK AMONGST THE RICE FIELDS AS NIGHT BEGINS TO CHASE THE LIGHT AWAY
THERE IS NO NOISE TO PERMEATE THESE MOMENTS. THE SOUNDTRACK IS ALL VISUAL.
WE STOP IN THIS RANDOM VILLAGE FOR LUNCH
BETTY

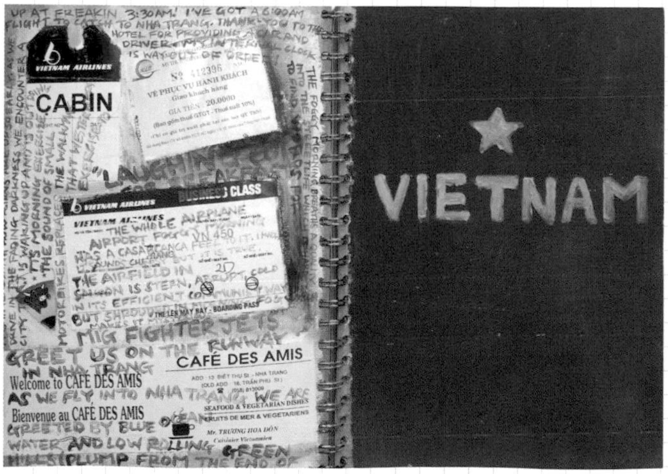
VIETNAM AIRLINES
CABIN
CAFÉ DES AMIS
Welcome to CAFÉ DES AMIS
Bienvenue au CAFÉ DES AMIS
VIETNAM

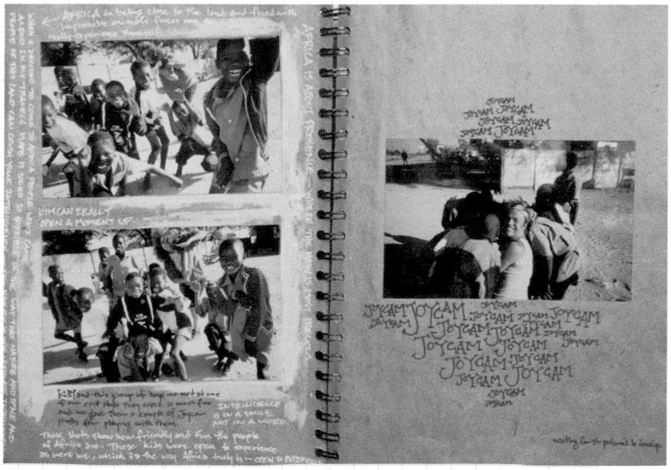
KIM CAN REALLY OPEN A MOMENT UP.
JOYGAM

LYLE OWERKO

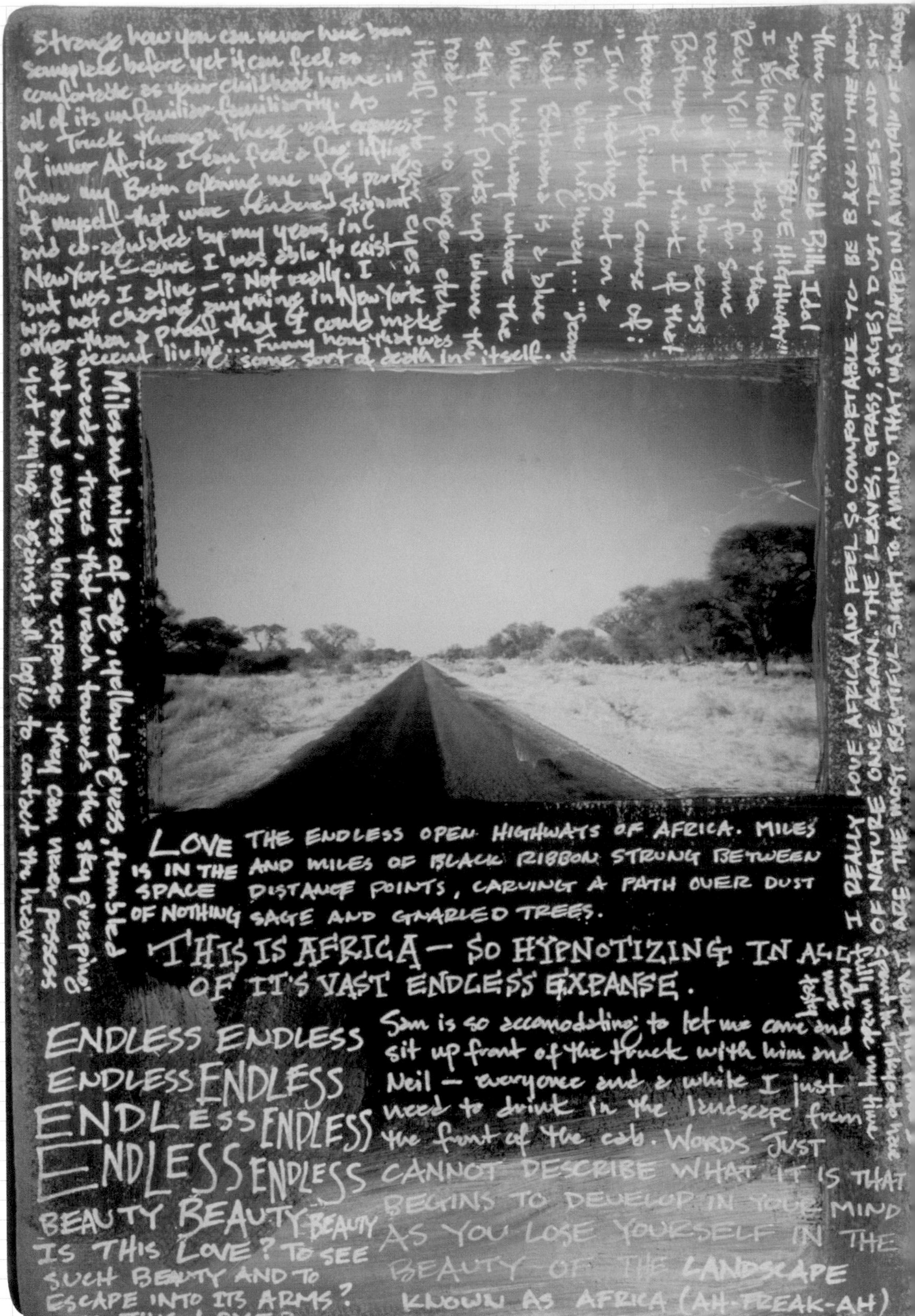
Strange how you can never have been someplace before yet it can feel so comfortable as your childhood home in all of its unfamiliar familiarity. As we truck through these vast expanses of inner Africa I can feel a fog lifting from my brain opening me up to parts of myself that were rendered stagnant and co-regulated by my years in New York — sure I was able to exist but was I alive —? Not really. I was not chasing anything in New York other than a proof that I could make decent living... Funny how that was some sort of death in itself.
There was this old Billy Idol song called "Blue Highway." I believe it was on the "Rebel Yell" album for some reason as we blow across Botswana I think of that teenage friendly course of: "I'm heading out on a blue blue highway..." seems that Botswana is a blue highway where the sky just picks up where the road can no longer etch itself into our eyes.
I REALLY LOVE AFRICA AND FEEL SO COMFORTABLE TO BE BACK IN THE ARMS OF NATURE ONCE AGAIN. THE LEAVES, GRASS, SAGES, DUST, TREES AND SKY ARE THE MOST BEAUTIFUL SIGHT TO A MIND THAT WAS TRAPPED IN A MOUNTAIN OF IMAGES
Miles and miles of sage, yellowed grass, tumbled weeds, trees that reach towards the sky & vast and endless blue expanse they can never possess yet trying against all logic to contact the heavens.
LOVE IS IN THE SPACE OF NOTHING
THE ENDLESS OPEN HIGHWAYS OF AFRICA. MILES AND MILES OF BLACK RIBBON STRUNG BETWEEN DISTANCE POINTS, CARVING A PATH OVER DUST SAGE AND GNARLED TREES.
THIS IS AFRICA — SO HYPNOTIZING IN ALL OF IT'S VAST ENDLESS EXPANSE.
ENDLESS ENDLESS ENDLESS ENDLESS ENDLESS ENDLESS ENDLESS ENDLESS
BEAUTY BEAUTY BEAUTY
IS THIS LOVE? TO SEE SUCH BEAUTY AND TO ESCAPE INTO ITS ARMS? IS THIS LOVE?
Sam is so accomodating to let me come and sit up front of the truck with him and Neil — everyonce and a while I just need to drink in the landscape from the front of the cab. WORDS JUST CANNOT DESCRIBE WHAT IT IS THAT BEGINS TO DEVELOP IN YOUR MIND AS YOU LOSE YOURSELF IN THE BEAUTY OF THE LANDSCAPE KNOWN AS AFRICA (AH-FREAK-AH)

VISIONS OF BOTSWANA

→ The fact that people exist here seemingless without grass or much foliage is almost beyond comprehension. We are driving along the fringe of the Kalihari desert as we pass through these communities built amongst dust — erected as some sort of touching statement to the human spirit — standing guard to the last vestiges of a civilization built on the nomadic spirit. It's hard to find words for a scene beyond any basis of existence that I could compare this to. Even as I want to compare this to the American Indian I can't 'cause there is no comparison. This is so completely different.

Somewhere today Barbara says: "THE END OF THE WORLD IS A VERY VERY BIG PLACE." Yes she is correct, cause we are in a very big place that is starting to seem like it is the end of the world 'cause I do not know what could possibly begin here.

SCENES FROM THE WINDOW OF THE TRUCK AS WE PASS THROUGH MILES AFTER MILES OF DESERT. EVERY ONCE AND A WHILE WE WOULD PASS A VILLAGE CLINGING TO LIFE AMIDST THIS DUST BOWL — I COULD WATCH OUT OF THE WINDOW FOR HOURS MESMERIZED BY THE PASSING SCENERY.

I will never ever forget the image of the young boy running out of the swirling dust of his village to wave at us as we zoomed past. This flight of fancy will forever be etched in my mind as he gleefully waved at us putting all of his energy into a moment most of the people on the truck never even noticed or probably never even gave that much of a thought to — that moment is forever preserved in my mind.

Dust, Dust and more Dust. We are definitely in the middle of nowhere, however we have to say that the roads so far have been in great condition. It does make the trip a little easier and have given some of the distance that we have been covering.

LYLE OWERKO

/ LYNDA BARRY

Lynda Barry began using an Asian-style brush painting in her journals about five years ago. "I discovered I could write fiction in a more satisfying way by writing with a paintbrush very slowly," Barry says. "I started keeping my journal that way, too, and I was surprised by how many specific memories were embedded in these pages."

Barry, author of the weekly cartoon *Ernie Pook's Comeek*, now does the brushwork on a daily basis, working on pages torn from a legal pad. Though the thick, wet lines of the ancient brush might seem better suited to rice paper, Barry says she likes the combination of the gray against the yellow. The paper's ordinariness also helps her to think of the practice as "messing around."

The slow style is the opposite of how she's long thought it best to go about writing and drawing. Getting it out quickly is supposed to circumnavigate a person's internal editor. But Barry has found that going slowly "invites more back-of-the-mind images." She continues, "Often something completely unsuspected appears and surprises me. That's what I love most."

Barry's published work is fairly personal. In addition to Marlys, her scrappy hero who bears a resemblance to Barry, she has called her graphic novels "autobifictionalography." Given its intimate nature, one might presume that Barry's journals have been central to her work. But until she took up the brush, the journals she'd been keeping since age thirteen proved largely unhelpful. "All I ever did was complain or worry while writing very fast," she explains. "When I try to reread them, my eyes just bounce away from the pages and pages of pissed-off handwriting."

The newer pages, however, serve as a wellspring. Ideas percolate for weeks and months. When she goes back through her journal and finds the same story reappearing months apart, often with no active memory of having done so, it gives her faith that a story is worthwhile. "The journal pages are what attracts the stories—kind of like humming bird feeders," Barry muses.

She begins each morning by working at her journal and returns to it whenever she feels stuck. The pages help Barry return to her "groove" if she falls out of it and keep the dreaded censor at bay. Whenever an errant thought gets stuck in her head, disrupting her work flow, she writes it in the journal. She finds that the slow, deliberate process of painting the words lets them soak into her creative unconscious.

Barry's love of journals comes not from a teacher or famous artist but from Woolworth's. "I always loved to look at paper and pens and office supplies there and saw these diaries with locks on them—five-year diaries where you write three sentences a day. I always wanted to fill one of those up. I still have fantasies that I might yet do it."

MARCH 23th 2003
GEESE Flying NORTH
THISTLE IS COMING UP
Grackles in the YARD
RUMSFELD SAYS SHOCK AND AWE PART OF WAR IS NOW OVER
information roller coaster
STARS BRIGHT IN GROVE TONIGHT
MICHAEL MOORE SPEAKS OUT AGAINST THE WAR AND WAS BOOED OFF THE STAGE
ONE WRONG TURN INTO OBLIVION

HE CHANGED INTO A LION THEN A SNAKE THEN A FISH
EAVENLY UPERNATURAL NIMAL I LOVE YOU SO
MARCH 23 200
MATSUOKA

THAT ITSELF IS ITSELF ITSELF IS SELF EVIDENT
MARCH 23 2004
SOMETIMES PETTING IT TO KEEP THE IMAGE DOWN UNDER
PETTING IT UNTIL A PICK PICTURE COMES CLEAR
MOVE THE BRUSH AROUND

TODAY is OCTOBER 31ST 2002
This morning ONE HUNDRED BLACKBIRDS AND ONE HUNDRED CROWS IN THE DOWED CORNFIELD
BAHAY KUBO
AI BUHAY
MASA-KIT
SA PILAPINAS, DOW
ALING MA
I START AND THEN RUN OUT OF GAS WALKING TURNS OUT TO BE JUST AS FAST JUST AS SLOW
HEY WINKY

JANUARY 5TH 2004
"THE CLOCK IS TICKING, AND MARS WAITS FOR NO ONE"
TV - NOVA
ABCDEFGHIJKLMNOPQRSTUVWXYZ
SNOW TODAY
WALK IN GROVE - COLD
DOGS GET BATH
"LANDING ON MARS HAS NEVER BEEN
YEAH NUTHA SHOT PLEASE

/ ERICA BOHANON

Erica Bohanon can fill a sketchpad in a month. She favors orange Rhodia pads from France with their gridded pages, though recently she's been dallying with unlined journals because of the sense of freedom they provide her. She uses pencil, ballpoint, sometimes a roller-ball—nothing too fancy. The most important thing is to keep the hand moving. In just five seconds, she can scribble the bare form of a chair, her hand quickly repeating the familiar lines. Tops, she'll spend ten minutes on a sketch.

Looking at the pages of chairs, tables, stowaway beds, and lamps dashed onto the pads in these daily exercises, *obsessive compulsive* comes to mind. After all, on many pages Bohanon is drawing essentially the same chair again and again and again. Of the quick-handed sketches, the young furniture designer enthuses, "I find it's so important to keep jotting down ideas, even if they're the worst ideas in the world. Each one leads to something bigger and better. *Everything* derives from that little scribble jotted down on a napkin or in a sketchbook."

As a little girl Bohanon played with the big sheets of drafting paper one of her relatives, an architect, gave her. She spent hours drawing her dream house; her favorite part was designing and placing the furniture. The journals did not start until she began studying design in college. During one class, blandly titled "Presentation Techniques," she noticed that she drew a lot more than her classmates and decided to compile her sketches for an assignment. The result was several large screen prints covered in sketches. Hand-colored, the furniture sings, bops, and chirps around the page. The sheer volume provides a sense of movement and delightful mayhem not imparted on the daily journal pages.

Bohanon liked the screen prints so much she's incorporated them into her journal-keeping process, making a new one about every six months. "They're part of the generative process," she explains. They help me see where I'm coming from, and then they lead to more sketches."

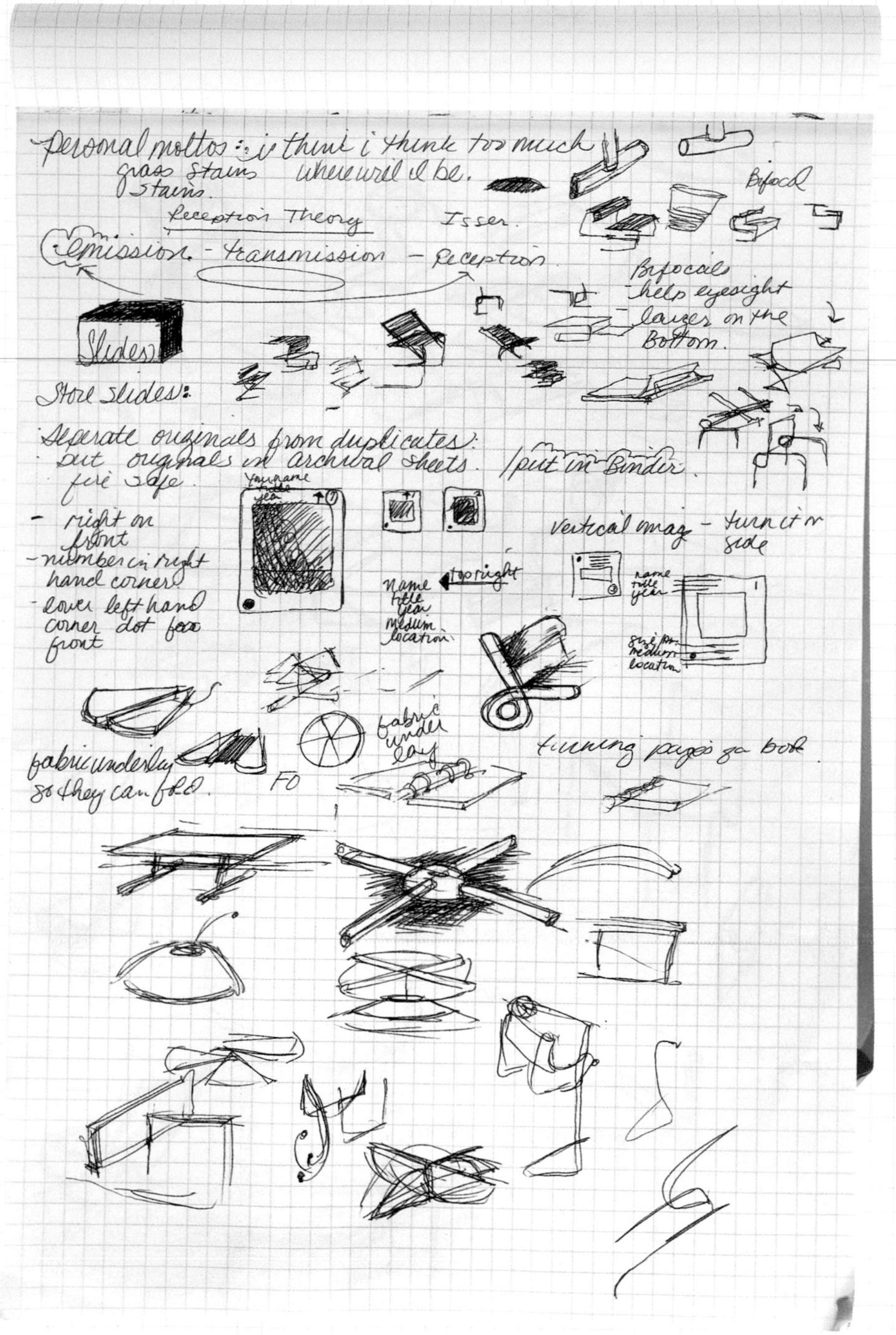

personal mottos: i think i think too much
grass stains
stains.
where will i be.
Bifocal
Reception Theory
Isser.
Emission - transmission - reception
Bifocals
helps eyesight
lenses on the
Bottom.
Slides
Store slides:
Seperate originals from duplicates:
put originals in archival sheets.
/put in Binder.
fire safe.
- right on front
- number in right hand corner.
- lower left hand corner dot face front
name
title
year
medium
location
top right
vertical mag - turn it on side
fabric under lay
fabric underlay so they can fold.
FO

ERICA BOHANON

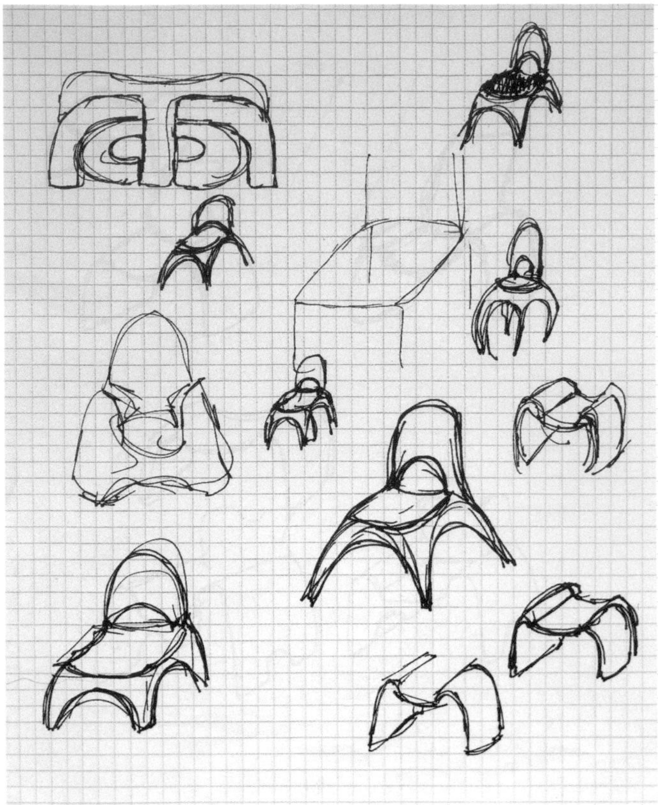

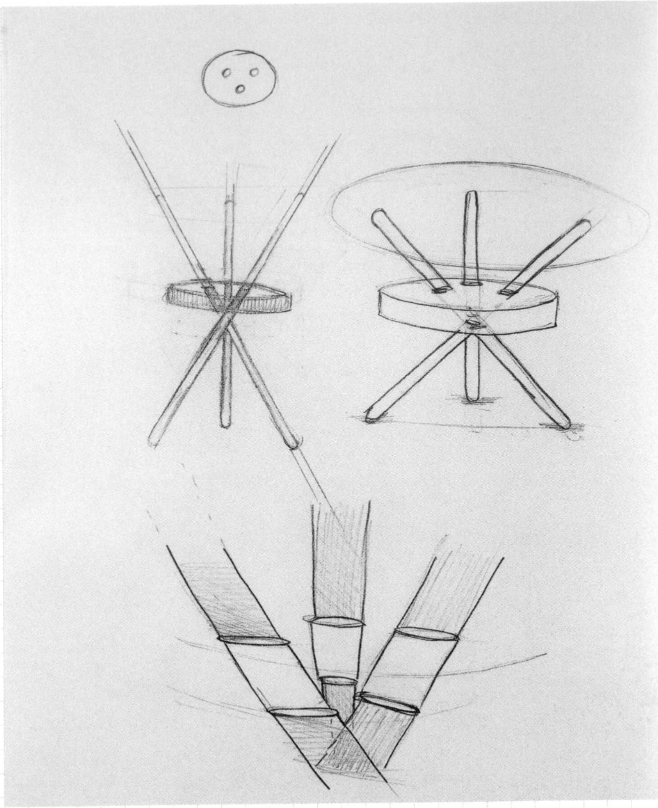

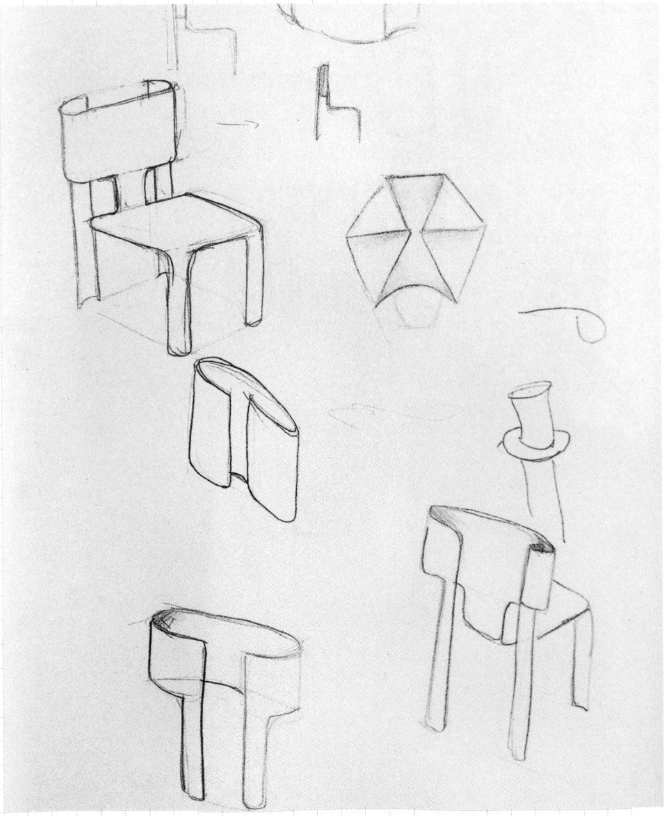

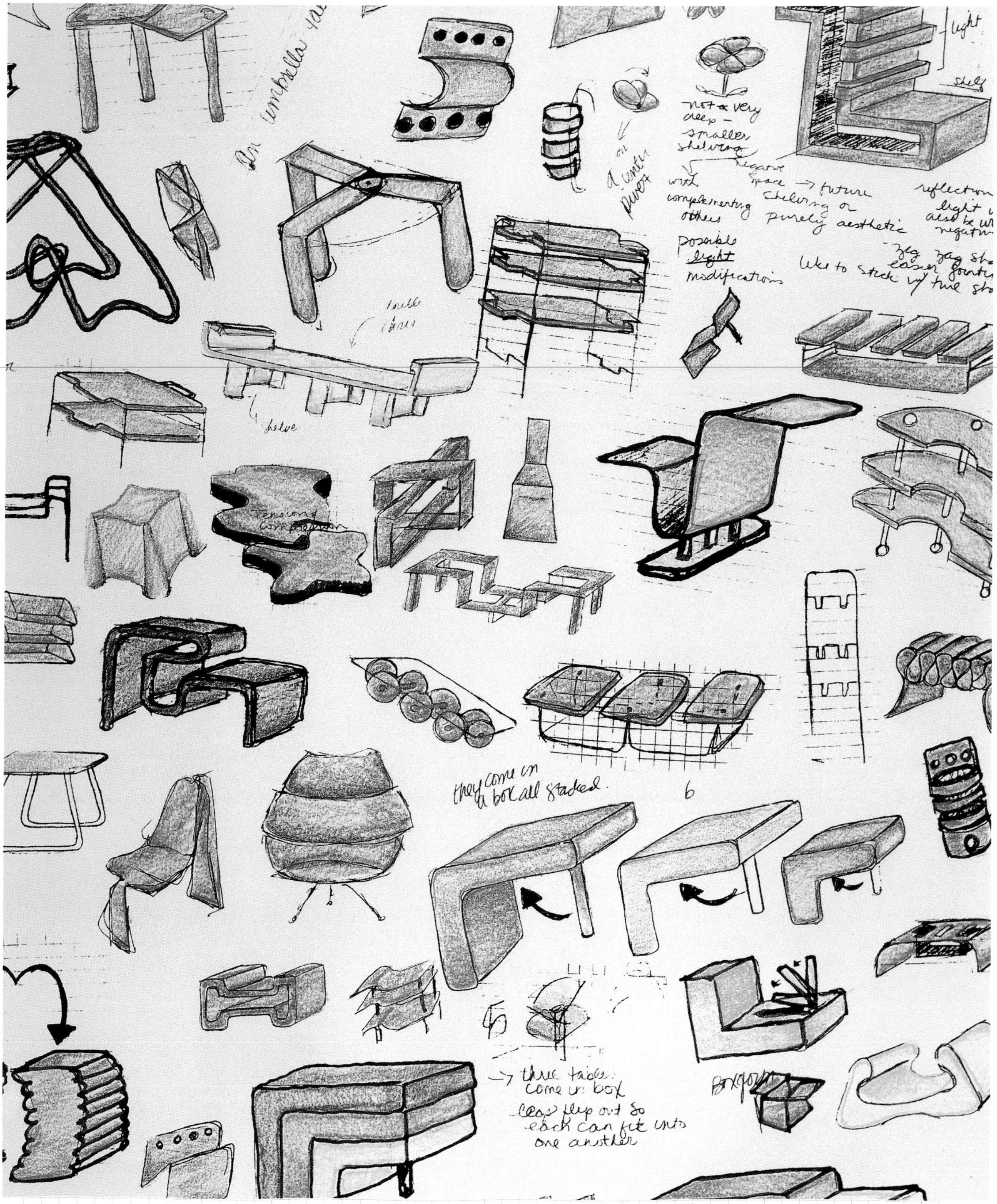

ERICA BOHANON

/ ERWIN BOER

Erwin Boer solves mathematical puzzles on airplanes. When others are immersed in trashy novels, he is figuring out theoretical problems—in pen.

The cognitive scientist and engineer studies the interaction of humans and machines for Nissan with a consortium of universities. His journals are a crucial tool in his demanding, frequent-flyer lifestyle. "I always start one intending it to be neat," he says, emitting a self-deprecatory laugh, "but it never happens." Although his journals do not mirror the tidiness of his professors' lab books, which he so admired, they are not without order.

Boer's obvious pleasure with life and elegant style belie any scientist geekiness. Still, he has some eccentric traits, such as the elaborate computerized filing system he created to tame a plethora of professionally related information. His journals are numbered at the top of each page, providing a discrete numerical record by which a search program can locate, along with the contents of CDs, DVDs, and papers from academic conferences. On the title page of each journal, he tries to create an index.

Entering Boer's journals provides an inkling of life inside the scientist's mind. The books are dense and tangled, filled with handwritten numbers, notes, and drawings of enigmatic figures. He keeps two different-size journals: smaller ones that serve as running to-do lists and larger ones in which to process ideas, brainstorm, and dream. He used to write short poems in them but has not had time lately. Additionally, he uses a computer stylus, especially for meetings. "My thoughts jump too fast. Writing things down helps me to remember them."

The Dutch-born Boer, who works in the U.S., Europe, and Japan, often goes to a café with a notebook in hand for several hours of thinking and creative work. He can fill a notebook in about a month with ideas that could ultimately result in papers. By the time a thought reaches that state, though, he's bored by it. "Once you've had that spark, that 'Oh, so that's it!' moment, it's no longer interesting," he shrugs.

There are probably few scientists who take such material delight in their journals. Boer is undoubtedly an aesthete. He likes fountain pens and the soft, handmade paper of Italian-bound journals. Sometimes, he confesses, he takes out his journals not to locate a figure—as would be the case for most scientists—but to simply enjoy their look and feel. "It's walking in memory land," he smiles.

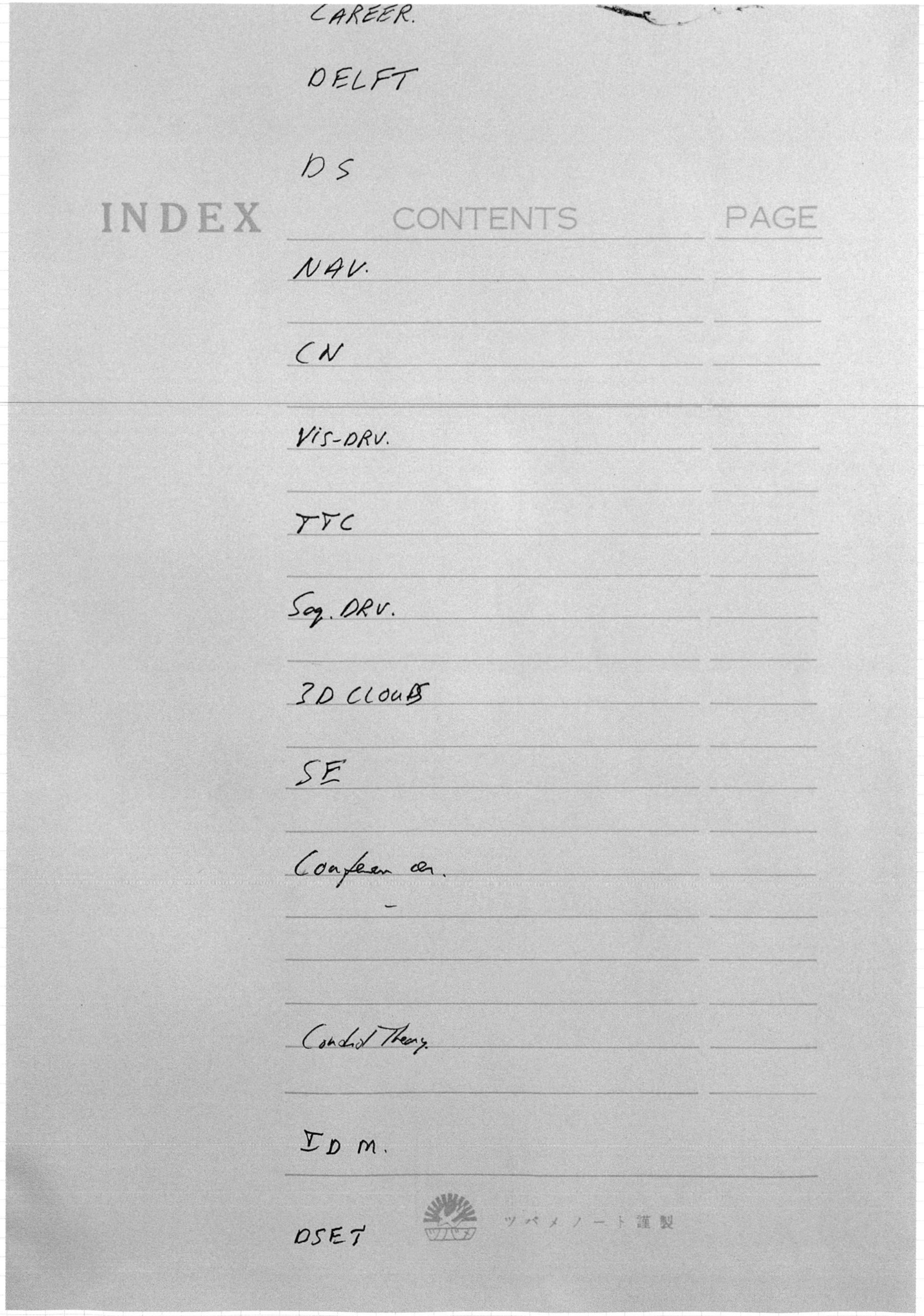
CAREER.
DELFT
DS
INDEX
CONTENTS
PAGE
NAV.
CN
VIS-DRV.
TTC
3D CLOUDS
SE
Control Theory.
IDM.
DSET
ツバメノート謹製

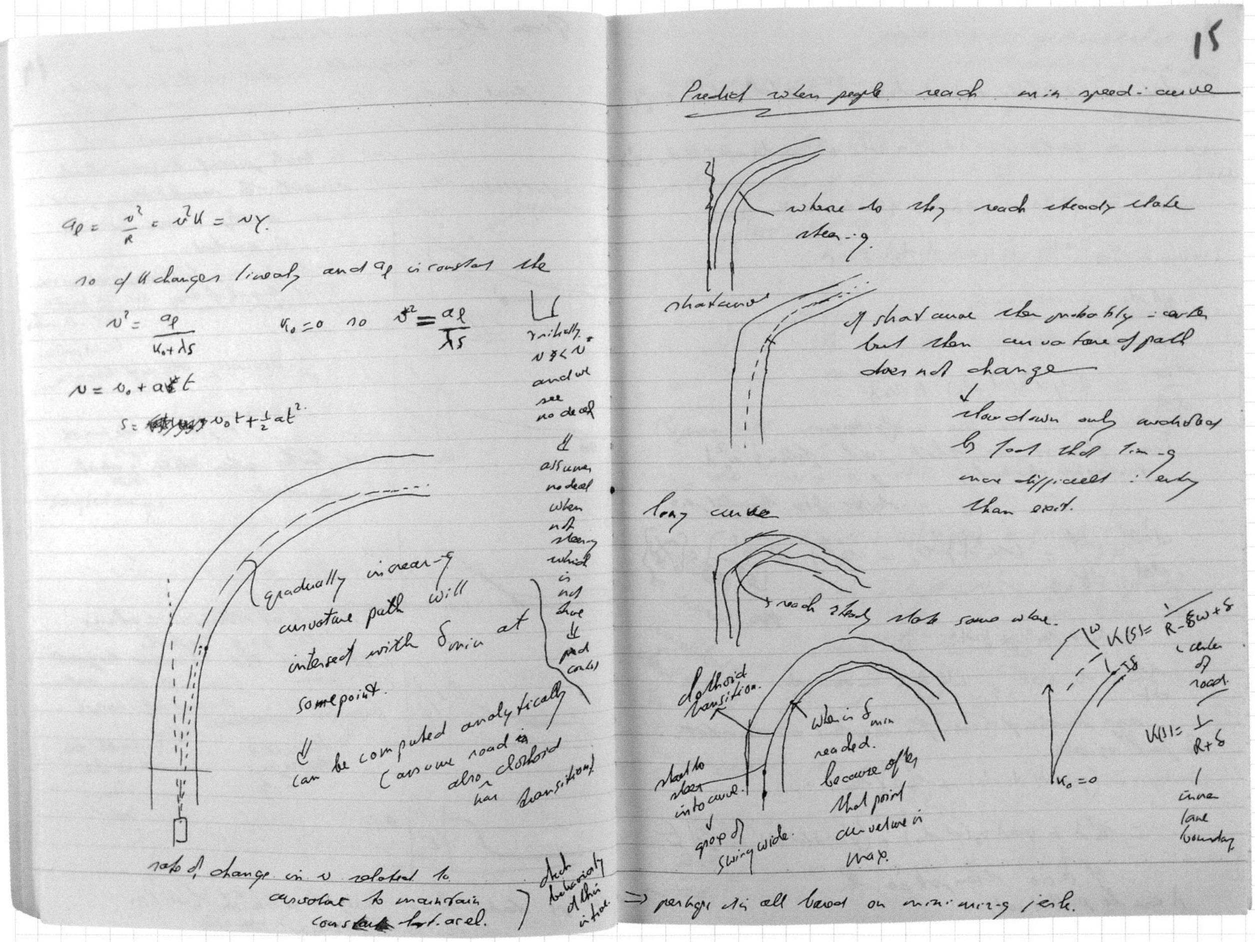
15
gradually increasing curvature path will intersect with δ min at some point.
can be computed analytically
clothoid transition.
long curve
perhaps it's all based on minimizing jerk.

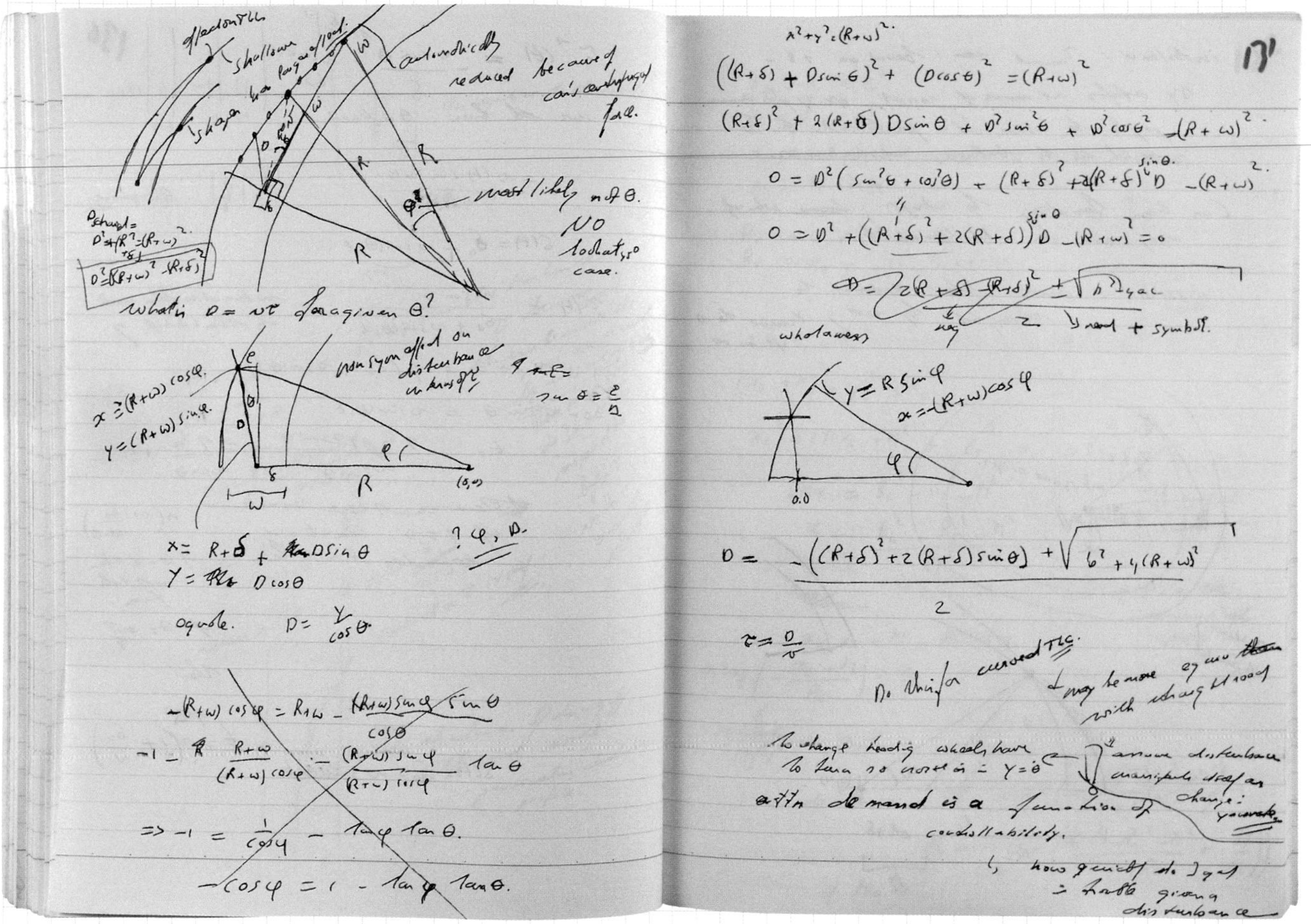
reduced because of
most likely
To change heading wheels, have
controllability.

ERWIN BOER

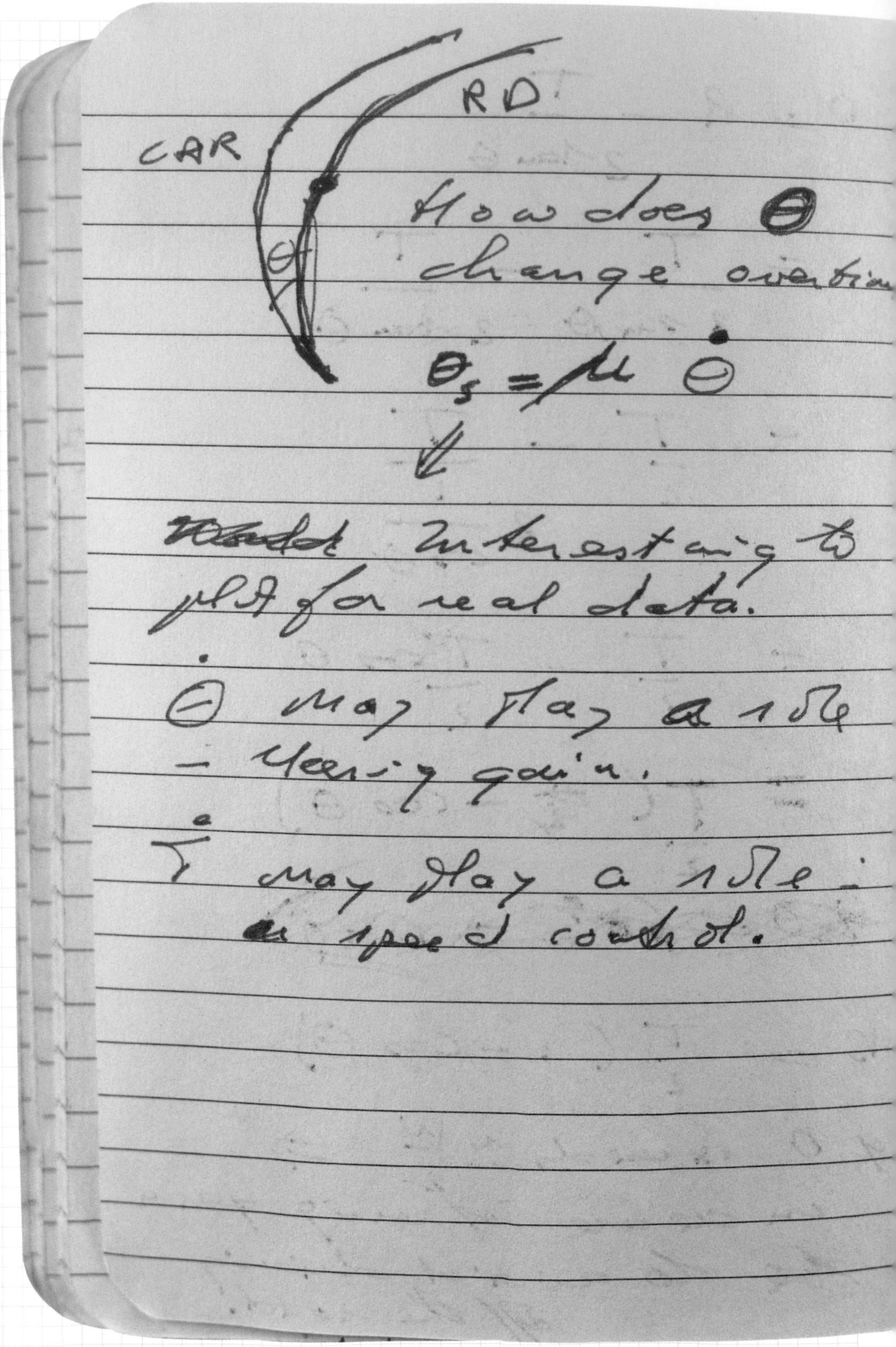
CAR
RD
How does θ
change overtime
Interesting to
plot for real data.
θ̇ may play a role
- steering gain.
may play a role:
a speed control.

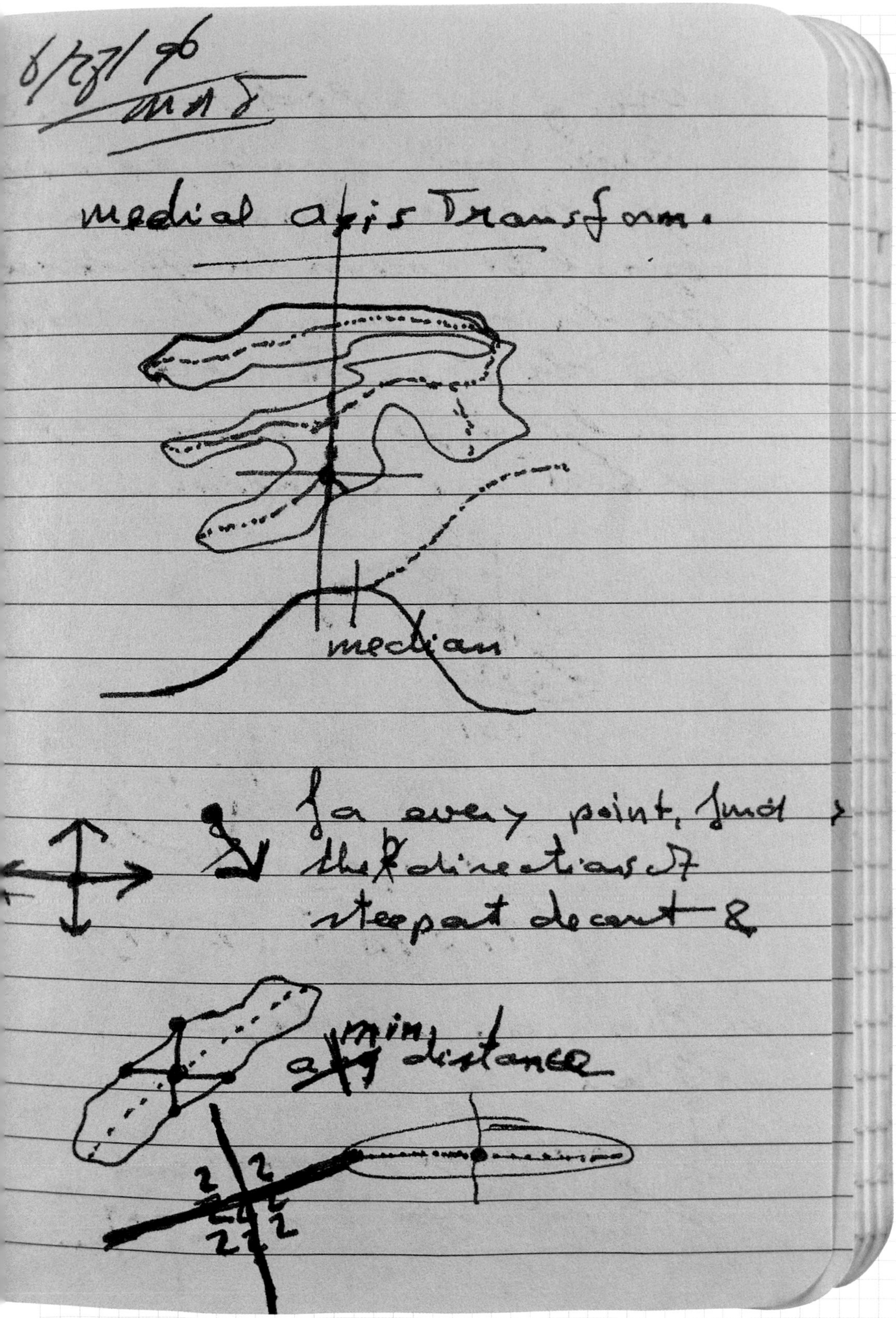
6/27/96
medial axis Transform.
median
for every point, find the directions of steepest decent &
min distance

/ DAVID BYRNE

Most of David Byrne's notebooks have a random feel—ideas coming in and out of focus. They are not continuous in the way a journal dedicated to the development of a lengthy project can be. Rather, they are the bulletin board where intriguing language, ideas, and snapshots get pinned for inspiration or possible future use. Given that Byrne has substantial credits to his name as a songwriter, film score composer, director, and visual artist, it is a complex bulletin board, indeed.

While visiting Japan in the early 1980s, Byrne chose a small notebook in which to collect impressions. He attended traditional theater performances —Kabuki, Noh, and Bunraku—as well as Japanese fashion shows, which he found "mind-blowing" in their theatricality. Over dinner one night a friend noted how everything needs to be bigger on stage, referring to the gestures, movements, and facial expressions of the kinds of performances Byrne had been seeing. "Hearing him say that," Byrne recalls, "I doodled down in response a graphic version of a western business suit that was simply, well, bigger. Not only bigger but flatter, much like the Noh theatre."

It was, of course, the Big Suit that would become the band's visual trademark and also provide the kernel for *Stop Making Sense,* the landmark concert film and tour of the same name. The simple line drawing is less elaborate than many phone scribbles or cocktail napkin maps. It is hard, then, to believe that what was born from such brevity would provide fuel for so many people's creative consciousness.

"I obviously was thinking of the whole show as being more presentational," explains Byrne of the suit and the concert. "Unlike naturalistic Western theater, this show would be more Brechtian, more Eastern, more revealing of its working and stage devices. To me, all this is implied in this little sketch."

Though most pages of his journal are related to music, Byrne is clearly a visual thinker, as the suit sketch indicates. There are ideas for how to notate Theremin music, the world's first electronic instrument, via different lengths of squiggly lines, and various LP cover designs. In the case of the album cover for *Speaking in Tongues*, when a design by artist Robert Rauschenberg proved too expensive to produce, Byrne scrambled to devise one: "We had to come up with a cheap alternative super quick. I ended up designing it by painting, collaging, and letter-pressing text directly onto blank album covers that I had lying around the house." The imagery sprang from his reading of Joseph Campbell at the time.

Not surprisingly, Byrne's notebooks also contain phrases for lyrics or titles. Perhaps the most interesting of them in terms of the subject of journaling comes from the Talking Heads' song, "Life During Wartime": "Burn all my notebooks. What good are notebooks? They won't help me survive." The songwriter frequently jots down phrases he has overheard in conversation or from the media, clumps of words that sound absurd or enigmatic when taken out of context. Covering a page, they include arrows and other private symbols that were meaningful at the time but are now lost even to Byrne. Looking at such a page today, he says, "I added to them at various times, so there are different pens being used, and sometimes I'd underline it in red.... The jottings are more than just a list of phrases—their placement and visual relationships could be 'read' on another level, implying more meaning that just the text could impart."

Byrne has not changed to an electronic organizer partly because the spatial relationship of words and drawings on a page is so vital to his understanding of an idea: "These things are like concrete poetry: the way the words *look* is as important as what they say."

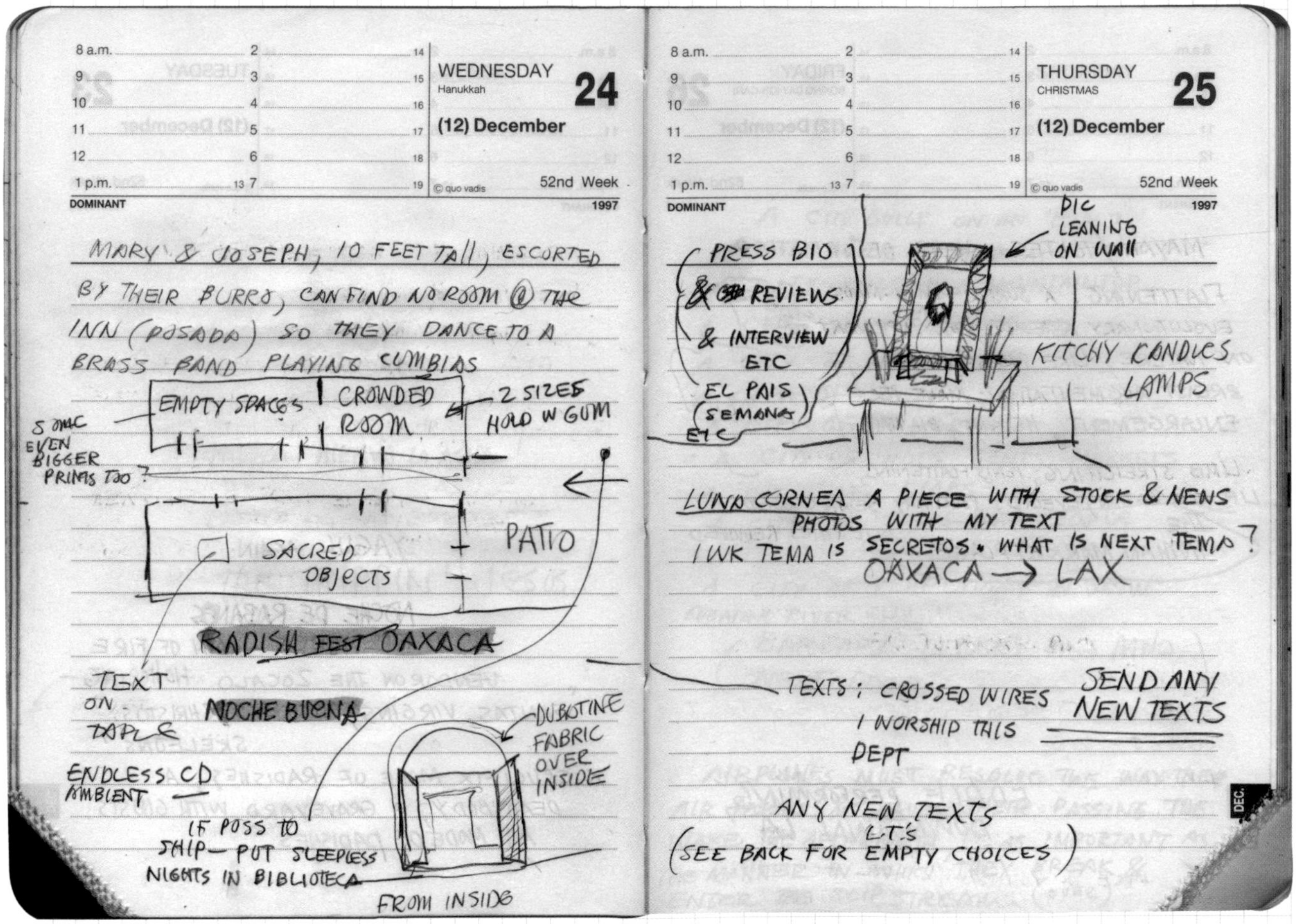
WEDNESDAY
Hanukkah
24
(12) December
52nd Week
1997
MARY & JOSEPH, 10 FEET TALL, ESCORTED BY THEIR BURRO, CAN FIND NO ROOM @ THE INN (POSADA) SO THEY DANCE TO A BRASS BAND PLAYING CUMBIAS
EMPTY SPACES
CROWDED ROOM
2 SIZES HOLD W GUM
EVEN BIGGER PRINTS TOO?
SACRED OBJECTS
PATIO
RADISH FEST OAXACA
TEXT ON TABLE
NOCHE BUENA
DUBOTINE FABRIC OVER INSIDE
ENDLESS CD AMBIENT
IF POSS TO SHIP — PUT SLEEPLESS NIGHTS IN BIBLIOTECA
FROM INSIDE
THURSDAY
CHRISTMAS
25
(12) December
52nd Week
1997
PRESS BIO
REVIEWS
& INTERVIEW ETC
EL PAIS
SEMANA
ETC
PIC LEANING ON WALL
KITCHY CANDLES
LAMPS
LUNA CORNEA A PIECE WITH STOCK & NEWS PHOTOS WITH MY TEXT
1 WK TEMA IS SECRETOS • WHAT IS NEXT TEMA?
OAXACA → LAX
TEXTS: CROSSED WIRES
I WORSHIP THIS DEPT
SEND ANY NEW TEXTS
ANY NEW TEXTS
(SEE BACK FOR EMPTY CHOICES)

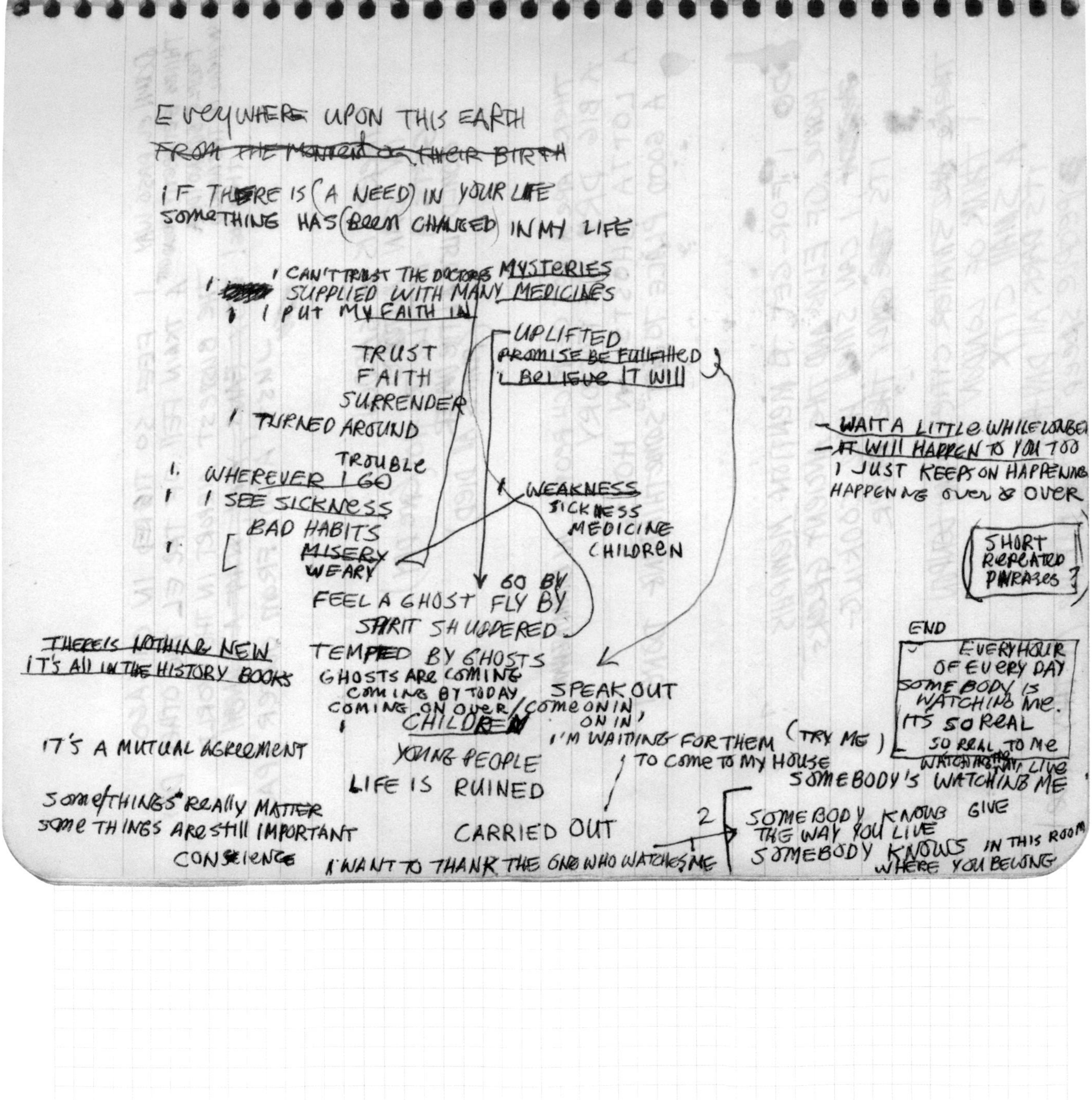

EVERYWHERE UPON THIS EARTH
~~FROM THE MOMENT OF THEIR BIRTH~~

IF THERE IS (A NEED) IN YOUR LIFE
SOMETHING HAS (BEEN CHANGED) IN MY LIFE

I CAN'T TRUST THE DOCTORS MYSTERIES
SUPPLIED WITH MANY MEDICINES
I PUT MY FAITH IN

UPLIFTED
~~PROMISE BE FULFILLED~~
I BELIEVE IT WILL

TRUST
FAITH
SURRENDER

I TURNED AROUND

TROUBLE
WHEREVER I GO
I SEE SICKNESS
BAD HABITS
MISERY
WEARY

WEAKNESS
SICKNESS
MEDICINE
CHILDREN

GO BY
FEEL A GHOST FLY BY
SPIRIT SHUDDERED

- WAIT A LITTLE WHILE LONGER
- ~~IT WILL HAPPEN TO YOU TOO~~
I JUST KEEPS ON HAPPENING
HAPPENING OVER & OVER

SHORT REPEATED PHRASES ?

~~THERE'S NOTHING NEW~~
IT'S ALL IN THE HISTORY BOOKS

TEMPTED BY GHOSTS
GHOSTS ARE COMING
COMING BY TODAY
COMING ON OVER / COME ON IN,
ON IN'
CHILDREN

SPEAK OUT

I'M WAITING FOR THEM (TRY ME)
TO COME TO MY HOUSE

END
EVERY HOUR
OF EVERY DAY
SOMEBODY IS
WATCHING ME.
IT'S SO REAL
SO REAL TO ME
WATCHING THE WAY, LIVE
SOMEBODY'S WATCHING ME

IT'S A MUTUAL AGREEMENT

YOUNG PEOPLE
LIFE IS RUINED

SOME THINGS REALLY MATTER
SOME THINGS ARE STILL IMPORTANT
CONSCIENCE

CARRIED OUT

I WANT TO THANK THE ONE WHO WATCHES ME

2
SOMEBODY KNOWS GIVE
THE WAY YOU LIVE
SOMEBODY KNOWS IN THIS ROOM
WHERE YOU BELONG

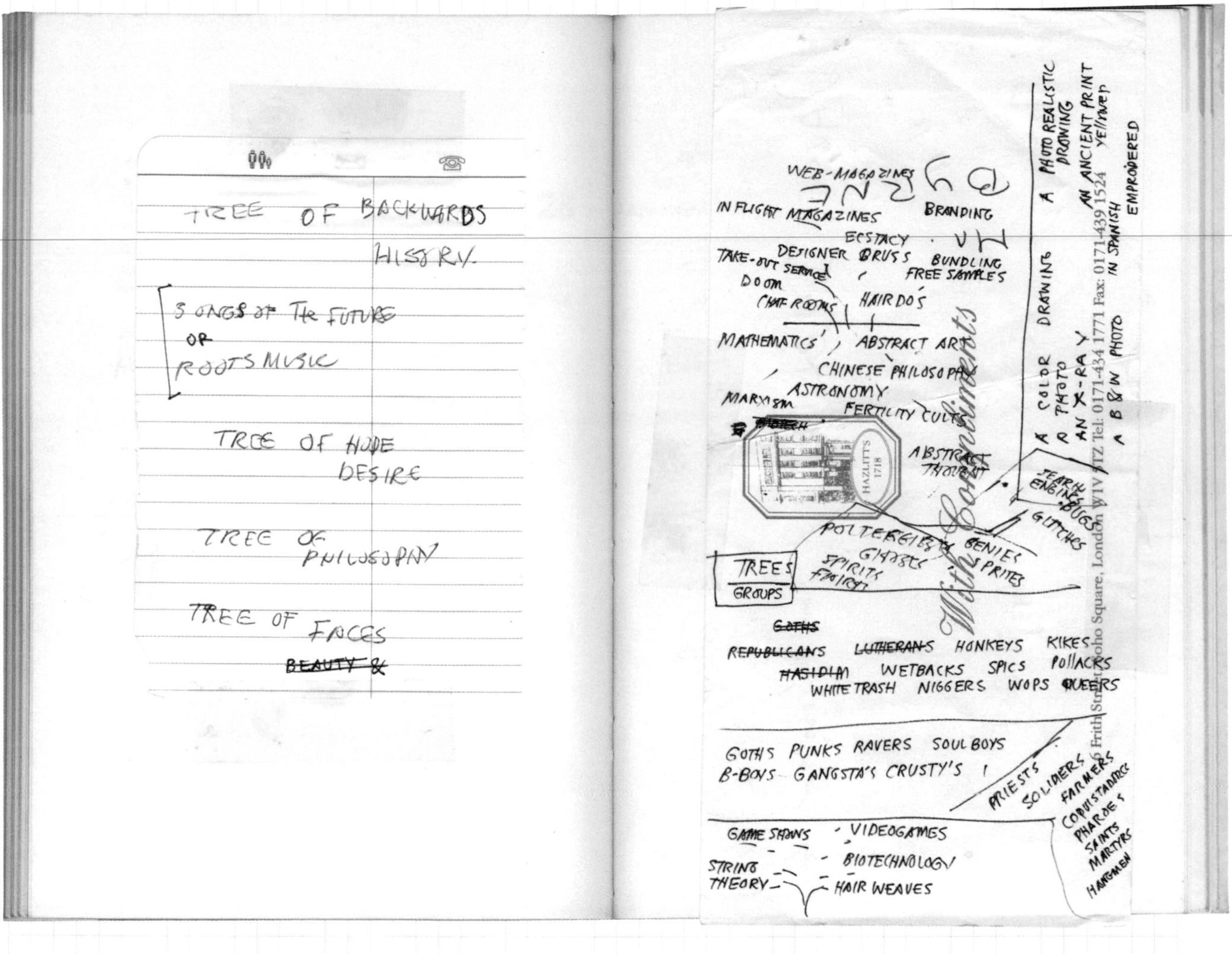
TREE OF BACKWARDS
HISTRY
SONGS OF THE FUTURE
OR
ROOTS MUSIC
TREE OF HOPE
DESIRE
TREE OF
PHILOSOPHY
TREE OF FACES
BEAUTY &
WEB-MAGAZINES
IN FLIGHT MAGAZINES
BRANDING
ECSTACY
DESIGNER DRUGS
BUNDLING
FREE SAMPLES
TAKE-OUT SERVICE
DOOM
CHAT ROOMS
HAIR DO'S
MATHEMATICS
ABSTRACT ART
CHINESE PHILOSOPHY
ASTRONOMY
MARXISM
FERTILITY CULTS
HAZLITT'S 1718
ABSTRACT THOUGHT
SEARCH ENGINES
BUGS
GLITCHES
POLTERGEISTS
GENIES
GHOSTS
SPRITES
SPIRITS
FAIRIES
TREES
GROUPS
GOTHS
REPUBLICANS
LUTHERANS
HONKEYS
KIKES
HASIDIM
WETBACKS
SPICS
POLLACKS
WHITE TRASH
NIGGERS
WOPS
QUEERS
GOTHS PUNKS RAVERS SOUL BOYS
B-BOYS GANGSTA'S CRUSTY'S
PRIESTS
SOLIDERS
FARMERS
CONQUISTADORES
PHAROES
SAINTS
MARTYRS
HANGMEN
GAME SHOWS
VIDEOGAMES
STRING THEORY
BIOTECHNOLOGY
HAIR WEAVES
A PHOTO REALISTIC DRAWING
A COLOR DRAWING
A PHOTO
AN X-RAY
AN ANCIENT PRINT YELLOWED
A B&W PHOTO
IN SPANISH
EMBROIDERED
With Compliments
6 Frith Street, Soho Square, London W1V 5TZ Tel: 0171-434 1771 Fax: 0171-439 1524

DAVID BYRNE

/ THE 1,000 JOURNALS PROJECT

It is too bad the journals that are part of the 1,000 Journals Project do not have tiny, hidden video cameras attached to them. The images that would come back from the journeys would be as fascinating as the books' contents. Reminiscent of the Grateful Dead anthem "what a long, strange trip it's been," one journal was stowed in a cave (and may still be there), another was stolen at gunpoint, and one traveled throughout Brazil and Ireland before returning to the United States, where it made its way up the Eastern seaboard.

That latter one was Journal #526, the only book thus far to be returned to Brian Singer, the San Francisco–based graphic designer who began launching blank black journals in August 2000. By January 2003 Singer had set all one thousand journals adrift. The stamp inside each cover offers the following instructions; "Take this journal and add something to it. Stories, photographs, drawings, opinions. Anything goes." The rest is up to the finder.

The project was inspired by bathroom-wall graffiti, an interest that dates back to Singer's college days. He was intrigued by the commercial nature of the messages, a coming together of virtual strangers. After trying to work out the logistics of putting blank books in bathroom stalls, he landed on the idea of traveling journals. Within weeks he was designing and producing the first batch.

But why a thousand? "A few days after the idea hit me," Singer says, "I knew it had to be a thousand. It had to be that big in order to get any back." The journals' whereabouts are tracked on the website Singer maintains, 1000journals.com, where people who have come into contact with a journal can post a scan on the site and report about a book's location. Singer is often surprised when a previously unheard-from journal pops up, while another that has been steadily accounted for disappears.

Journal #526 had only been sighted five times when it was returned to Singer nearly full of images and writing in August 2002. "I had no clue it was almost done," he says. "So when it showed up in a velvet bag that someone had made for it, I had the biggest grin on my face!"

In addition to the book's physical journeys, Singer is interested in the creative journeying they inspire in those who come into contact with them. He says he "created the project for the Average Joe to rediscover his love of painting and art." On the website, he quotes from a book about creativity, *Orbiting the Giant Hairball* by Gordon MacKenzie, that points out how a class of kindergarteners will all raise their hands when asked if they are an artist but only about a third of sixth graders will do so. "What happens to us growing up?" Singer wonders. "We begin to fear criticism and tend to keep our creativity to ourselves."

Although the covers are professionally designed, the contents inside are a hodgepodge of writing, collage, politicizing, and simple drawings. Based on comments he's received via e-mail, Singer's goal of reigniting people's creative spark has been successful. He is told frequently that someone has gone out and bought a journal and started drawing again after a thirty-year hiatus.

As a graphic designer, Singer (who goes by the moniker "someguy" on the website) sometimes feels like everything he does is driven by profit margins—which can really sap a guy's creativity. The 1,000 Journals Project is an antidote to that, something totally devoid of funding and advertising. *And without rules*. Intrigued by the possibilities, Singer jokes, "I think it would be great if one journal came back all blue."

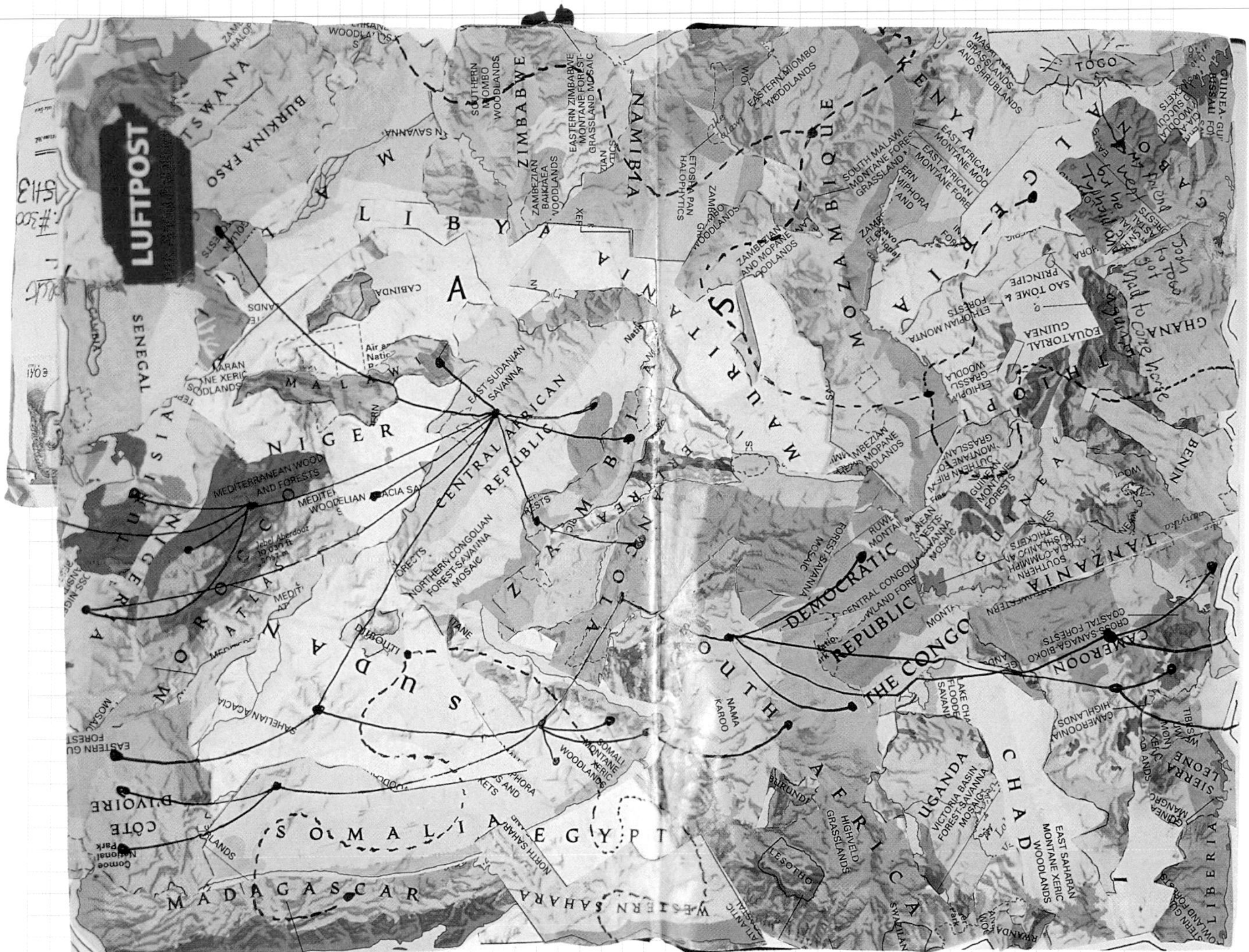

No. 438
1 TAKE THIS JOURNAL AND ADD SOMETHING TO IT. STORIES, PHOTOGRAPHS, DRAWINGS, OPINIONS. ANYTHING GOES.
2 VISIT THE WEB SITE AND TELL EVERYONE WHERE YOU FOUND IT. IF POSSIBLE, SCAN WHAT YOU ADDED AND SEND IT TO US.
3 IF THE JOURNAL IS FULL, EMAIL US, AND WE'LL ARRANGE FOR ITS' RETURN. CONTENTS WILL BE SHARED WITH THE WORLD.
4 IF THE JOURNAL ISN'T FULL, GO TO THE SITE AND CONNECT WITH SOMEONE WHO WANTS IT, OR GIVE IT TO A FRIEND/STRANGER.
Ex • LIBRIS
~~Yours~~ & Mine
FOLLOW ME
ME TOO
BOO
438
WWW.1000JOURNALS.COM
438
THIS JOURNAL BELONGS TO SOMEONE ELSE. CONTENT VOLUNTARILY CONTRIBUTED TO IT BECOMES THE SOLE PROPERTY OF SOMEGUY AND MAY BE PUBLISHED IN A COMPILATION OR AS SELECTED WORKS. IT MAY BE EDITED (ESPECIALLY DEATH THREATS) SO DON'T FUCK AROUND. (FEEL FREE TO FUCK AROUND.) CREDIT GIVEN WHERE CREDIT IS DUE.
EMAIL: SOMEGUY@1000JOURNALS.COM COPYRIGHT ©2000

Topic:
Notes:
are you listening

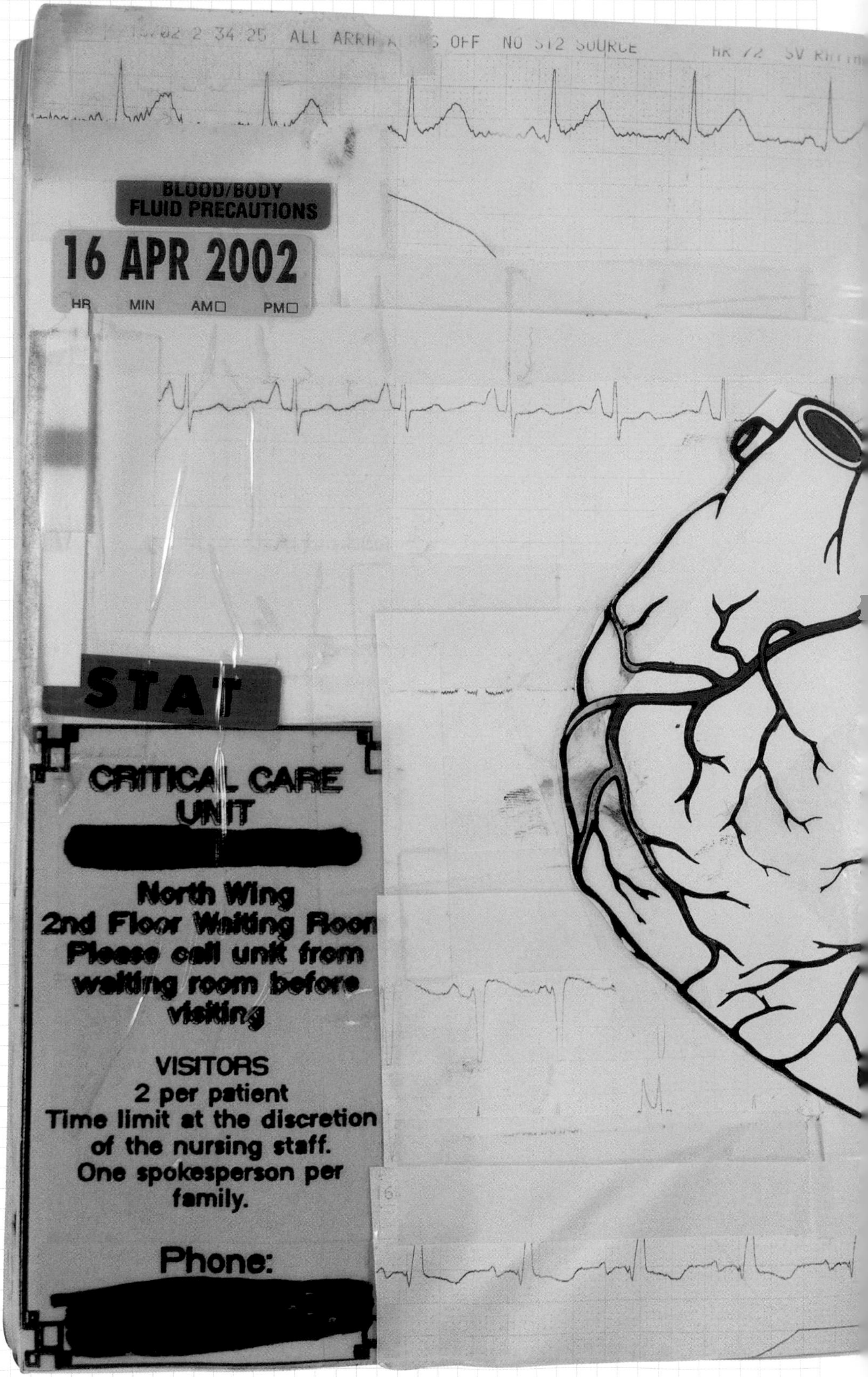
BLOOD/BODY
FLUID PRECAUTIONS
16 APR 2002
HR MIN AM☐ PM☐
STAT
CRITICAL CARE
UNIT
[redacted]
North Wing
2nd Floor Waiting Room
Please call unit from
waiting room before
visiting
VISITORS
2 per patient
Time limit at the discretion
of the nursing staff.
One spokesperson per
family.
Phone:
[redacted]

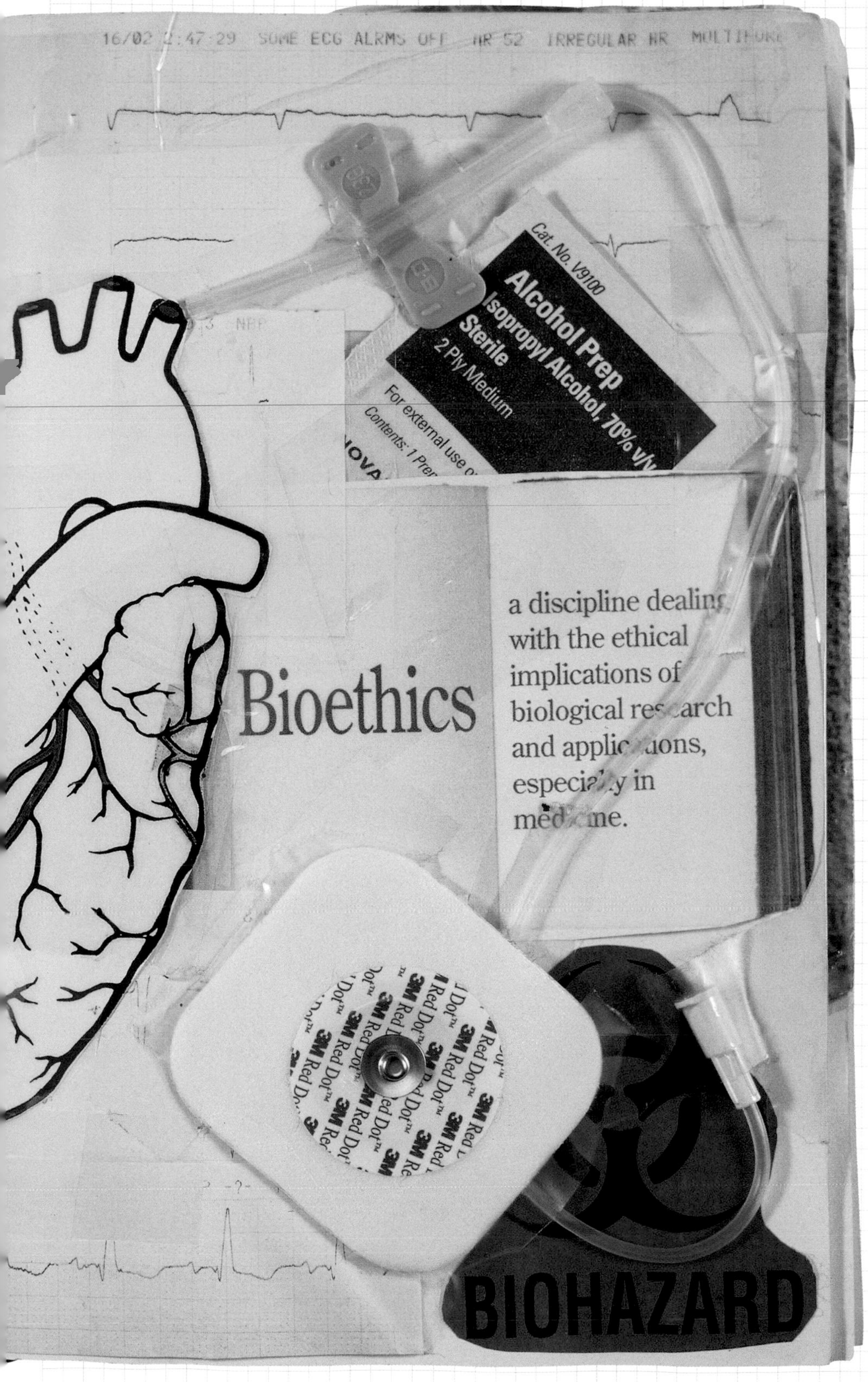
16/02 2:47:29 SOME ECG ALRMS OFF HR 52 IRREGULAR HR
Cat. No. V9100
Alcohol Prep
Isopropyl Alcohol, 70%
Sterile
2 Ply Medium
For external use
Bioethics
a discipline dealing
with the ethical
implications of
biological research
and applications,
especially in
medicine.
3M Red Dot™
BIOHAZARD

/ ANDREW SWIFT

One of Andrew Swift's favorite memories from a trip to Honduras with a medical mission was of a team performing a cesarean section. "There was an older physician and a team of scrub nurses with whom he'd worked for years," recalls Swift, who once thought he'd go to medical school but turned to a career in medical illustration instead. "Not once did they talk about the surgery; they talked about their kids' soccer games, their families. It was like ballet. *Flawless*."

What appealed to him most about that scene, from which he made a favorite sketch of one of the doctor's hands making an incision, was the craft involved. The team had done so many surgeries together that they were utterly in sync with the process, the instruments, the patient, and each other. It all flowed. At its best, says Swift, drawing can be a similar experience. But it takes many sheets of paper to get there.

Swift came to this realization through an unlikely route. After three years in the Peace Corps working as an illustrator, he applied to a medical illustration program. "I thought I drew *perfectly*. I figured they'd snap me right up," he recalls. Instead, they told him to go back to school and learn to draw.

Taking their advice, he enrolled in every art class possible at a nearby community college. Then, he spent ten months in New York, crashing on a friend's couch and studying day and night at the Arts Student League. He drew constantly. Midway, he went home for a visit and took along every scrap of paper on which he'd drawn. "It was such a huge amount of paper it was burdensome," he remembers.

Clearly he could not keep it all. So he got in the habit of culling his drawing collection every few weeks, going through the stacks of scrap paper, napkins, and paper bags on which he draws. The keepers get taped together into a homemade folder, smallest image to largest. The others are tossed.

The kind of automatic drawing Swift admires is essential for certain kinds of medical illustration. Teaching oneself to be able to remember something and draw it back faithfully is a learned skill that he relies on, for example, when accurately portraying how kidneys sit in the body—at an angle, not up and down—or how tissue looks when being tugged by a suture.

Swift, a professor of medical illustration, recently had a rare opportunity to accompany a medical mission to a hospital in Honduras where he spent ten days in the labor and delivery ward. Because some of his training overlaps that of medical students, he was allowed to scrub in for several procedures. The pace was grueling. He spent one entire night with the resident in charge of deliveries, a twenty-two-year-old named Carla, who operated all night without a break. When it was time for the morning meeting and she did not have her paperwork finished, the physician in reprimanded her.

Through it all, Swift drew as much as he could. He relied on several blank sheets of paper folded in quarters, kept in his breast pocket. Sometimes, as with the team doing the cesarean, he could make a quick gesture sketch on the spot. Other times, he drew later from memory. His favorites are those that look fresh and not overworked. All of the drawings put him back in the moment. Though spontaneous, they are proof that practice *does* make perfect.

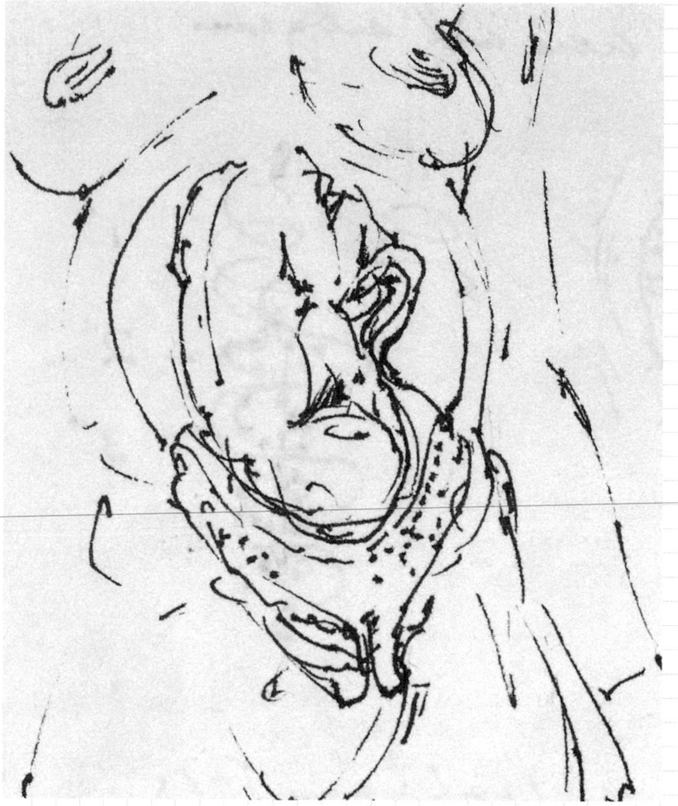

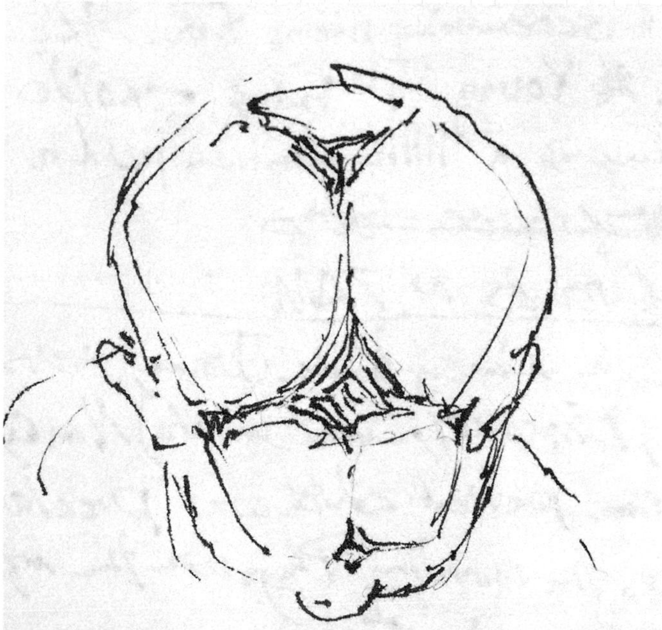

/ JOHN CLAPP

"My journals are a collection of things I'm curious about," John Clapp says. As a children's-book illustrator and art professor at San Jose State University, those things tend to be related to the visual vocabulary. A recent reading of a book by an Oxford neuroscientist, for instance, led him to jot some notes about classroom use of emotional intelligence versus rational intelligence. A page or two later there's a drawing inspired by a magazine article he read about Toni Morrison.

Hoping to become a comic-book artist, Clapp started keeping a sketchbook as early as seventh grade. He now has twenty books from his adult years, which he keeps on a shelf in his office. In addition to a running daily journal, he maintains a small one for every children's book he illustrates. They help him to remember a project in chronological order: "a nice little artifact at the end of the process."

He tries to be proactive about the journal, making a daily drawing of some kind. Recently he set himself the task of drawing portraits of writers. Halfway into a clunky likeness of Aristotle, he grew bored and began playing in the margins with a loose sketch based on something he'd just read about Shel Silverstein. Abandoning the initial exercise altogether, he followed Silverstein, trying to figure out how the illustrator-cartoonist worked. Clapp calls this deconstruction of another artist's style a "forensic approach" and likens it to "trying on someone else's hat to see how you look."

Clapp considers his books to be journals, sketchbooks, and diaries all in one. Still, he is the first to admit they are slim on intimate details. He has been greatly influenced by one of his colleagues, Barron Storey, whose books Clapp calls "aggressively personal." By comparison, Clapp's journals tend toward the observational. "I'd like them to be more personal. I try sometimes to be more reflective, but if you keep a journal for a long time, it's just like handwriting. It returns to who you are."

Clapp frequently reminds students to let go of their egos. Loosely quoting the painter Frank Auerbach, he says that style is not about having a program; it is about how one responds in a crisis. In other words, your immediate, intuitive reactions are your style, and learning to act on intuition allows an artist to circumvent his or her ego. "A journal," Clapp comments, "is the friendliest place an artist can practice being honest with himself, which is a scary thing to learn how to do."

Channel Self-Destructive Behavior (Be Absurd)
MR. EXPRESSO
THE ONLY TIME HE EVER SITS STILL
IS WHEN HE'S WATCHING WATCHING THE FLOWERS WATCHING YOU
THE IDEA IS TO RESPOND BEFORE YOU START TO THINK ABOUT IT.
AUTOMATIC OBSERVATION
A WRITE A BOOK
SHOW OFF YOUR SKILLS
GO THROUGH THE DOOR
THE BEAUTY OF EXCESS ENERGY
WRITE A BOOK
WRITE A BOOK

"Please bring your seats to an upright position..."
AA flight 202 to New York – 10.29.03 (Society of Illustrator's Show)
Got to stop all the editing! Let it rip.
Looking forward to seeing Michael, and tomorrow night – David Saylor + the Scholastic crowd – Jerry Pinkney – Maybe Jon Muth.
Feeling the bravery of drawing again – the automatic quality. Still want to paint every page in some way. Add it later.
Evacuation Routes
757
self-esteem – "The worst sickness known to
man or woman, because it says"
Gate 15 –
10.29.03
6)
MUZAK IS MAKING ME CRAZY

Dummies
Work on Eishwarts while CT is out...
Go Beyond the narrow audience —
general audience.
More you can do — Not art Specific —
"de-mystify" the creative process
changing the way you Think.
"Answer those questions..."
Not an art book —
Not been done. —
Martin Sexton - Lounge-ey Singer
Lunch w/ Harcourt people at "Dakoto"
Kia
Barb Fisch
Ellen (Vicki Tisch replacement)
This world — your world — becomes what you believe.
It Reflects your views, making you see what you expect to see.
Your expectations manifest themselves.
The club has made me much more conscious of, and forgiving, of, people and their faults, political leanings and opinions. The crux being that most everyone I meet — the intelligent people — have reasons for what they believe. A Good & Decent character is more important than anything else.
Good day with Kia — saw the seals at La Jolla Cove's kiddie cove
Dinner at "Aloha Sushi" Hawaiian Grill.
Shining is going to be reviewed by Ebony Magazine.
Leopard Sharks at the Scripp's Aquarium

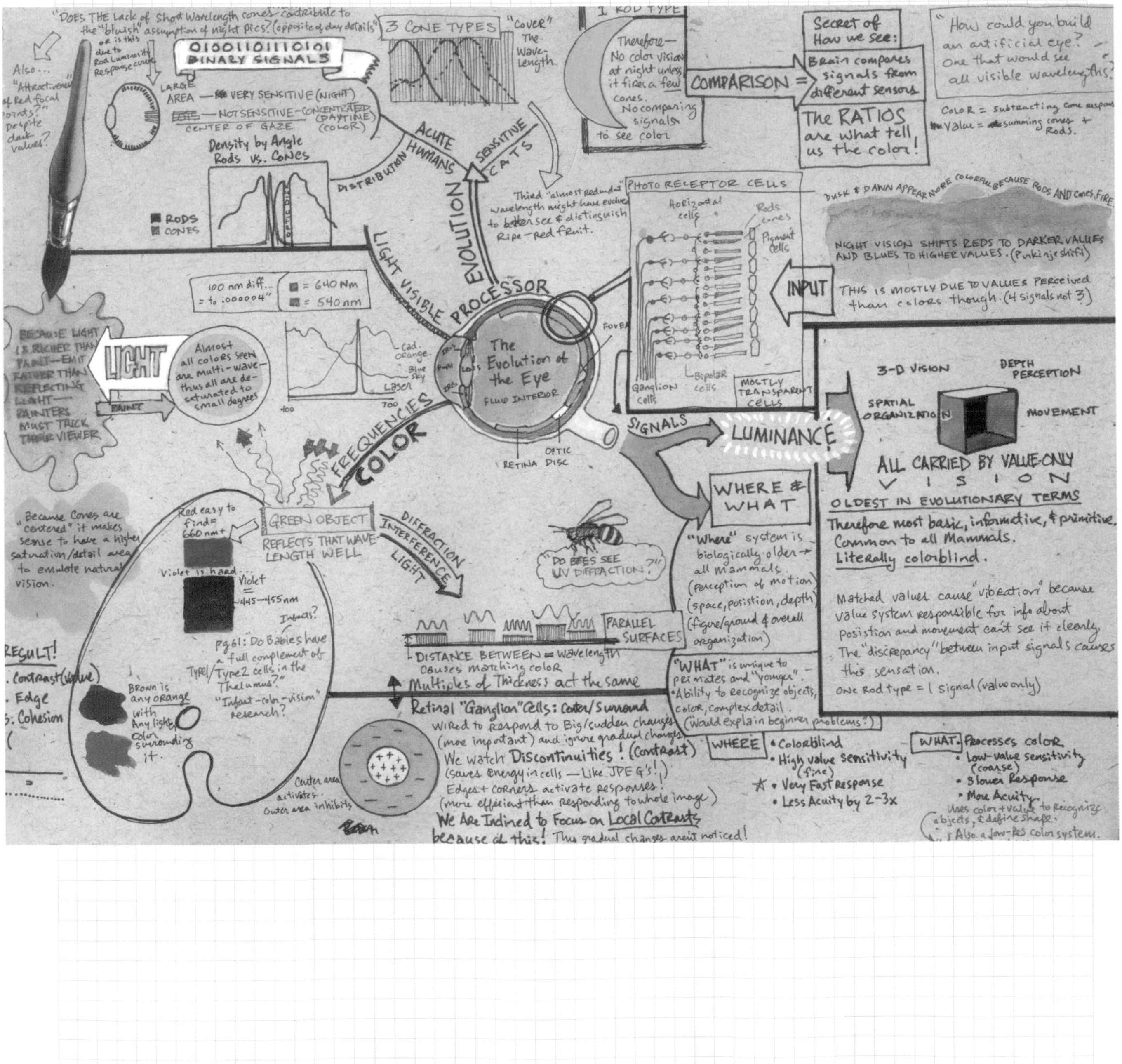
"DOES THE Lack of Short Wavelength cones contribute to the "bluish" assumption of night pics? (opposite of day details)"
or is this due to Rod Luminosity Response curve
Also... "Attractiveness of Red focal points?" Despite dark values?
0100011011110101 BINARY SIGNALS
LARGE AREA — VERY SENSITIVE (NIGHT)
NOT SENSITIVE — CONCENTRATED (DAYTIME) (COLOR)
CENTER OF GAZE
Density by Angle Rods vs. Cones
RODS
CONES
DISTRIBUTION
ACUTE HUMANS
SENSITIVE CATS
EVOLUTION
3 CONE TYPES
"Cover" The Wavelength
1 ROD TYPE
Therefore— No color vision at night unless it fires a few cones. No comparing signals to see color
COMPARISON =
Secret of How we see:
Brain compares signals from different sensors
The RATIOS are what tell us the color!
"How could you build an artificial eye? One that would see all visible wavelengths?"
COLOR = subtracting cone responses
Value = summing cones + Rods.
Third "almost redundant" wavelength might have evolved to better see & distinguish Ripe-red fruit.
PHOTO RECEPTOR CELLS
Horizontal cells
Rods cones
Pigment cells
Ganglion cells
Bipolar cells
MOSTLY TRANSPARENT CELLS
DUSK & DAWN APPEAR MORE COLORFUL BECAUSE RODS AND Cones FIRE.
NIGHT VISION SHIFTS REDS TO DARKER VALUES AND BLUES TO HIGHER VALUES. (Purkinje shift)
INPUT
THIS IS MOSTLY DUE TO VALUES Perceived than colors though. (4 signals not 3)
LIGHT VISIBLE PROCESSOR
100 nm diff... = to .000004"
= 640 Nm
= 540 nm
BECAUSE LIGHT IS RICHER THAN PAINT—EMIT RATHER THAN REFLECTING LIGHT— PAINTERS MUST TRICK THEIR VIEWER
LIGHT
PAINT
Almost all colors seen are multi-wave— thus all are de-saturated to small degrees
Cad. orange
Blue sky
LASER
400
700
The Evolution of the Eye
FLUID INTERIOR
FOVEA
RETINA
OPTIC DISC
FREQUENCIES
COLOR
SIGNALS
LUMINANCE
3-D VISION
DEPTH PERCEPTION
SPATIAL ORGANIZATION
MOVEMENT
ALL CARRIED BY VALUE-ONLY VISION
OLDEST IN EVOLUTIONARY TERMS
Therefore most basic, informative, & primitive. Common to all Mammals. Literally colorblind.
Matched values cause "vibration" because value system responsible for info about Position and movement can't see it clearly. The "discrepancy" between input signals causes this sensation.
One Rod type = 1 signal (value only)
WHERE & WHAT
"Where" system is biologically older → all mammals. (Perception of motion) (space, position, depth) (figure/ground & overall organization)
"WHAT" is unique to primates and "younger". • Ability to recognize objects, color, complex detail. (Would explain beginner problems.)
WHERE • Colorblind • High value sensitivity (fine) • Very Fast Response • Less Acuity by 2-3x
WHAT • Processes color • Low-value sensitivity (coarse) • Slower Response • More Acuity. Uses color + Value to Recognize objects, & define shape. Also a low-res color system.
"Because Cones are "centered" it makes sense to have a higher saturation/detail area to emulate natural vision.
Red easy to find= 660 nm+
Violet is hard...
Violet 445—455nm
Pg 61: Do Babies have a full complement of Type1/Type2 cells in the Thalamus?" "Infant-color-vision" research?
Brown is any orange with Any lighter color surrounding it.
GREEN OBJECT
REFLECTS THAT WAVELENGTH WELL
DIFFRACTION INTERFERENCE LIGHT
"DO BEES SEE UV DIFFRACTION?"
PARALLEL SURFACES
DISTANCE BETWEEN = Wavelength causes matching color
Multiples of Thickness act the same
RESULT!
. Contrast (value)
. Edge
. Cohesion
Retinal "Ganglion" Cells: Center/Surround
Wired to respond to Big/sudden changes (more important) and ignore gradual changes.
We watch Discontinuities! (Contrast)
(saves energy in cells — Like JPEG's!)
Edges + corners activate responses! (more efficient than responding to whole image)
Center area activates. Outer area inhibits
We Are Inclined to Focus on Local Contrasts because of this! Thus gradual changes aren't noticed!

Book Notes
1. Observation Skills
2. Creating Form using Line
3. Using Light
4. Using Perspective.
overlapping
Line Weight
Interior Corners
Accents
Crisppublications –
"The Universal Traveler"
"ISBN: 1-56052-679-3
Don Koberg & Jim Bagnall
W.W. Watts
"An American Rhetoric"
WHERE ARE THEY MAKING MOST OF THE CUTS?
Holland opened the door.
the building hummed
Kathleen Geib
Toni Morrison
"Invention, the spontaneous generation of new Rules, is central to art" — John Gardner.

JOHN CLAPP

04 / CREATION

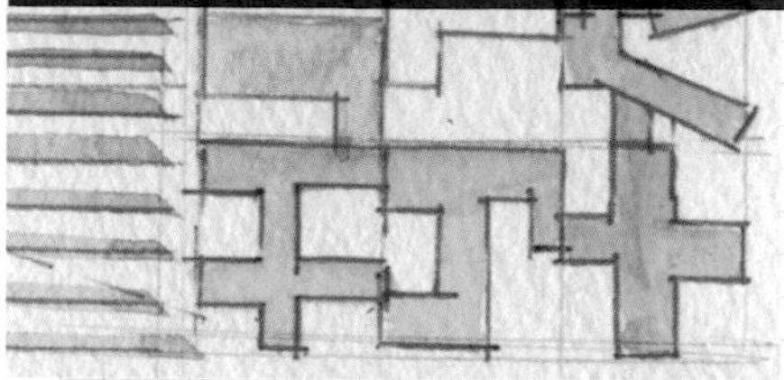

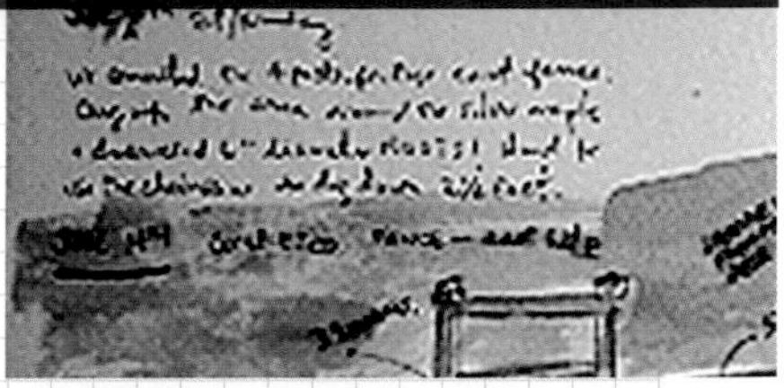

/ CREATION

"The public is rarely permitted to take a peep behind the scenes," wrote Edgar Allan Poe, "at the vacillating crudities, of the true purpose seized at the last moment, at the wheels and pinions, the tackle for scene shifting, the step ladders and demon traps, the red paint and black patches." Though it may not always be the gory scene suggested by Poe in a journal, one can look as though through a window at the imperfections and seeming meanderings that ultimately lead to a finished product.

The journal records the process, which John Dewey and his descendents, the poststructuralists, valued over the product. In his famed lecture, *Art as Experience*, Dewey argued that the value of art is not as a relic, a museum piece to be admired from afar, but as an aesthetic experience. "With respect to the physical materials that enter into the formation of a work of art, everyone knows that they must undergo change. Marble must be chipped; pigments must be laid on canvas; words must be put together. It is not so generally recognized that a similar transformation takes place on the side of 'inner' materials, images, observations, memories and emotions. They are also progressively re-formed; they, too, must be administered. This modification is the building up of a truly expressive act."

A journal of creation serves as witness, scribe, and memory. It is a continuing dialog of the creative impulse from inkling to eventual realization. At its completion (whether the pages are filled or not depends on the person and the project; sometimes a half-filled journal is inexorably complete), a journal is a record of a creative passage, providing proof that the greatest pleasure is often connected to the making, not to the end product. The work we do in it is like fertilizer, producing rich soil for yet more creative sprouts. "Ideas come from just creating, the action of taking a picture, seeing the image, and then reworking it into something completely different," photographer Robert ParkeHarrison says.

If process is, as Dewey believed, the more interesting aspect of creativity, then the journal itself is the art. Or, as Adrienne Rich has said, "The notes for the poem are the only poem."

The artists in this section all rely heavily on their journals, viewing them as crucial tools. Architect Steven Holl refers to the drawings and watercolors, which inform the buildings that follow, as seed-germs. Inspired by his brother to keep a more detailed record of his painting process, Mike Roberts is now having nearly as much fun with his bookmaking as with his painting. Julie Baugnet's seasonal tracking of her garden helps her develop an urban plot. ParkeHarrison's journals are full-circle affairs, documenting the sparks, process, and aftermath of every photographic series he and his wife produce. Likewise, landscape architect Thomas Oslund's books include client meetings, phone numbers, initial sketches, and scenes that move him. Quilt maker Denyse Schmidt's journals help her achieve the spontaneity she seeks for all her work. Filmmaker Mike Figgis's journals are filled with conceptual ideas; and yet, as is true of all the contributors in this section, they retain a highly personal purpose for him as well: "It's the only truly frank conversation I can ever have."

/ STEVEN HOLL

At dawn, with a cup of green tea in hand, Steven Holl sets out his watercolors and a spiral-bound journal. He has followed this routine for more than twenty years, having learned to value the creative spark that comes prior to the day's unfolding energy.

What he paints varies on his mood and the tenor of the day; perhaps a formal study or a light study may appear. Often, these early morning creative stretches "mark the beginning concepts for a building," the architect says.

Holl has drawn and painted as long as he can remember; his mother still has several paintings done during early elementary school. In addition to the watercolor journal, he also maintains a journal in which he notes his "impressions of spaces and places, ideas, concepts, criticisms, reflections." He carries these with him at all times, relying on them for inspiration especially during his frequent travels. Begun in Rome in 1970 when he studied there, Holl says, "the journals have allowed a continuous process, a dialog with ideas, quotes and spontaneous captured intuitive thoughts."

By way of the journals' continuity, he cites his book *Questions of Perception: A Phenomenology of Architecture*. Written in 1993, Holl explored how "sense perceptions are a crucial measure of architecture." The topic has not loosened its hold on him, however, as a June 2004 journal entry demonstrates: "I marked a Zen Buddhist ordering of perception in six categories: eye consciousness, ear consciousness, olfactory consciousness, tongue consciousness, body consciousness, and mind consciousness."

Although Holl's thirty-five–person design office relies on the "fastest and highest resolution computer drawings to develop [a] project," he maintains that the initial drawings—the fusion of brain, mind, and hand—are essential to the process. Regarding the significance of drawing, he refers to Louis Sullivan's concept of the "seed-germ," and says, "Like the soul or initial spirit of a project, its presence at the beginning is crucial."

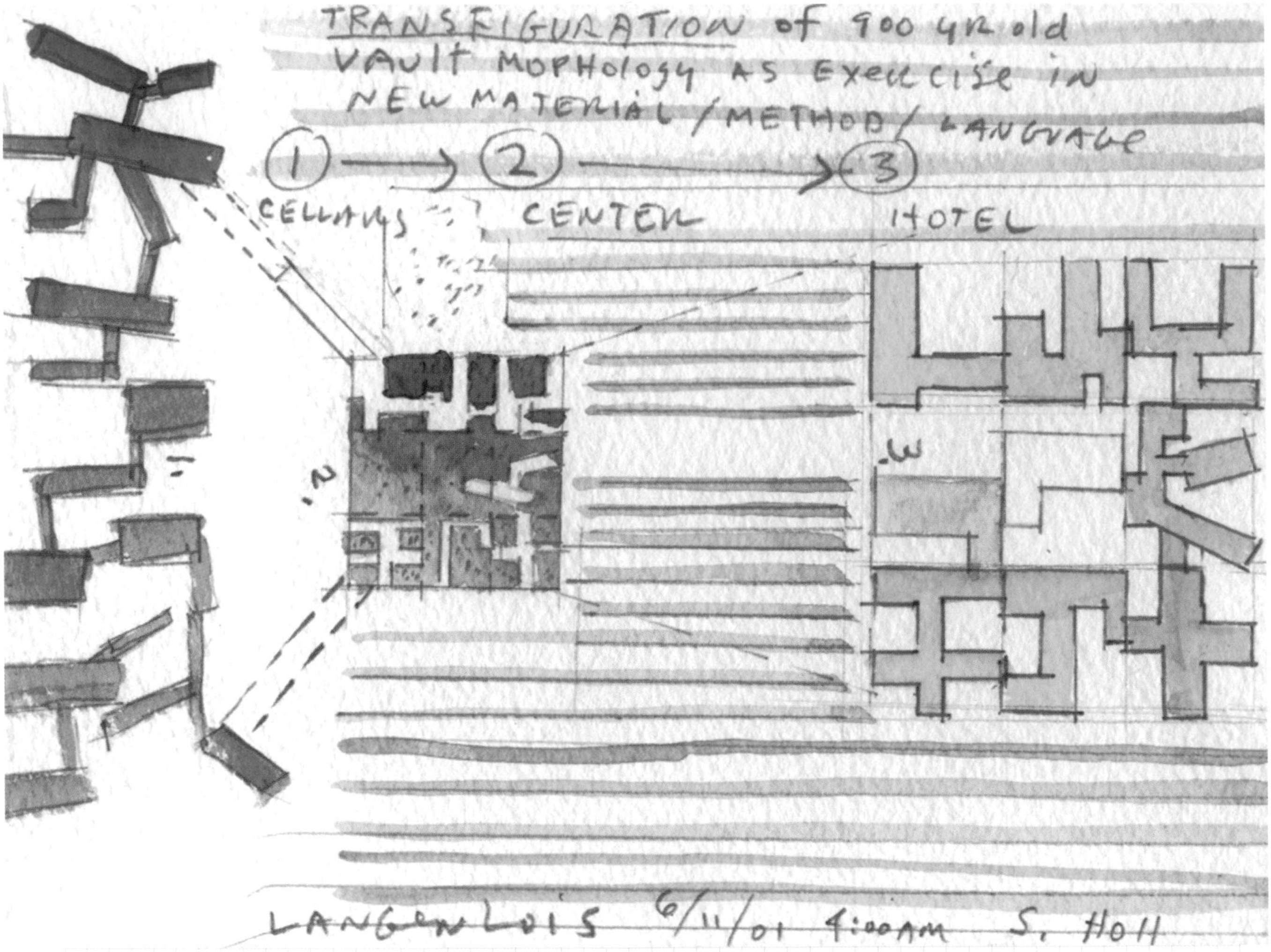
TRANSFIGURATION of 900 YR old
VAULT MOPHOLOGY AS EXERCISE IN
NEW MATERIAL / METHOD / LANGUAGE
1
2
3
CELLARS
CENTER
HOTEL
LANGENLOIS 6/11/01 4:00AM S. HOLL

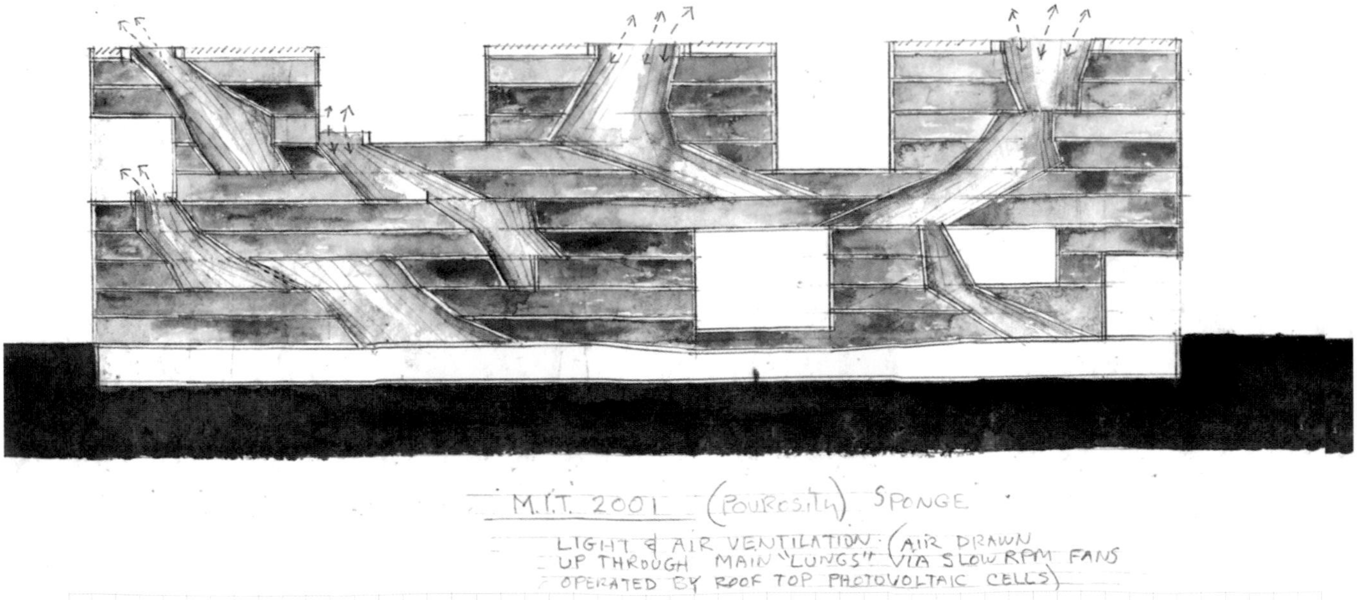
M.I.T. 2001 (POUROSITY) SPONGE
LIGHT & AIR VENTILATION (AIR DRAWN
UP THROUGH MAIN "LUNGS" VIA SLOW RPM FANS
OPERATED BY ROOF TOP PHOTOVOLTAIC CELLS)

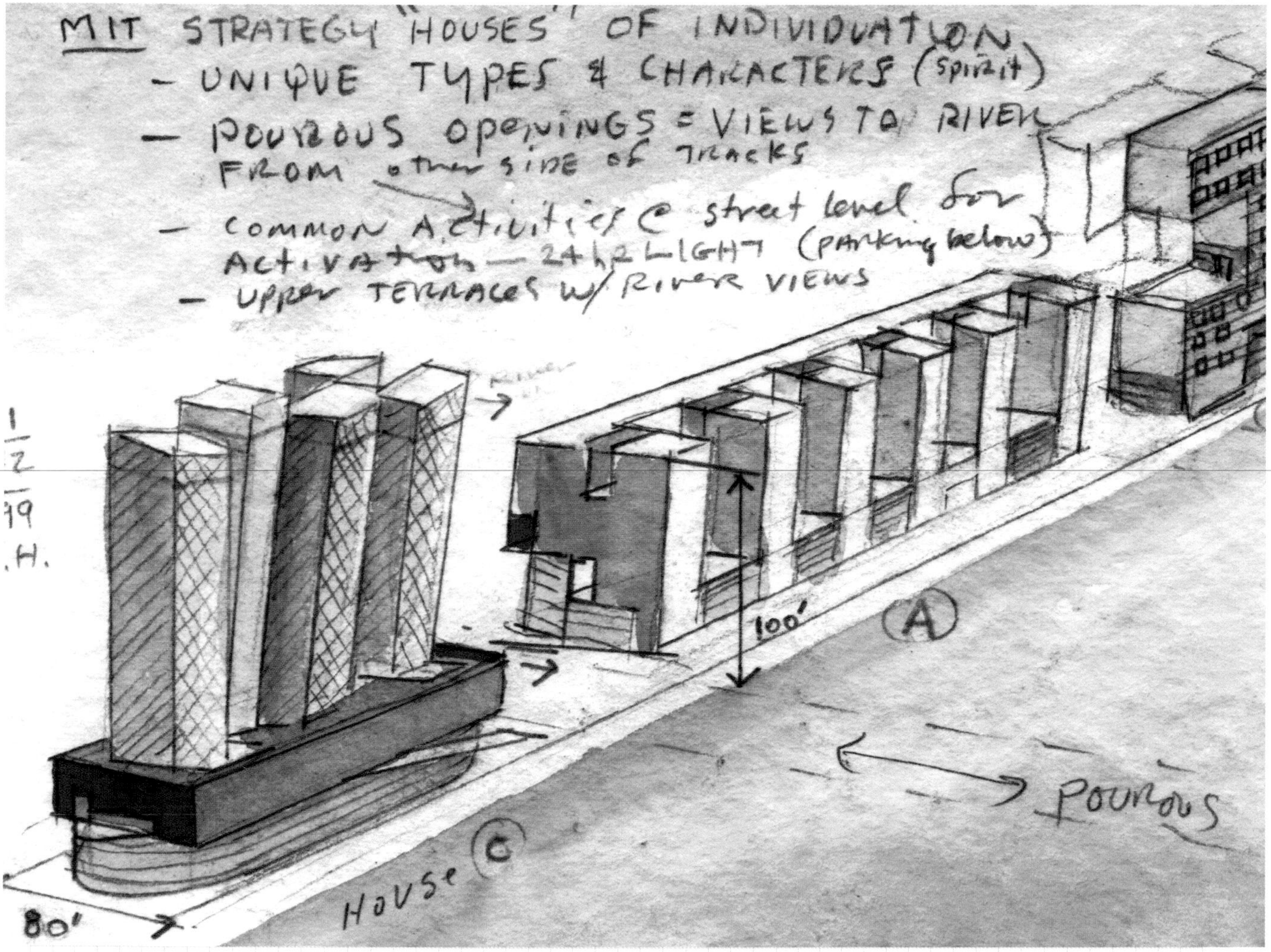
MIT STRATEGY "HOUSES" OF INDIVIDUATION
- UNIQUE TYPES & CHARACTERS (spirit)
- POUROUS OPENINGS = VIEWS TO RIVER FROM other side of TRACKS
- COMMON ACTIVITIES @ street level for ACTIVATION — 24 hr LIGHT (parking below)
- UPPER TERRACES w/ RIVER VIEWS
100'
A
POUROUS
HOUSE C
80'

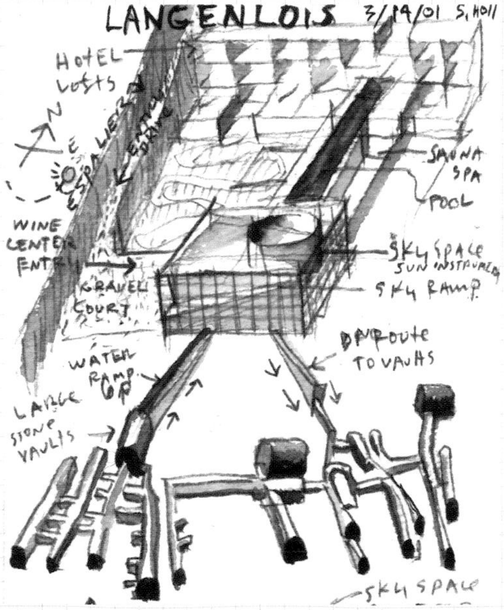
LANGENLOIS 3/19/01 S. HOLL
HOTEL LOFTS
N
SAUNA
SPA
POOL
WINE CENTER ENTRY
SKY SPACE
SUN INSTRUMENT
SKY RAMP
GRAVEL COURT
DRY ROUTE TO VAULTS
WATER RAMP UP
LARGE STONE VAULTS
SKY SPACE

3 TYPES OF LIGHT GATHERING:
① Reflected indirect
② Direct
③ THRU WATER LENSE
WATER
FUTURE ADDITION
WATER SOUNDS @ DROPS IN SECTION
Public Fountain EDGE
VIEWS OUT TO SCULPTURE
WATER RECIR... TO TOP PO... from HE...
GLASS LENSES (ICE) into The LANDSCAPE OF WATER GARDENS
Museum Shop
Public PLAZA
PARKING Below
Problem
CONE OF VISION
GALLERY OF ROOMS:
BASIC PLAN OF GALLERIES
Below = 3 circulation potent...
NELSON ATKINS ADDITION: A VISION OF LENSES IN THE GARDEN FOUNTAINS
(KANSAS CITY'S FOUNTAINS SURPASS ROME)

/ MIKE ROBERTS

The earliest journal of any kind painter Mike Roberts can recall keeping is the receipt stubs held together by metal rings that he had for his childhood paper route. He still has one of these, but most of his other early journals—small, leather-bound lab books given to him by his engineer father and early painting sketchbooks—are gone, thrown away. "They felt like a nuisance at some point," Roberts sighs with regret. "What I wouldn't give for them now."

Roberts has made up for their loss by keeping a series of notebooks and journals, which he now binds himself. There are the "Walking Books" for doodles and ideas, which he keeps in the chest pocket of his signature bib overalls. Along with his wife and daughters, all artists, he keeps journals during family vacations. The miniature books are filled with receipts, mileage records, and at least one dead fly. And then there is the large, ledger-like tome that sits on the desk of his studio. He started the "Studio Log" in 1979 to note the day's events. "It has pretty basic information," he says. "*Made a frame. Started to gesso.* It keeps you moving. I can look at it and see, 'Well, Mike, you didn't work for two days, you'd better do something!'"

For more than a year, however, the Studio Log has been largely ignored, overshadowed by slender books corresponding to a single painting. Roberts adopted the new journals after the death of his older brother George, a printmaker who taught Roberts how to paint. After George's death from cancer in 2001, the task of cleaning out his studio fell to Roberts. "I [found] preparatory drawings that he'd done for a final print—five to seven of them per print," he remembers with awe. "And sketchbooks I'd never seen before. I had no idea he put such effort into a piece."

Affected by his brother's meticulous habits, Roberts decided to commence his own painting journals. Typically he had done a few thumbnails and sketches and then put it all down on the canvas to make adjustments as he went. Inspired by George, he now charts a painting from beginning to end.

Many of his paintings are both allegorical and personal, documenting family and friends. They're also mischievous. The first one to evolve from a journal was no different. "Pizza, Death and Painting" is an exploration of Roberts's attempt to go on the Atkins diet. The painting includes two images of Roberts, one in the guise of a skeletal pizza-delivery man. Trailing behind him is Frida Kahlo, of whom he pondered in the journal, "Frida suffered too. Why not put Frida in the painting?"

Roberts admits that the journals do not greatly affect his painting methods—at most he is more organized now. The greatest reward comes simply from making something different. "If you're not thinking of new things, you're stagnant," Roberts muses. "When you're a kid, you're excited, pulling new things off the shelf, trying something different. You still want that feeling when you're fifty-six. And the work is what gives it to you."

George would no doubt agree.

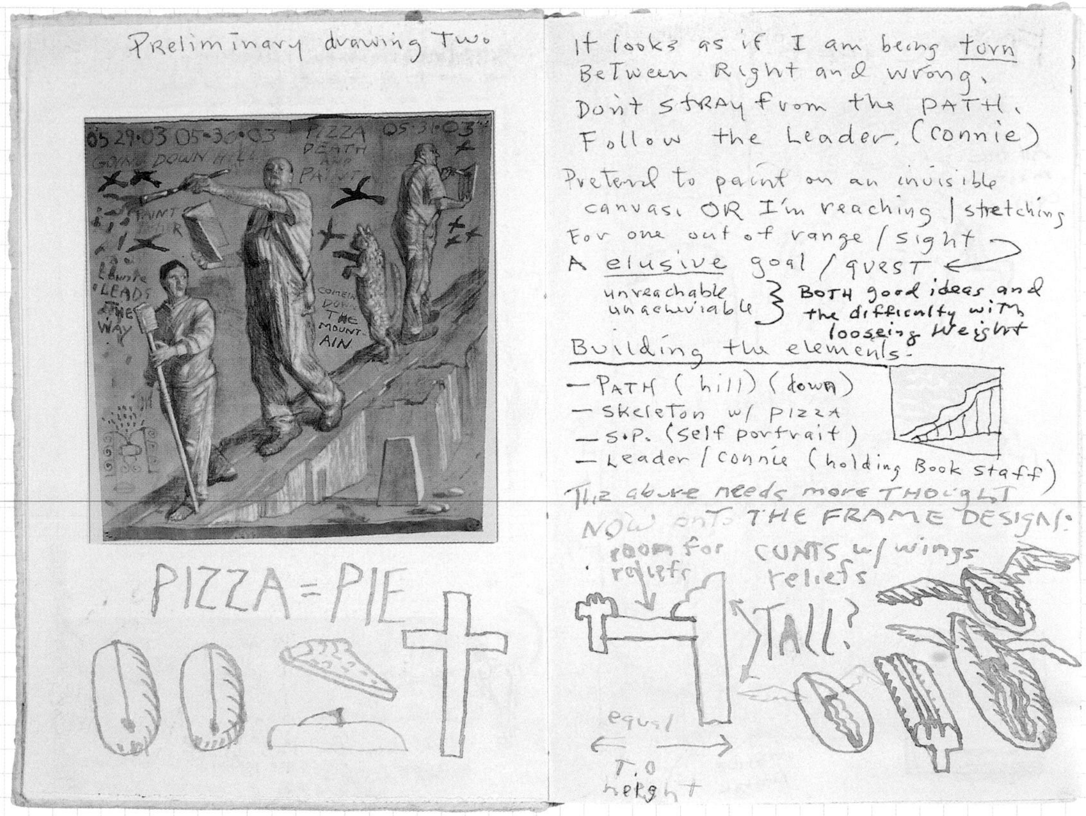
Preliminary drawing Two
05·29·03 05·30·03 PIZZA DEATH AND PAINTING 05·31·03
GOING DOWN HILL
COMING DOWN THE MOUNTAIN
PIZZA = PIE
It looks as if I am being torn
Between Right and wrong.
Don't stray from the PATH.
Follow the Leader. (connie)
Pretend to paint on an invisible
canvas. OR I'm reaching / stretching
For one out of range / sight
A elusive goal / QUEST
unreachable
unachievable
BOTH good ideas and the difficulty with loosing Weight
Building the elements -
— PATH (hill) (down)
— Skeleton w/ PIZZA
— S.P. (self portrait)
— Leader / connie (holding Book staff)
The above needs more THOUGHT
NOW onto THE FRAME DESIGN:
room for reliefs
CUNTS w/ wings reliefs
TALL?
equal
T.O height

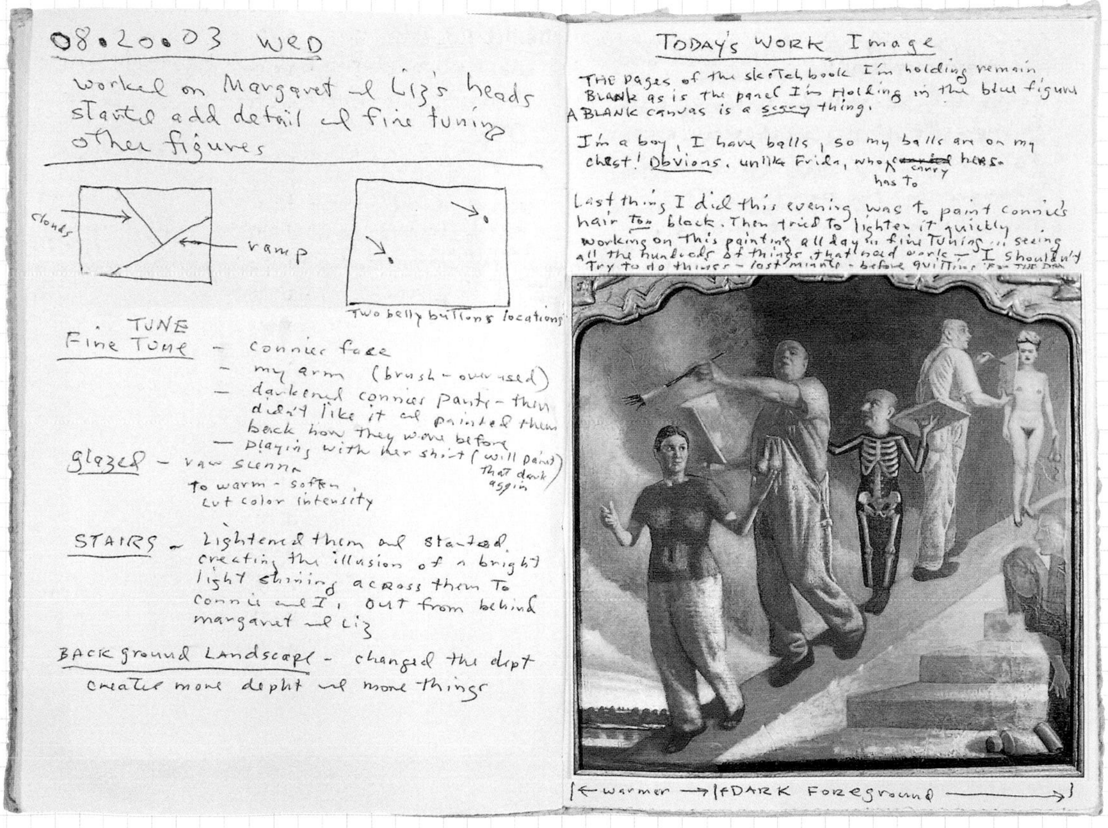
08·20·03 WED
worked on Margaret and Liz's heads
started add detail and fine tuning
other figures
clouds
ramp
Two belly buttons locations
TUNE
Fine Tume – connie's face
– my arm (brush – over used)
– darkened connie's pants – then didn't like it and painted them back how they were before
– playing with her shirt (will paint that dark again)
glazed – raw sienna
To warm – soften,
cut color intensity
STAIRS – Lightened them and started creating the illusion of a bright light shining across them To connie and I, out from behind margaret and Liz
BACKground Landscape – changed the dept
create more depht and more things
TODAY's WORK Image
THE pages of the sketchbook I'm holding remain
BLANK as is the panel I'm Holding in the blue figure
A BLANK canvas is a scary thing.
I'm a boy, I have balls, so my balls are on my
chest! Obvious. unlike Frida, who has to carry hers.
Last thing I did this evening was to paint connie's
hair too black. Then tried to lighten it quickly
working on this painting all day in fine Tuning ... seeing
all the hundreds of things that need work — I shouldn't
Try to do things – last minute – before quitting for the day
|← warmer →|← DARK Foreground →|

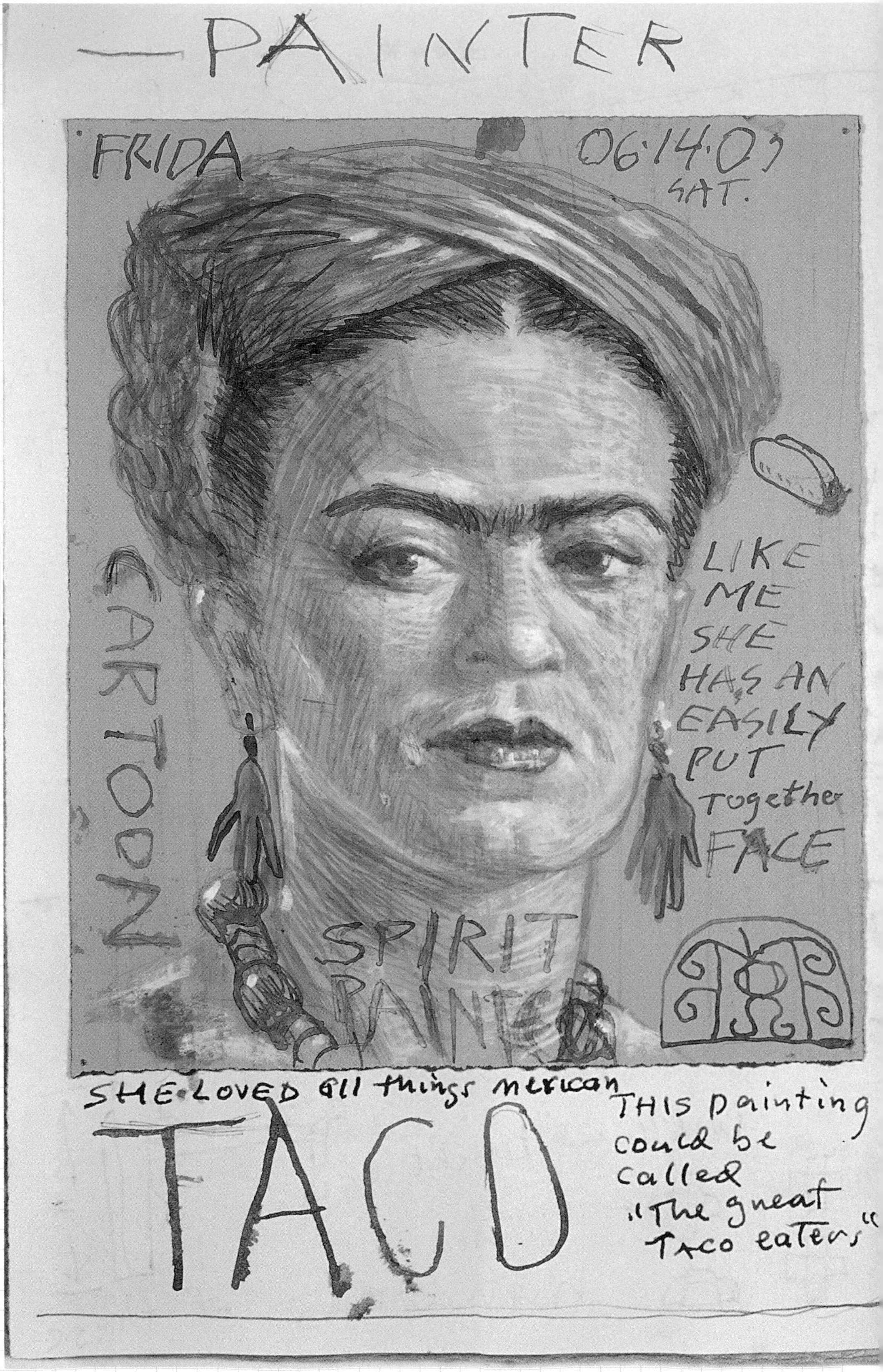
—PAINTER
FRIDA
06·14·03
SAT.
CARTOON
LIKE ME SHE HAS AN EASILY PUT together FACE
SPIRIT PAINT
SHE LOVED all things mexican
TACO
THIS painting could be called "The great Taco eaters"

PAINTER
06.12.03
HOW I SEE MY-SELF
SELF PORTRAIT - AT THE AGE OF 55
I LOVE MEXICAN FOOD
EATERS

/ JULIE BAUGNET

As a painter, Julie Baugnet is inclined to pay careful attention to the details of her garden. Reading Aldo Leopold's conservationist classic *A Sand County Almanac* inspired her to look beyond the artist's domain of color and textures to the physical phenomena in her backyard oasis. Compelled by Leopold's practice of phenology—the study of the chronological occurrence of natural events, such as bird migrations and flower blooming, and the comparison of dates of occurrence from year to year—she has noted and tracked her natural space in a more formal manner.

Baugnet has kept a variety of journals since attending art school in the 1970s, including one in which she drew only coffee cups. Currently she maintains two kinds of journal: one in which she plans paintings and the other a garden journal. She started it in 1997, the year she and her husband, landscape designer Carter Clapsadle, bought their home in St. Paul, Minnesota. The couple saw potential in the homely bungalow and quickly turned both the interior and yard into their living laboratory.

Baugnet's journal moves slowly, at a garden's pace. She averages about ten entries a season, documenting the life of the garden, including Leopold-like observations of the first crocuses and birds of the season, dinner parties, and garden visitors.

Although Baugnet sometimes adds one of Clapsadle's spontaneous sketches—usually plans and whims for the future—most of the documentation is hers. She keeps pockets in the journal for photographs and watercolors, which can be added at a later time. She has enjoyed, for instance, creating a photo-based sequence showing the garden's evolution from a ho-hum suburban plot into a celebration of prairie grasses.

While Baugnet's record is about close examination of a familiar space, its essential purpose is as a creative tool in the never-ending adaptation of that space. Being able to see when the tulips came up and the color of the crocuses in a certain section of the garden is indispensable information when trying to plan the spring planting during the dark winter months. Gardening in Minnesota, after all, takes faith. And a journal.

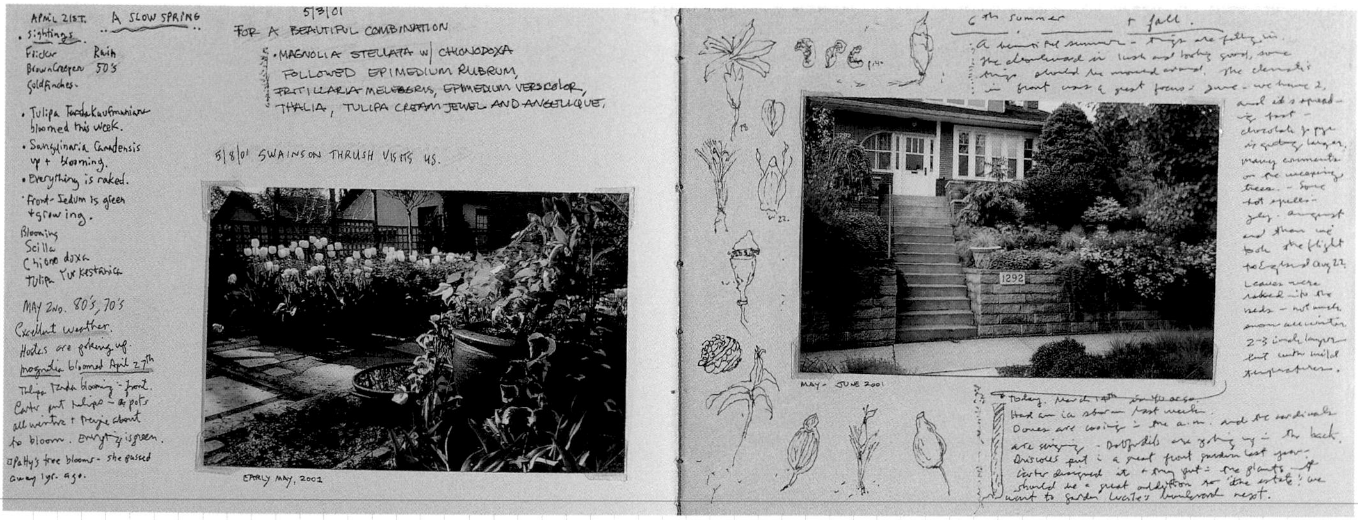
APRIL 21ST. A SLOW SPRING
5/3/01
FOR A BEAUTIFUL COMBINATION
MAGNOLIA STELLATA W/ CHIONODOXA
FOLLOWED EPIMEDIUM RUBRUM,
FRITILLARIA MELEAGRIS, EPIMEDIUM VERSICOLOR,
THALIA, TULIPA CREAM JEWEL AND ANGELIQUE.
5/8/01 SWAINSON THRUSH VISITS US.
EARLY MAY, 2001
6th summer + fall.
MAY - JUNE 2001
1292

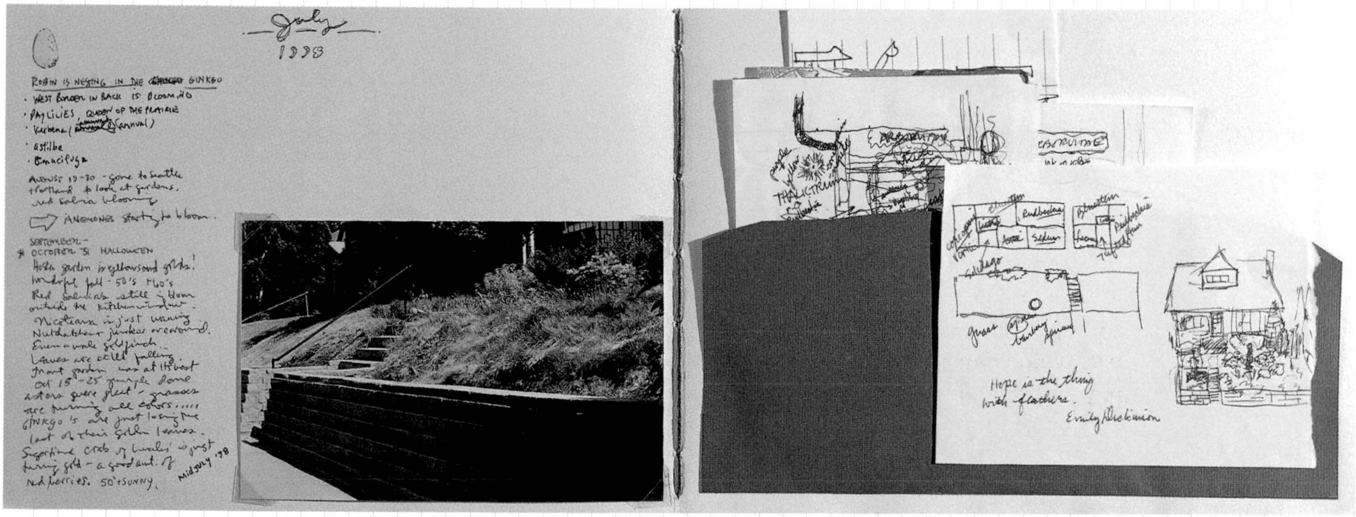
July
1998
ROBIN IS NESTING IN THE GINKGO
Hope is the thing
with feathers.
Emily Dickinson

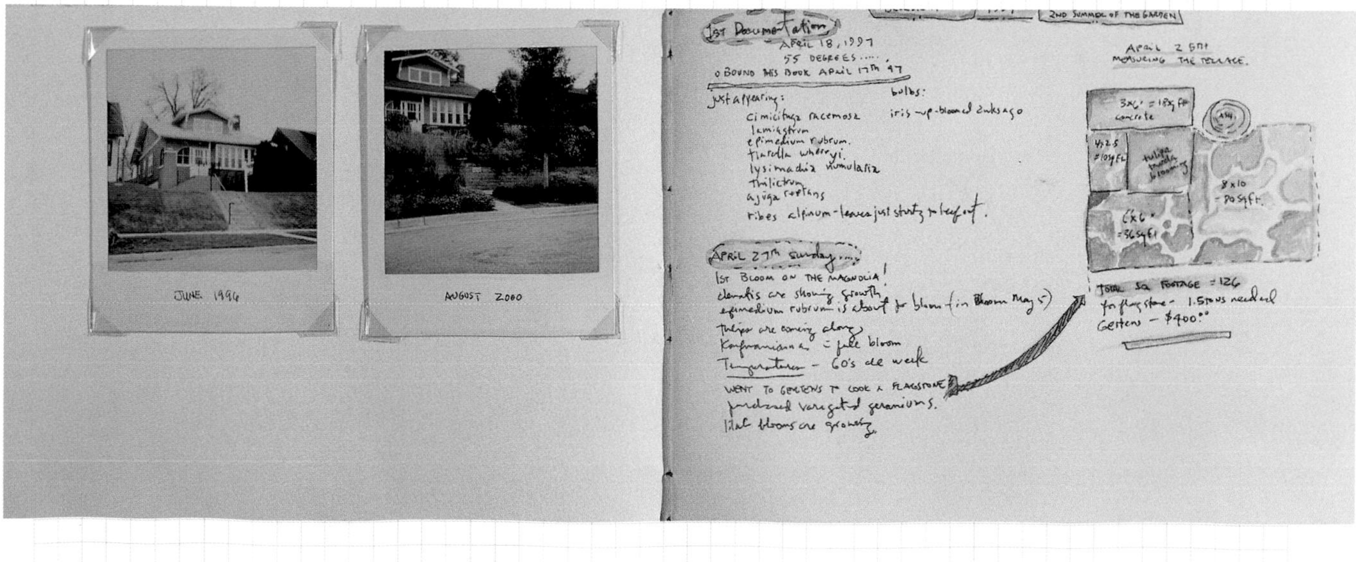
JUNE 1996
AUGUST 2000
1ST Documentation
APRIL 18, 1997
55 DEGREES.....
2ND SUMMER OF THE GARDEN
APRIL 27TH sunday
1ST BLOOM ON THE MAGNOLIA!
TOTAL SQ FOOTAGE = 126

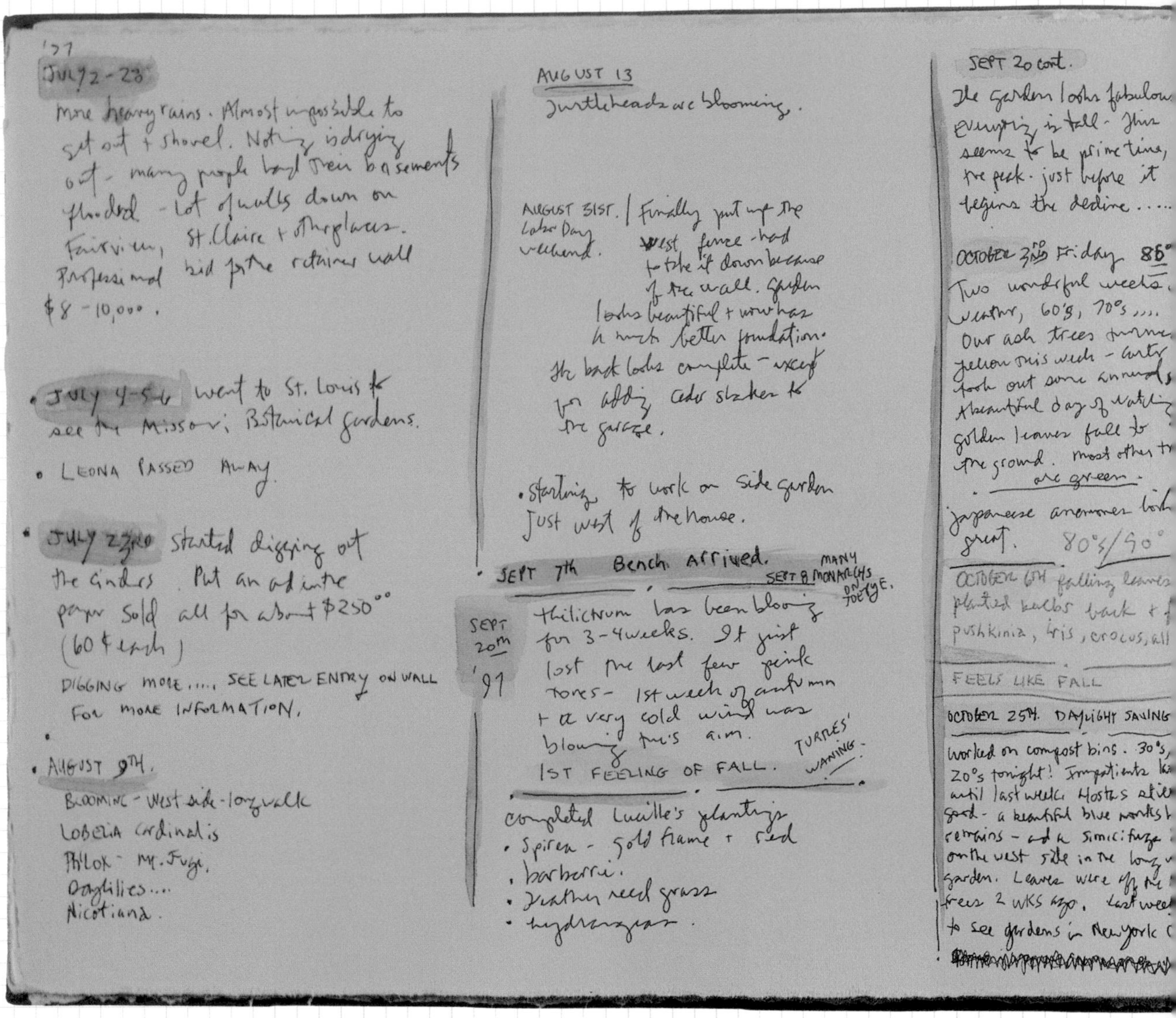

'97
JULY 2-28
More heavy rains. Almost impossible to get out + shovel. Nothing is drying out - many people had their basements flooded - lot of walls down on Fairview, St. Claire + other places. Professional bid for the retainer wall $8-10,000.

• JULY 4-5-6 went to St. Louis to see the Missouri Botanical gardens.

• LEONA PASSED AWAY.

• JULY 23RD Started digging out the cinders. Put an ad in the paper sold all for about $250^{00} (60¢ each)
DIGGING MORE..... SEE LATER ENTRY ON WALL FOR MORE INFORMATION.

• AUGUST 9TH.
BLOOMING - West side - long walk
LOBELIA cardinalis
Phlox - Mt. Fuji.
Daylilies....
Nicotiana.

AUGUST 13
Turtleheads are blooming.

AUGUST 31ST. Labor Day weekend. | Finally put up the west fence - had to take it down because of the wall. Garden looks beautiful + now has a much better foundation. The back looks complete - except for adding cedar stakes to the garage.

• Starting to work on side garden just west of the house.

• SEPT 7th Bench Arrived. SEPT 8 MANY MONARCHS ON JOE PYE.

SEPT 20th '97 Thalictrum has been blooming for 3-4 weeks. It just lost the last few pink tones - 1st week of autumn + a very cold wind was blowing this a.m.
1ST FEELING OF FALL. TURTLES' WANING.

Completed Lucille's plantings
• Spirea - gold flame + red
• barberries.
• feather reed grass
• hydrangeas.

SEPT 20 cont.
The garden looks fabulous. Everything is tall - This seems to be prime time, the peak - just before it begins the decline.....

OCTOBER 3RD Friday 85°
Two wonderful weeks. weather, 60's, 70's.... Our ash trees turned yellow this week - Curtis took out some annuals. A beautiful day of watching golden leaves fall to the ground. most other trees are green.

Japanese anemones look great. 80's/90's

OCTOBER 6TH falling leaves planted bulbs back + ... pushkinia, iris, crocus, all...

FEELS LIKE FALL

OCTOBER 25TH. DAYLIGHT SAVING...
Worked on compost bins. 30's, 20's tonight! Impatiens ... until last week. Hostas still good - a beautiful blue monkshood remains - and a Simicifuga ... on the west side in the long ... garden. Leaves were off the trees 2 WKS ago. Last week ... to see gardens in New York C...

NOVEMBER 2. SUNDAY. '98
Woke up to light snow.
The garden looks great.
Blue monks hood is still in bloom.

November 13th. THURSDAY.
1st substantial snowfall..

JAN 9th – 1998
not much snow yet this winter – mild – 30's.... just a half inch of whiteness

February 15th
40's
Robins + morning doves are back!
melting, light rain.

FEBRUARY 2YTH
SUPPOSEDLY IT IS AN EL NIÑO WINTER – HARSH RAINS ON ALL COASTS, FLORIDA, CALIFORNIA, + IN THE EAST. THAT HAS MEANT very mild TEMPERATURES FOR THE MIDWEST. WE HAD BELOW ZERO FOR ONLY 1WK, THEN ITS BEEN IN THE 20'S + 30'S ALL JAN + FEB. CARDINALS ARE CALLING. LIGHT AT 6:40AM.

FEB 24, cont. 50'S / 40'S '98
WE CHECKED FOR CROCUS+SILA AND THEY'RE ALL WELL ABOVE GROUND BUT STILL UNDER THE BEAUTIFUL BROWN BED OF LEAVES SO GENEROUSLY GIVEN TO US BY THE SILVER MAPLE.

'97/'98

Next Entry ⇒ 4 PAGES
GO TO SPRING '98.

PHENOLOGY
phenological journal
1. The branch of science dealing with the relations between climate + periodic biological phenomena...
[climate as it relates to the plants, birds etc].

JULIE BAUGNET

/ ROBERT PARKEHARRISON

Robert ParkeHarrison's photographs are eerie narratives of life in a world slightly like ours but also entirely different. A single character—ParkeHarrison himself, dressed always in a simple dark suit and white shirt—perches on a ladder with giant feathery wings attached to his arms or sews a gaping piece of earth with a giant needle. With their seemingly mocha-splattered glaze and dim lighting, the photographs can be mistaken for sepias of an earlier era; but their environmental storylines are utterly current.

For ParkeHarrison, who creates the behemoth photographs (they are as large as four by five feet) with his wife Shana, his journals are one of the most important tools in their making. The books are circular in nature, representing all stages of a photograph's making, from initial spark to printing to the ceremonial cleaning of the studio.

The couple completes about ten photographs over the course of a year, each image adding to their fifteen-year-long visual narrative. At the beginning of each series, ParkeHarrison says, "there's always a very uncomfortable feeling of not knowing where you're going." He pulls out past journals so that he and Shana can review what they have done in the past. "It's reassuring to see how we were able to start at point A and progress to a final series of work."

The source images ParkeHarrison collects and pastes into the journals—everything from old photographs collected on library visits (he often roams the stacks, pulling down random books like a game of exquisite corpse) to advertisements—provide inspiration in the early stages. The images, photocopied and pasted into the journal, share space with his writing. Though he says he has a difficult time with language, the writing helps him to find the center of a piece. In pages of penciled scrawl, he asks questions and offers possible answers.

An image begins to take shape in his mind, almost entirely as a result of the seeking process in his journal, allowing him to go into the field to take Polaroid test shots of possible locations. Props, such as a giant typewriter ball, are assembled next. Once a final version of the image comes into focus, it informs the progress of other images in the working series.

ParkeHarrison is unabashedly "obsessive" about his journal keeping. He has nearly forty books and even admits to writing in journals—smaller ones he calls the "satellite journals"—while driving. As compared with his wife's creative style, which he considers to be focused and precise (she keeps no journal), ParkeHarrison describes himself as scattered. "I need to work through something with my hands, whether on the page or in the studio. I run around going, 'I don't know what's going on!' That's when writing helps me to snap into place," he explains, laughing at his mental disarray.

The payoff is a rich compilation of ideas, the majority of which never get pursued to finality. Like many artists, he fears losing his creative drive. The journals are an ounce of prevention against that: "They're priceless to me because they contain so many ideas that were never pursued. It's very therapeutic to go back and read how my thoughts developed over time." Developed, not unlike a photograph.

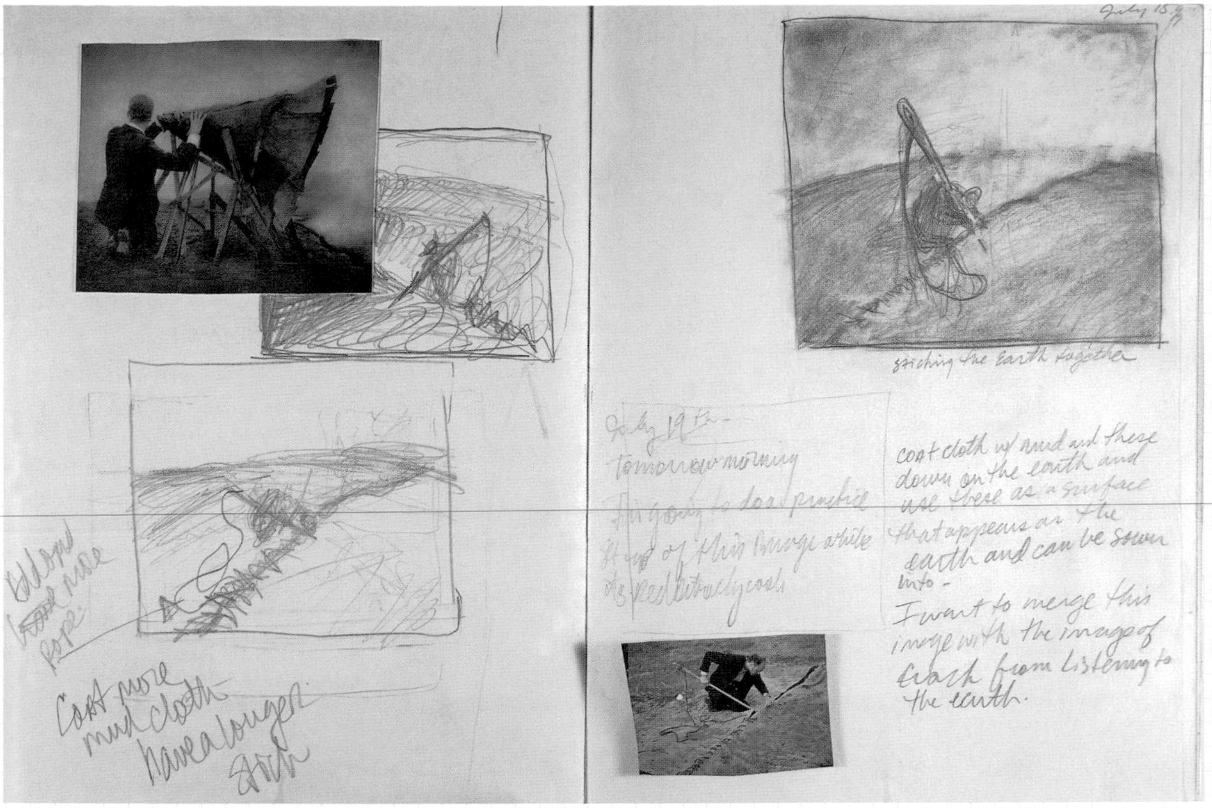
stiching the Earth together
coat cloth w/ mud and these
down on the earth and
use these as a surface
that appears as the
earth and can be sewn
into -
I want to merge this
image with the image of
crack from Listening to
the earth.
Coat more
mud cloth
have a longer

Catapult a Ball of Junk - or myself into space -
June 5
I want this transfusion image, to be very
Frankenstein - taking from life and into another
one - Very Frightening -

June 7th
make trees taller and thicker
Add more trees
use white powder
white sheet wider and farther back
extend sheet longer to show in foreground

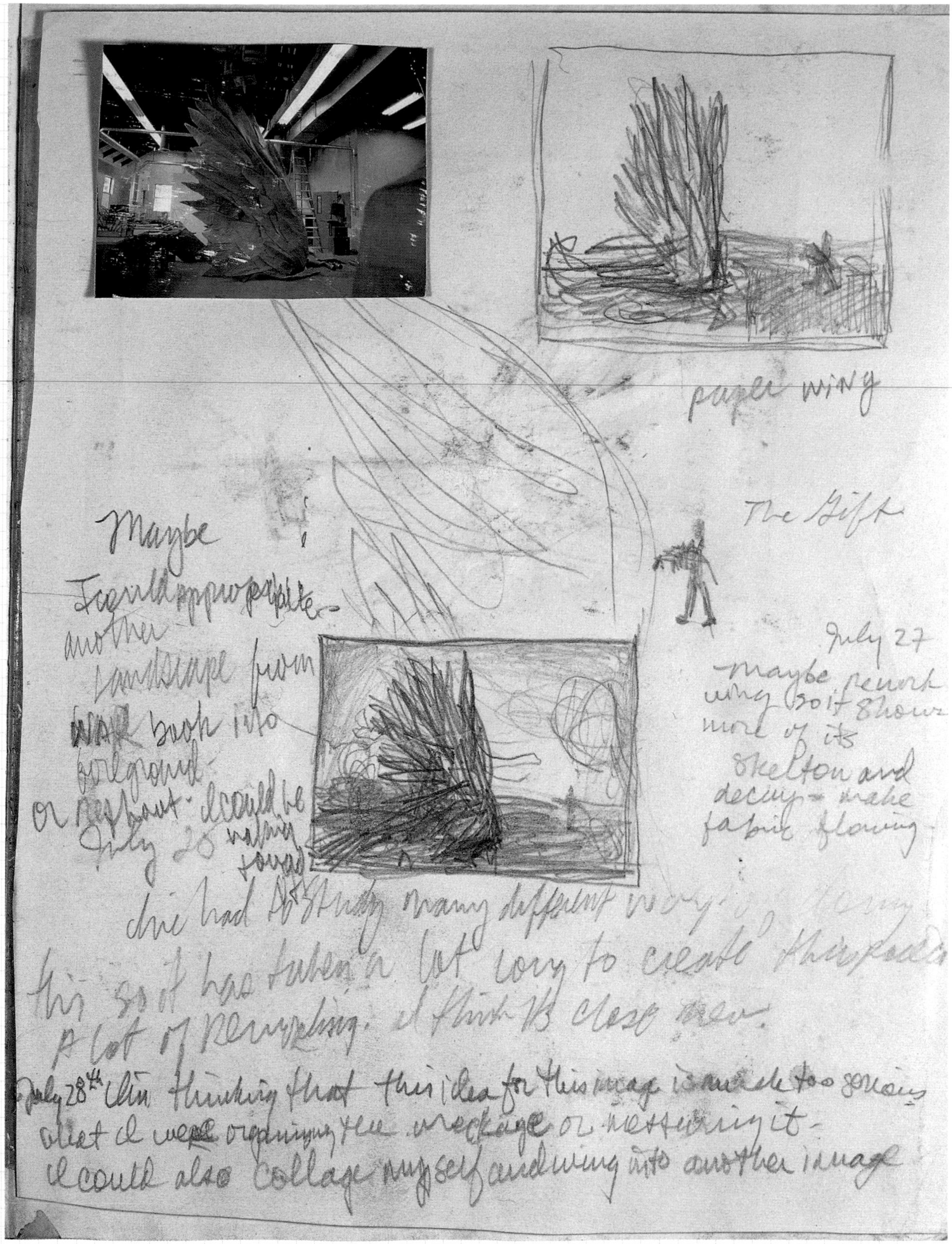
paper wing
The Gift
Maybe
another
landscape from
back into
foreground
July 20
July 27
maybe rework
wing so it shows
more of its
skelton and
decay - make
fabric flowing
July 28th I'm thinking that this idea for this image is much too serious
I could also collage myself and wing into another image

/ THOMAS OSLUND

"It's a one-stop shop," landscape architect Thomas Oslund says of the black-bound blank books he has been carrying with him since he was an undergraduate. At first the books were more about replicating others' ideas. Now they reflect the cycle of his varied projects, which include corporate gardens, memorials, golf courses, and vineyards. Drawings for a specific site give way to meeting notes and questions jotted during phone calls. There are sketches from his travels and occasional drawings by his children. He jokes that they reflect his ADD tendencies: "I'm a huge multitasker."

Although it has become something of a lost art in architecture, superceded by computers and the rise of architectural software, Oslund is dedicated to drawing. One of his first bosses was an architect who believed that working drawings should be able to hold their own against any other art. When you work solely on the computer, Oslund says, you are missing a crucial physical connection to the creative process: "The computer screen removes you from the process. You're not physically touching something, your hand isn't moving across the paper. There's a tactileness that's absolutely essential to the making of something."

Oslund's inspirations are formidable. In college he loved going to Harvard's rare-book library to look at the sketchbooks of the masters, such as Le Corbusier or Frederick Law Olmsted. Later, when he won the Rome Prize and spent a year in Italy, he had the opportunity to see several of da Vinci's codices. Each of these works provided windows into the creative process: "Looking at journals is a lot different than looking at a finished drawing. You start to see and almost understand how the ideas evolved into a final product."

Oslund keeps his process transparent for clients and others involved on a project to see. He has a keen awareness of the allure of creativity and says that, probably because of our reliance on technology and most people's distance from their own artistic talents, drawing is a bit magical. "I sit down and draw in front of my clients," he says, "and they're often very curious about it. It's something of a mystical talent."

He feeds his creativity by traveling and returning to the original purpose of his journals: to record inspiration. In Glacier National Park, he did a watercolor of a mountain landscape. His daughter Ingrid, now twelve, felt it was not complete and added a small skier to one of the slopes. On a trip to Norway he drew a carved mortise-and-tendon church whose style predates the Vikings. Fondly recalling the superb craftsmanship, he says, "I just needed to remember that one."

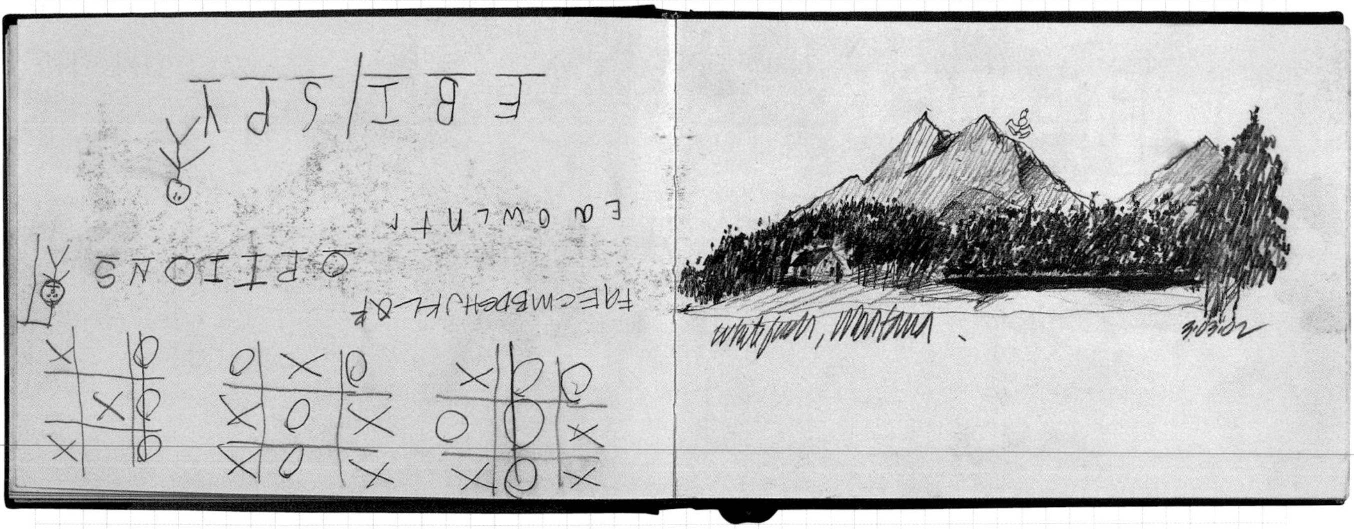
whitefish, montana

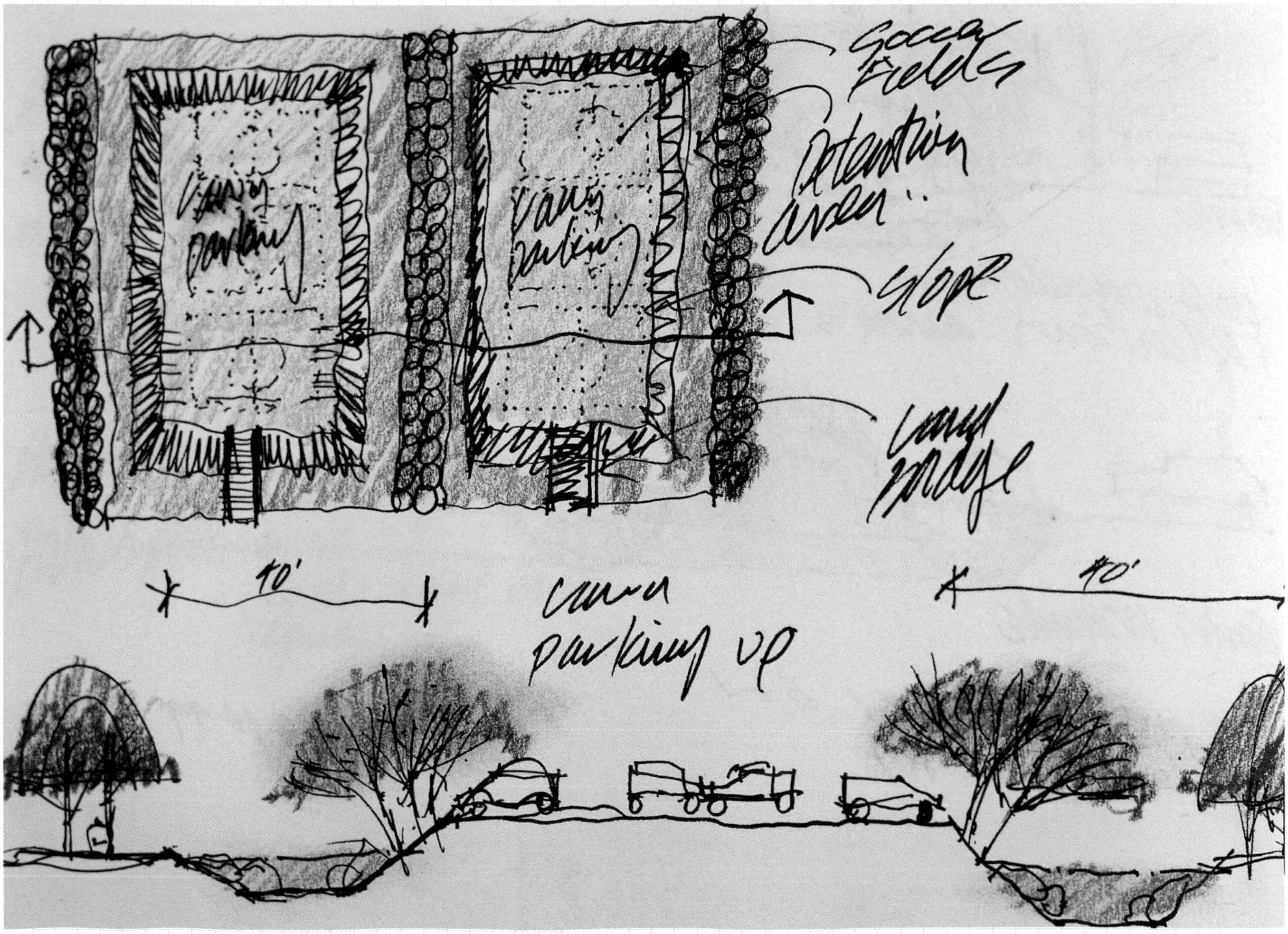
Soccer Fields
Detention area..
slope
40'
40'

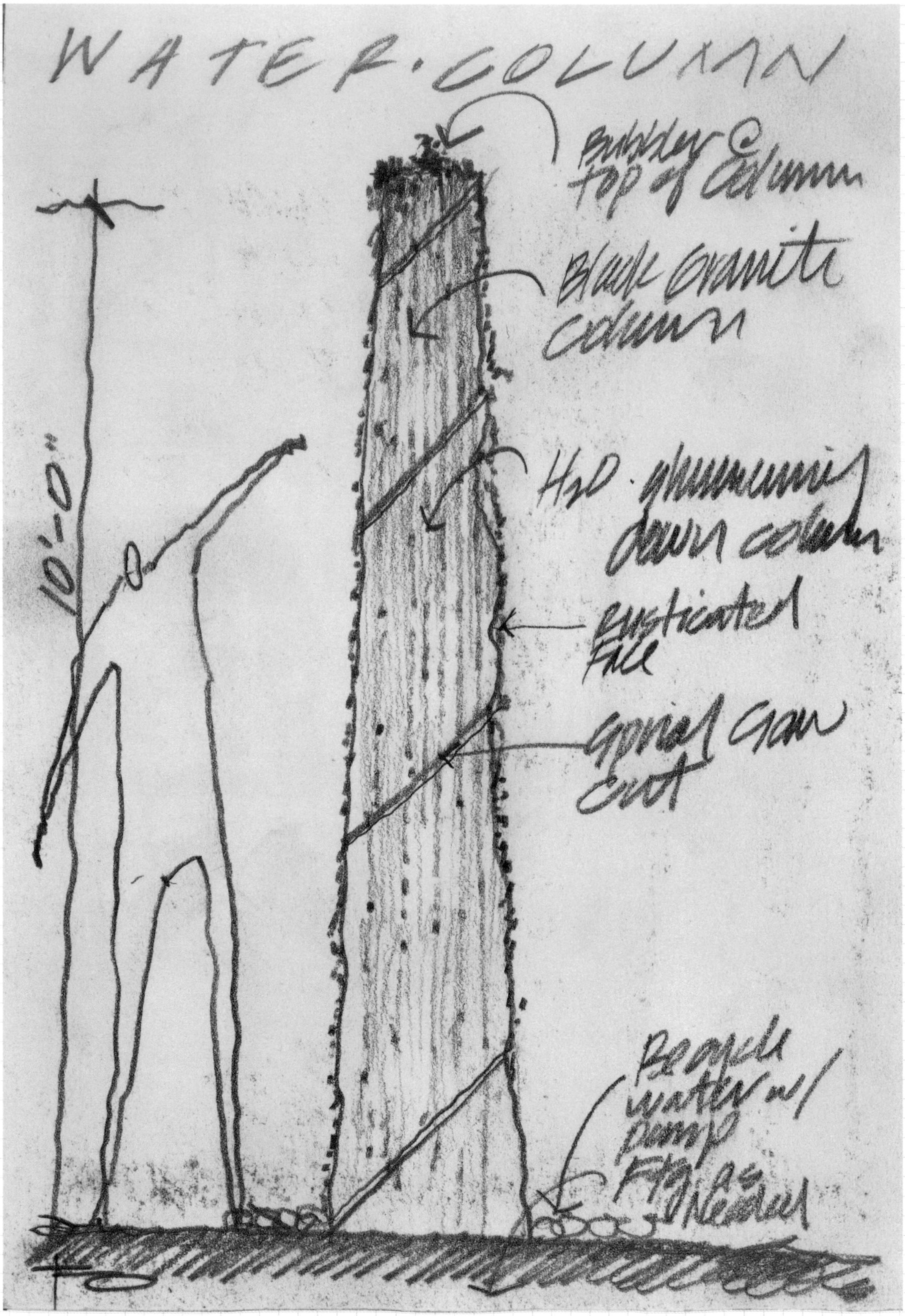
WATER·COLUMN
Bubbler @ top of column
Black Granite column
H2O
Rusticated Face
10'-0"

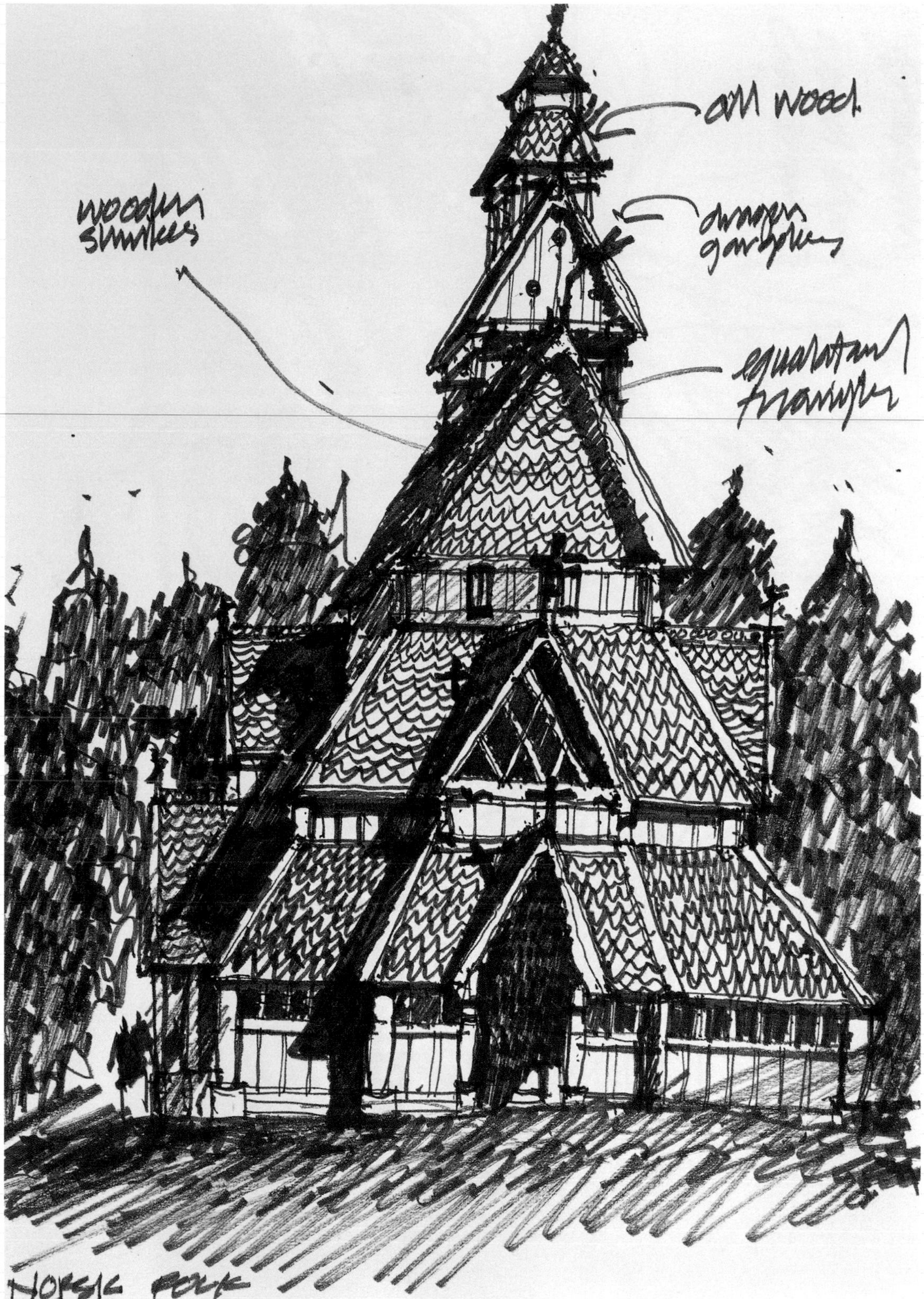
all wood.
wooden shingles
dragon gargoyles
equilateral triangles
Norsk Folk museum

/ DENYSE SCHMIDT

Descending from a long tradition of quilt making, Denyse Schmidt's creations have a quirky, decidedly contemporary spin without even a hint of hobby-store saccharine. Her journal pages are dotted with tiny renderings of the quilts, roughhewn sketches in colored pencil. Filled with saturated hues, one book has the deep colors of a New England fall: asters, cranberries, and pine. Another is summery and light with the colors of sherbet, lemonade, and babies' gingham blankets. Other pages comprise black-and-white sketches in which Schmidt works out the shapes of her quilts or drafts the prose she sometimes stitches into the pieces, such as "Tomorrow is Another Day."

The quilts first came to Schmidt as telephone doodles while she was working as a graphic designer: circles and squares repeated in a bold, graphic style. Gradually, they made their way from scrap paper into her journals. As the idea for a business devoted to quilt making emerged, the journals blossomed.

Between graphic brainstorms, Schmidt sticks in the stuff of life: musings over relationships, last-minute accounting, and taped-in quotes from tea bags. "Must stop with the nail biting," she admonishes herself on one occasion. It is this vulnerable, quirky side of Schmidt that comes through in the quilts. They marry creature comfort and high-art craftsmanship at a time when most textiles have a synthetic, Made-in-Sri-Lanka feel.

Schmidt's quilt-related journals were at their fullest when she was in the early stages of starting her business. They brimmed with new ideas and the headaches and challenges of an entrepreneurial undertaking. In recent years she has increasingly used a computer for design, and her journal keeping has declined. The hand-drawn element is still important enough, though, that she'll scan a drawing into the computer. She also pins things on the wall of her studio, so that she can gaze on them while designing, and the board operates as an extension of her journals. "I wish I had the discipline to take everything off it at the end of a season and add them to a journal," she says, a desire echoed by many contributors who rue lost ideas.

Schmidt finds her creative muse in many places, including the worlds of fashion and home décor, nature, and paintings. She likes the random composition of signs and shapes that happen unintentionally, such as on the backs of tractor trailers. Though she fills them more slowly, she still carries a journal with her most of the time—especially on her travels, which provide creative renewal—and has several in various stages of completion around the house. Returning to the personal notes and wanderings that coexist with the fanciful shapes and colors of her textile work, Schmidt says, "There's an emotional life attached to my journals. They're not just about work."

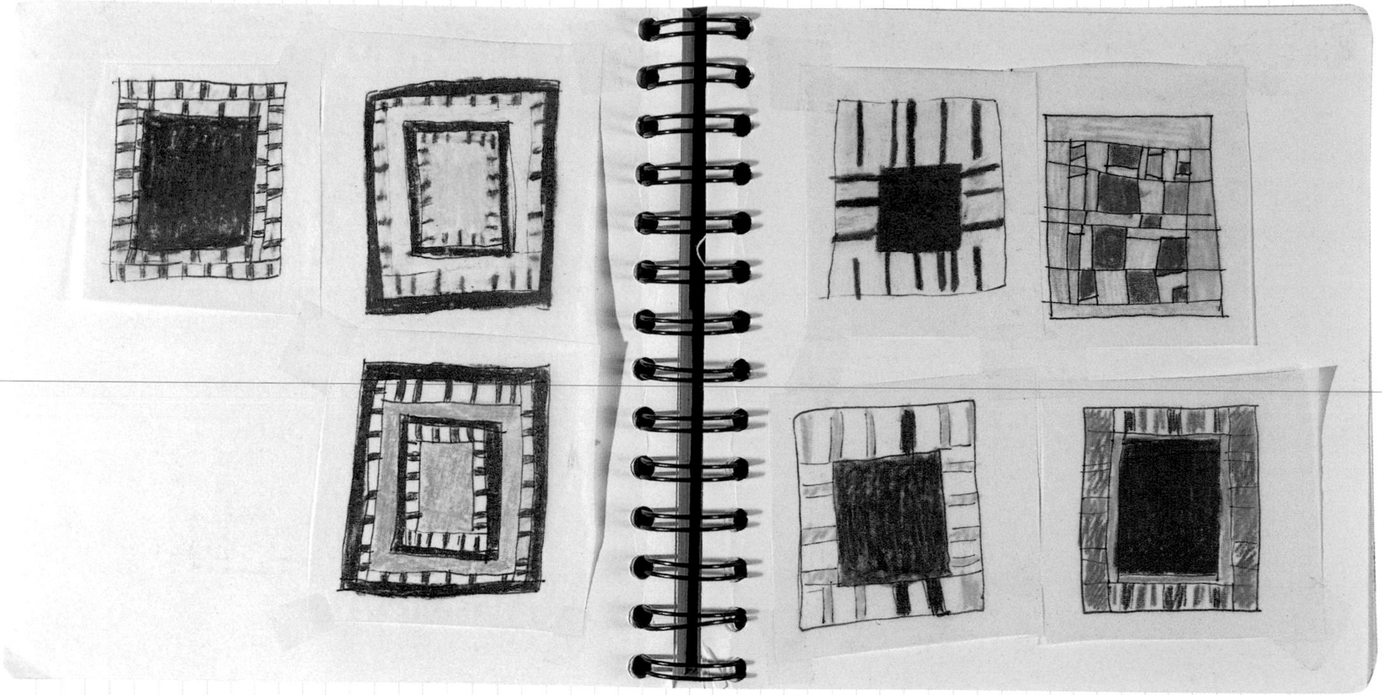

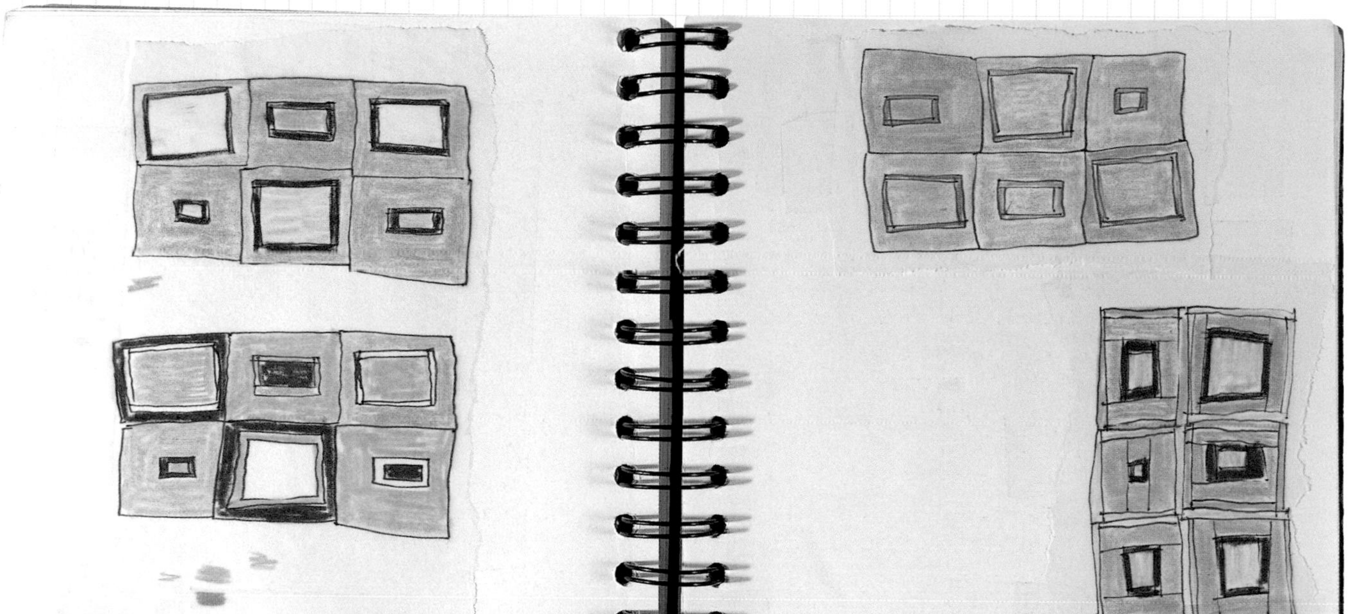

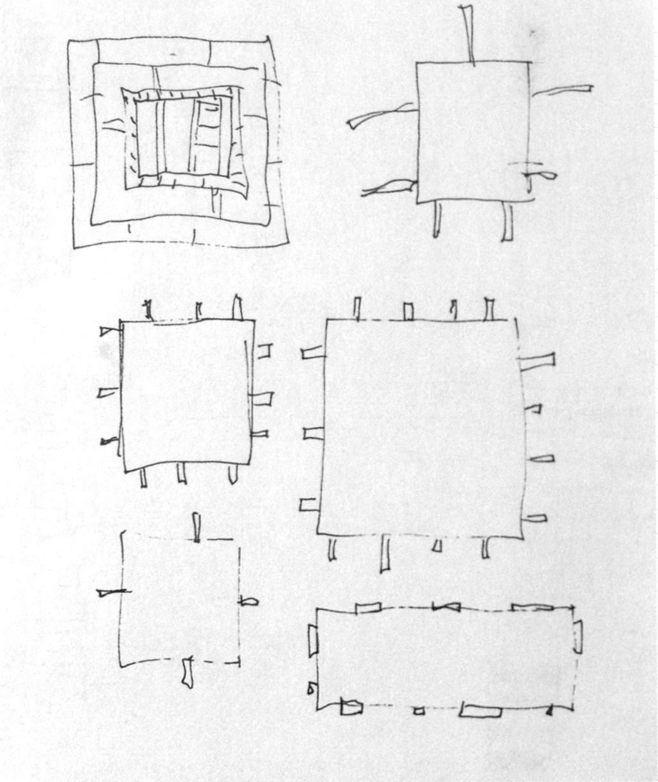

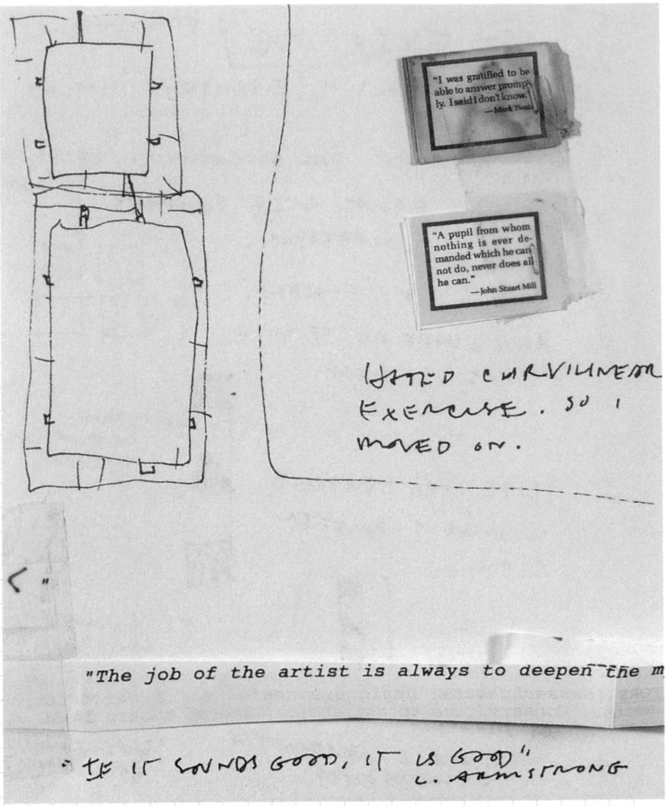
"I was gratified to be able to answer promp ly. I said I don't know." —Mark Twain
"A pupil from whom nothing is ever demanded which he can not do, never does all he can." —John Stuart Mill
HATED CURVILINEAR EXERCISE. SO I MOVED ON.
"The job of the artist is always to deepen the m
"IF IT SOUNDS GOOD, IT IS GOOD" L. ARMSTRONG

WHEEL OF FORTUNE/ PIE IN THE FACE
multi brights

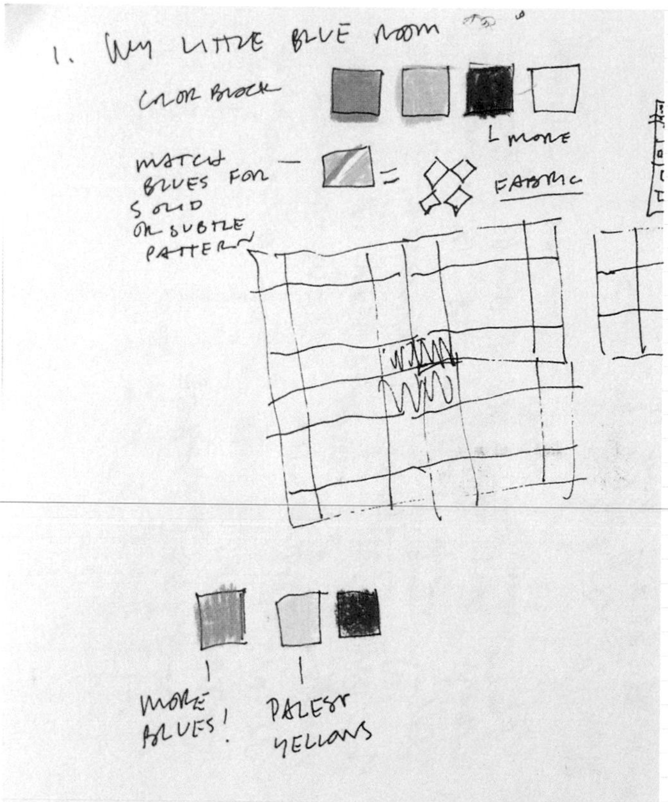
1. MY LITTLE BLUE ROOM
COLOR BLOCK
MORE
MATCH BLUES FOR SOLID OR SUBTLE PATTERN
FABRIC
MORE BLUES!
PALEST YELLOWS

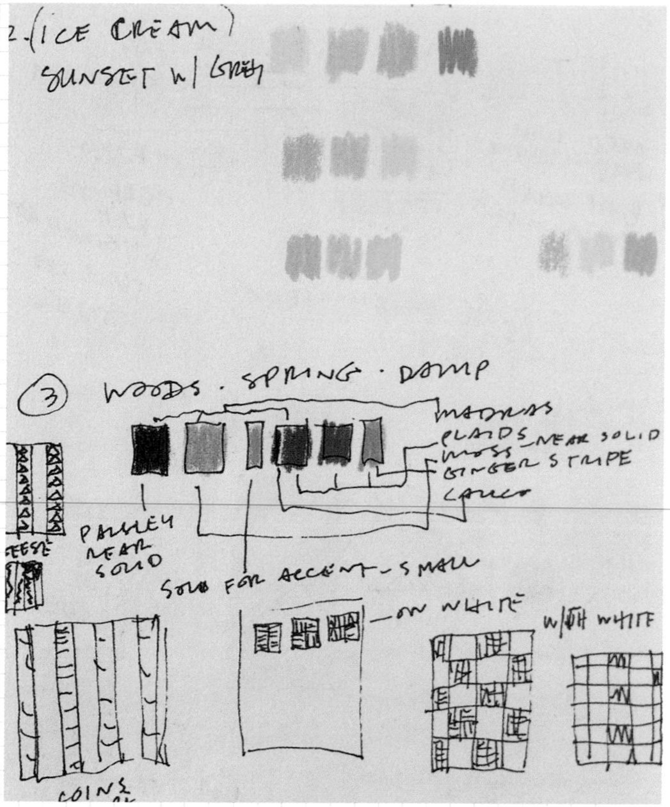
2. (ICE CREAM)
SUNSET W/ GREY
3 WOODS · SPRING · DAMP
MADRAS
PLAIDS
NEAR SOLID
GINGER STRIPE
PAISLEY NEAR SOLID
SOLID FOR ACCENT - SMALL
ON WHITE
WITH WHITE
COINS

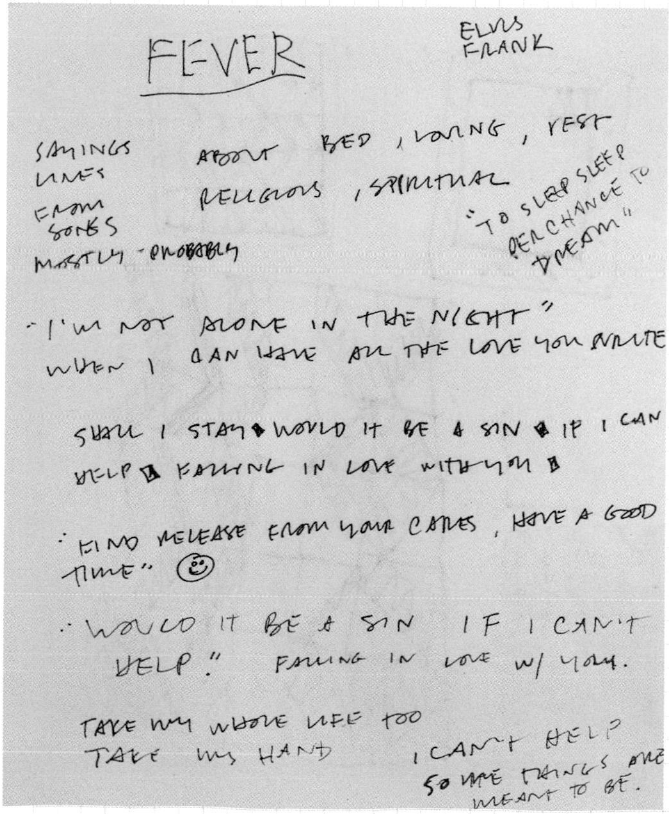
FEVER
ELVIS
FRANK
SAYINGS LINES FROM SONGS
MOSTLY - PROBABLY
ABOUT BED, LOVING, REST
RELIGIOUS, SPIRITUAL
"TO SLEEP SLEEP PERCHANCE TO DREAM"
"I'M NOT ALONE IN THE NIGHT"
WHEN I CAN HAVE ALL THE LOVE YOU WRITE
SHALL I STAY WOULD IT BE A SIN IF I CAN HELP FALLING IN LOVE WITH YOU
"FIND RELEASE FROM YOUR CARES, HAVE A GOOD TIME"
"WOULD IT BE A SIN IF I CAN'T HELP" FALLING IN LOVE W/ YOU.
TAKE MY WHOLE LIFE TOO
TAKE MY HAND
I CAN'T HELP
SOME THINGS ARE MEANT TO BE.

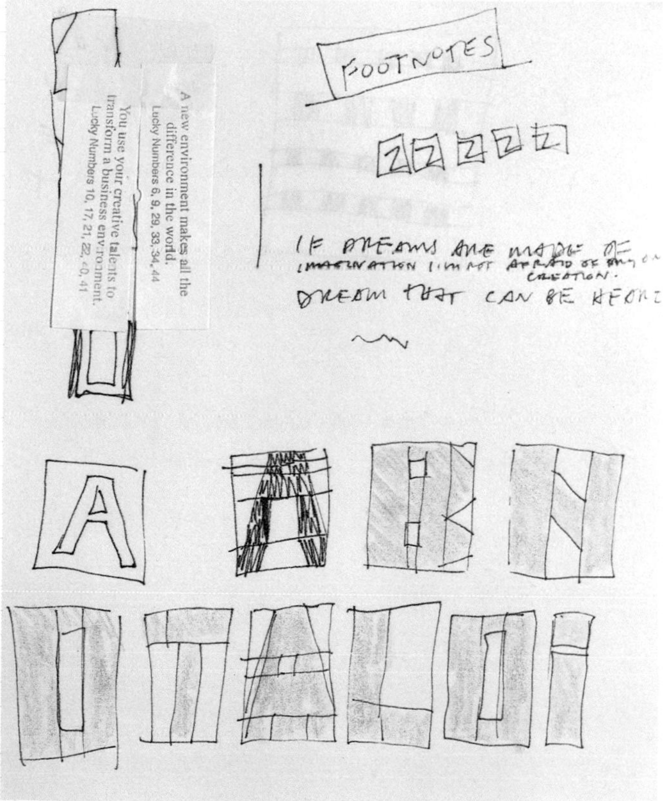
A new environment makes all the difference in the world.
Lucky Numbers 6, 9, 29, 33, 34, 44
You use your creative talents to transform a business environment.
Lucky Numbers 10, 17, 21, 22, 40, 41
FOOTNOTES
IF DREAMS ARE MADE OF
DREAM THAT CAN BE HERE

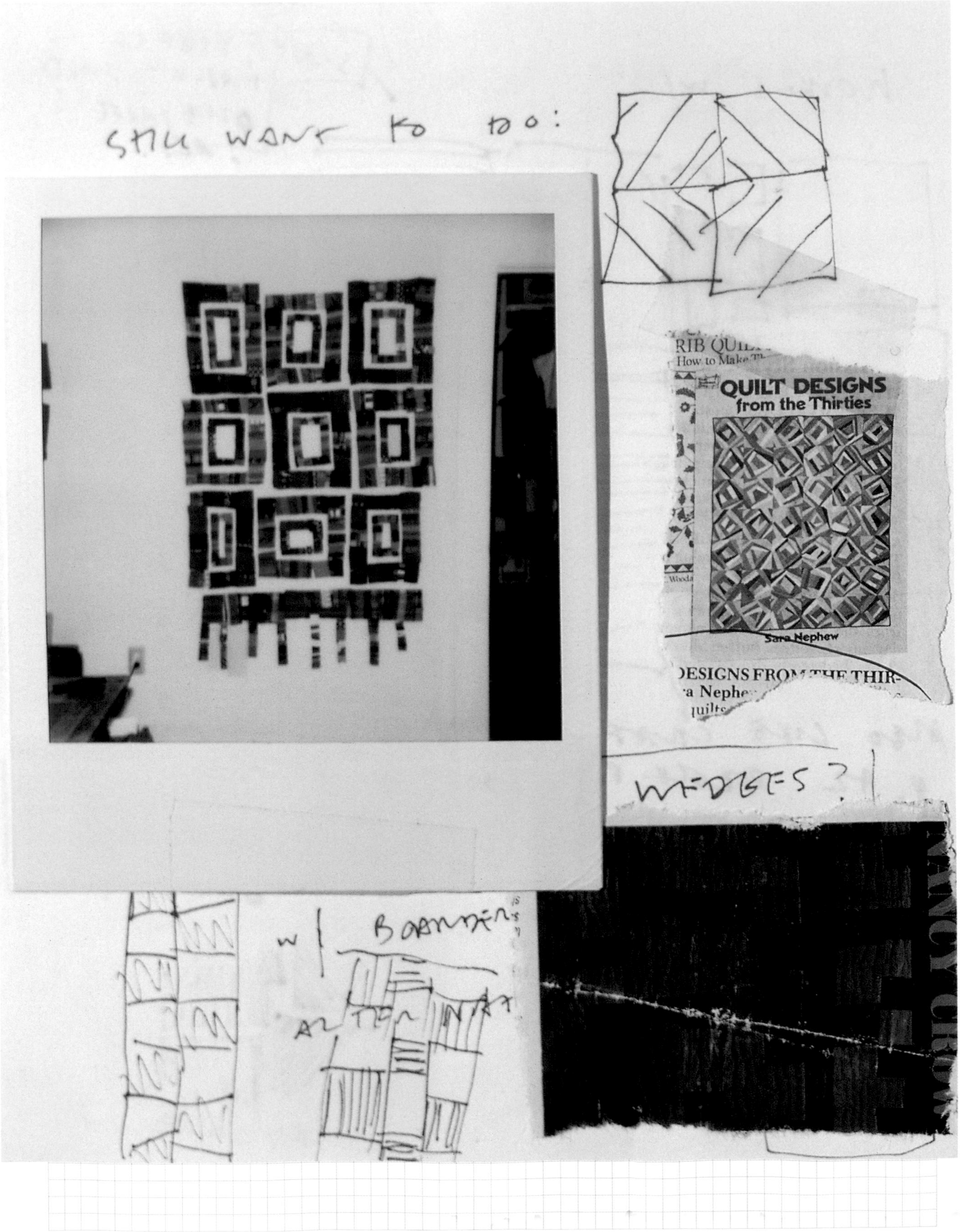
STILL WANT TO DO:
QUILT DESIGNS
from the Thirties
Sara Nephew
WEDGES?
NANCY CROW

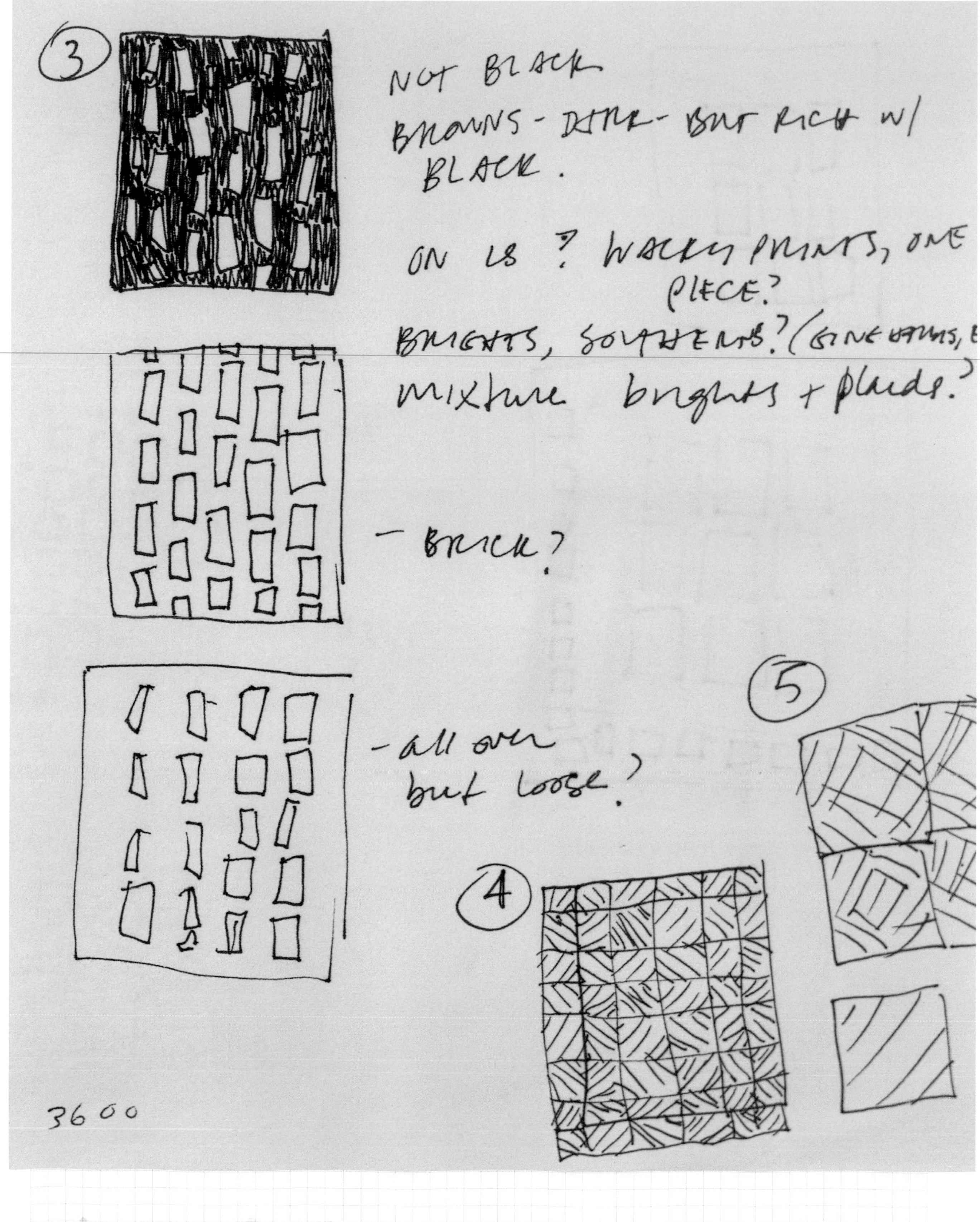
3
NOT BLACK
BROWNS - DIRT - BUT RICH W/ BLACK.
ON LS ? WACKY PRINTS, ONE PIECE?
mixture brights + plaids?
- BRICK?
- all over but loose?
5
4
3600

/ MIKE FIGGIS

Two things are clear about director Mike Figgis. First, he is a passionate but highly focused person who can freeze-frame multiple projects in order to concentrate on the one at hand. And, second, he values those things that make his life better and his art richer. His journals clearly serve such a purpose.

"I have a leather bag I take with me wherever I go," says Figgis. "Into it goes my travel docs, my camera, my small notebook, my phone..." He trails off, mentally checking his packing list. "Of those, the little notebook is by far the most important."

His "everyday journal" is where Figgis daydreams and reacts to the world. He calls it a "memory bank," and says, "I have a lot of ideas, and when I write them down psychologically my brain lets go of them. But then I forget them, so when I revisit them, it is quite a revelation." He also keeps notebooks specific to every current work-in-progress, which range from films to photography. He frequently refers to these for phone numbers, to-do lists, and other unembellished information. In addition, he's kept sketchbooks and dream journals.

What allows someone with such a ferocious creative energy to produce as much varied work as Figgis does is his organizational skill. He proudly calls himself "a very good librarian," when describing the shelf in his London home that holds all of his journals in sequence with notations on their spines. He says that he spends quite a bit of time cataloguing because "I work on the basis that if I have an idea, I need to resource it really quickly."

Not surprisingly, Figgis is particular about his materials. He is one of the few contributors who actually use the beautiful Italian journals that others either covet or keep unblemished on a shelf. He admits to having a soft spot for stationery stores and recently spent a "preposterous" amount on a leather-bound journal that will withstand travel. Pens are important, too. He has about 20 fountain pens and carefully selects three of different colors and widths for travel.

Figgis started keeping a journal in music school in the early 1970s, filling it with playlists and names of clubs for gigs. When he joined a performance art group, he was the scribe, writing down sequences. Gradually, drawings and collage elements found their way into the journals. The switch to film made the journal less of a tool for lists and planning and more "personal and self-searching."

For someone who lives so intensely in his head, generating, editing, tossing out and going on to new ideas in the time that most people are reading the front page of the morning paper, Figgis needs his journals to stay centered. "If I couldn't have that internal dialogue, I couldn't function." he comments of the journal's therapeutic role.

Because he is "always moving forward," he tends to pick up an old journal only when he's looking for something particular. For example, a current film echoes themes he explored years ago in a performance art piece causing him to search for threads in the old journal from those days. Sometimes he's humbled by his own former creative self: "I'll think I've had an original idea," he laughs, "but realize I already had it fifteen years ago!"

1)- Frances Farmer
2) New York.
3)- Script fragments
4)+ Hopper window
5)- Yellow cab
6)- Hotel Room
7). Songs.
8) Jazz dancers.
9)- Refugees
10) Cemetary
11) Skyscrapers.
12) Daily news.
13) LENOX HOTEL
DAILY NEWS
MOB BOSS
BLASTED IN
T.V. Set.

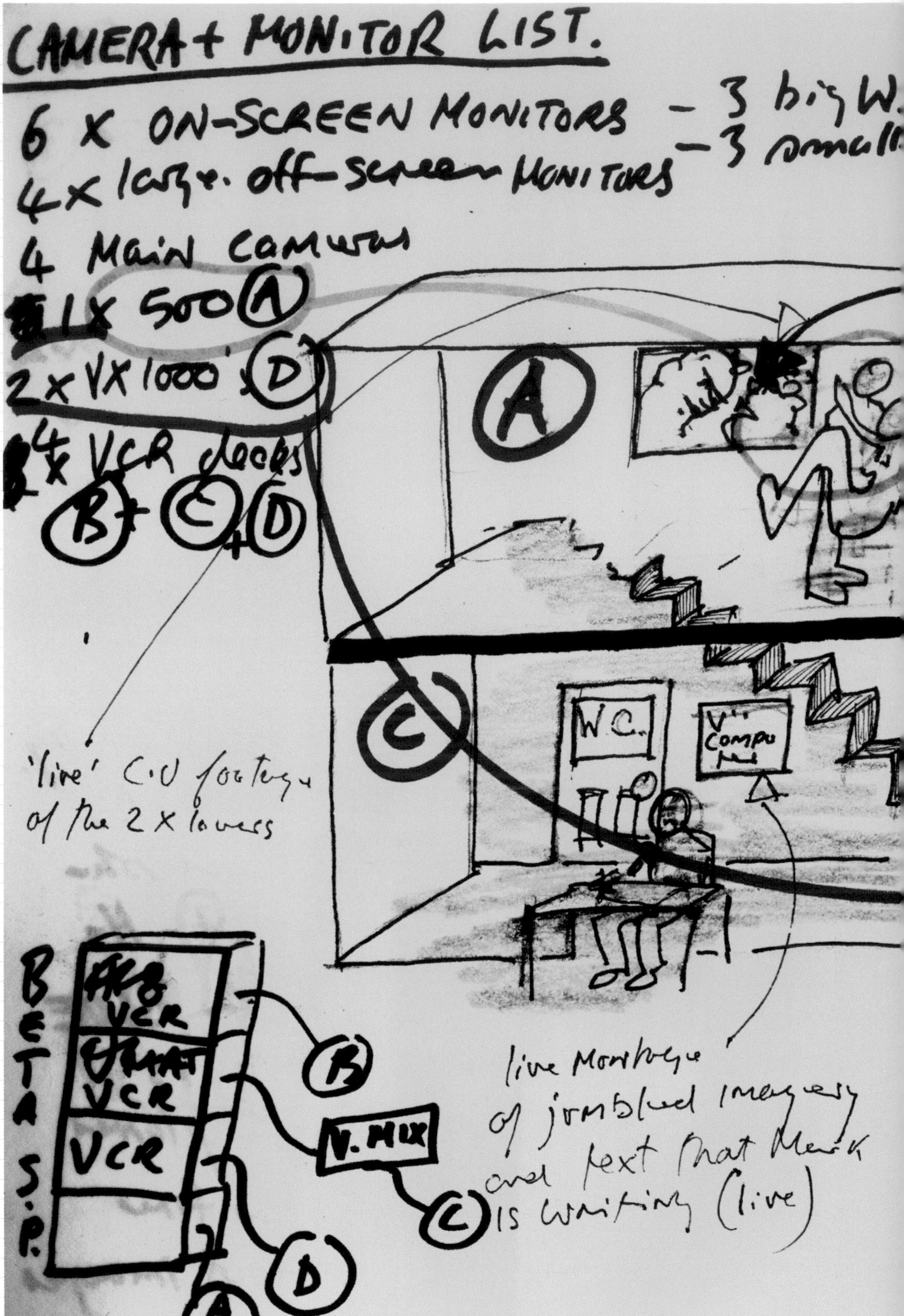
CAMERA + MONITOR LIST.
6 x ON-SCREEN MONITORS
4 x large off-screen MONITORS
4 Main cameras
1 x 500 A
2 x VX1000 D
4 x VCR decks
B + C + D
A
'live' C.U footage of the 2 x lovers
W.C.
V. MIX
live Montage of jumbled imagery and text that Mark is writing (live)
B E T A S.P.
VCR
VCR
VCR
B
C
D
A

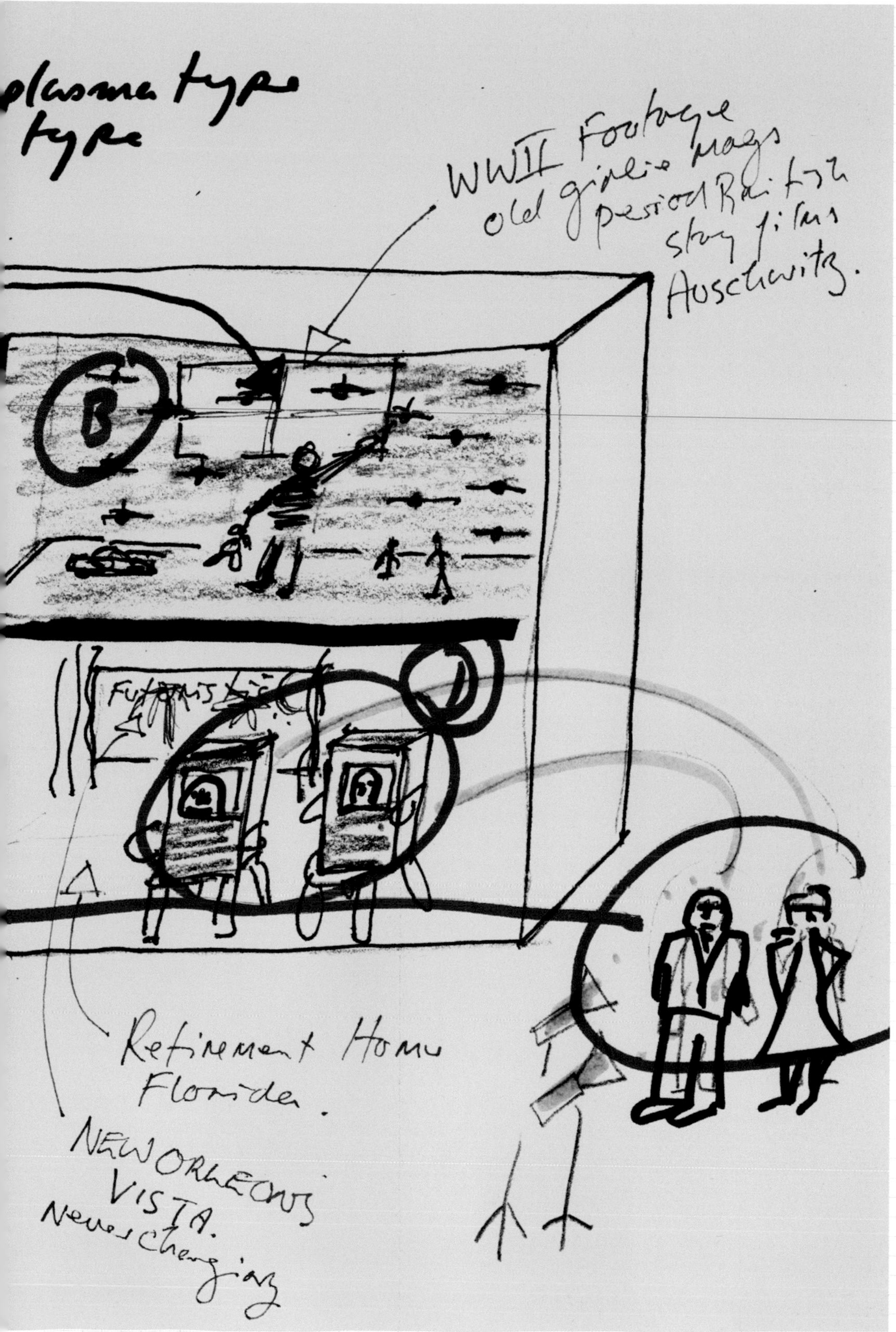
plasma type
type
WWII Footage
old girlie mags
stag films
Auschwitz.
Retirement Home
Florida.
NEW ORLEANS
VISTA.
Never changing

MIKE FIGGIS

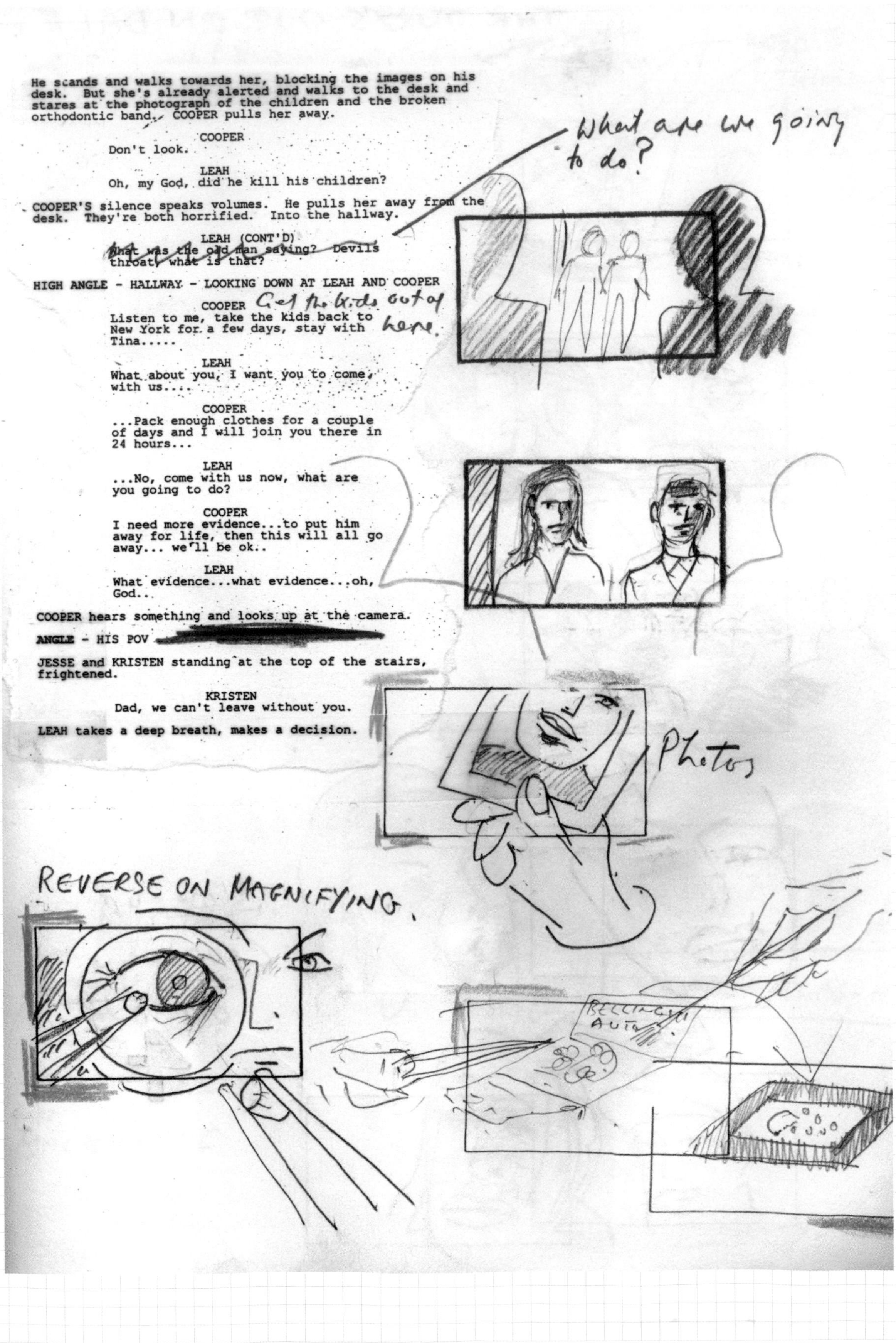

He stands and walks towards her, blocking the images on his desk. But she's already alerted and walks to the desk and stares at the photograph of the children and the broken orthodontic band. COOPER pulls her away.

COOPER
Don't look.

LEAH
Oh, my God, did he kill his children?

COOPER'S silence speaks volumes. He pulls her away from the desk. They're both horrified. Into the hallway.

LEAH (CONT'D)
~~What was the old man saying? Devils throat, what is that?~~

HIGH ANGLE - HALLWAY - LOOKING DOWN AT LEAH AND COOPER

COOPER
Listen to me, take the kids back to New York for a few days, stay with Tina.....

LEAH
What about you, I want you to come with us....

COOPER
...Pack enough clothes for a couple of days and I will join you there in 24 hours...

LEAH
...No, come with us now, what are you going to do?

COOPER
I need more evidence...to put him away for life, then this will all go away... we'll be ok..

LEAH
What evidence...what evidence...oh, God..

COOPER hears something and looks up at the camera.

ANGLE - HIS POV [redacted]

JESSE and KRISTEN standing at the top of the stairs, frightened.

KRISTEN
Dad, we can't leave without you.

LEAH takes a deep breath, makes a decision.

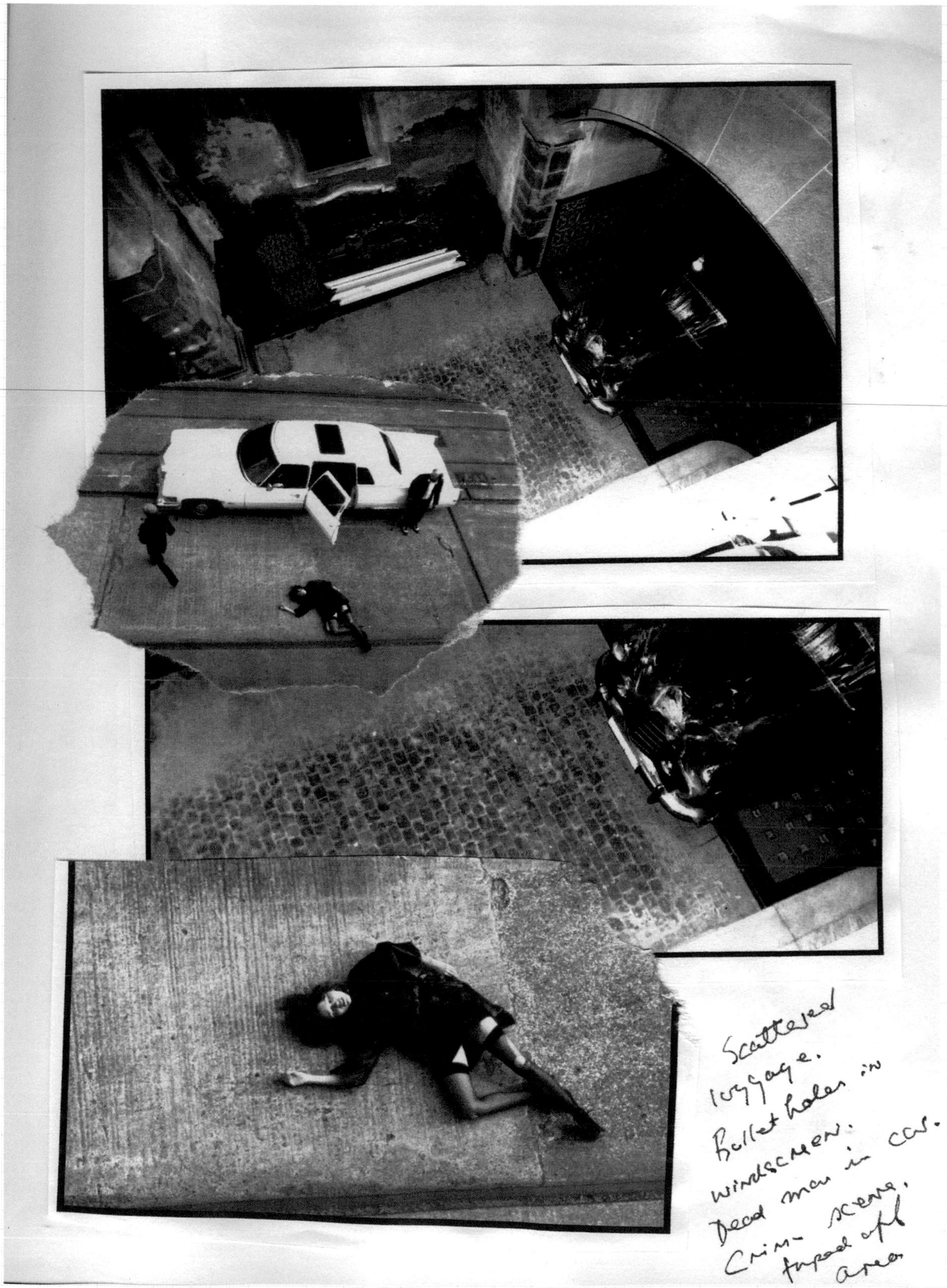
Scattered
luggage.
Bullet holes in
windscreen.
Dead man in car.
Crime scene.
taped off
area

ACKNOWLEDGMENTS

Trust is what this book hinges on—the trust of the thirty-one people in its pages to share their work not only with me but with the world. The majority of them mailed their journals to me (we all said private prayers to the FedEx gods), allowing me to read their books at leisure. Every time a journal arrived—sometimes floating free in a cardboard box or cosseted in layers of tissue and bubble wrap—it felt like an extreme privilege to become acquainted with its maker. Though I only had relatively brief telephone and email exchanges with most of the contributors, I count them all as friends and creative models. Many other people shared their journals with me as well, and I thank them for their interest in this project and their willingness to open their private lives to me. In order to find such an array of journal keepers, I relied on friends and their extended address books, people located online, and others interested in the topic that were willing to spread the word. The process made me a believer in six degrees of separation.

The people who helped this work spring from a series of passionate entries in my own journal to an actual book notably include Sally Wofford-Girand, my agent, and Princeton Architectural Press editors Mark Lamster and Jennifer Thompson. Dan Eldon and the many admirers of his art inspired this project, and I remain grateful to Kathy Eldon and Alan Rapp for allowing me to enter Dan's world; they both continue to buoy me, providing advice and perspective. My husband, Andrew Epstein, took most of the photographs in this book, sacrificing countless hours of his time. I know we will look back and be amazed that we did this with two children under the age of three. I am lucky to have some very talented friends whose feedback has been invaluable: chocolate cake all around for Megan Knight, April Lidinsky, Claudia McGehee, and members of my writing group (a.k.a., The Kate Vest Mystery gals). My extended family has helped to make this project possible in countless ways, as have Jessica Stokes, who cared so lovingly for my children; Flynn Larsen, who provided travel and research aid; John McKeone for his packing acumen; and Kevin Gunzenhauser who shared his photographic talents. I am also indebted to the Iowa Arts Council for a grant that assisted in the making of this book. My final thanks go to Andrew and our children, Bella and Tobey. You inspire me every day and remind me to laugh. This book may not rival *Madeline* in your present esteem, but know that it is all for you!

CONTRIBUTOR BIOGRAPHIES

Lynda Barry is a writer and cartoonist whose work has appeared all over tarnation. She was born in 1956 and lives on a farm somewhere in the profound Midwest.

Julie Baugnet is an associate professor of design at St. Cloud State University in Minnesota, where she teaches graphic design and foundations. She earned her BFA and MFA degrees at the Minneapolis College of Art and Design and also studied at the Croydon Polytechnic School of Art in London. She has exhibited her paintings extensively throughout the U.S. and is represented by Circa Gallery in Minneapolis.

United Press International has cited **Carol Beckwith** as "foremost among photographers who have recorded the cultures of Africa." She and Angela Fisher received multiple awards for their book *African Ceremonies*, including the United Nations Award of Excellence for their "vision and understanding of the role of cultural traditions in the pursuit of peace in the world." Their most recent book is *Faces of Africa* (National Geographic, 2004).

Sophie Binder is a self-employed designer living in St. Louis. Previously, she worked as a designer in the theme-park industry, first in her native France and then in the U.S. In 2001, she set off on a 14,000-mile bicycle trip through sixteen countries. She continues to bike and recently took up rock climbing.

Erwin R. Boer has researched human-machine interaction in a number of domains ranging from aviation and driving to scientific data visualization. He received his MS and Ph.D degrees in Electrical Engineering from Twente University of Technology in the Netherlands and the University of Illinois in Chicago, respectively. In 2001, Nissan offered him the opportunity to direct research in the area of intelligent driver support systems through close collaboration with a number of universities in the U.S., Canada, the Netherlands, and Japan.

Erica Bohanon was born in Peoria, Illinois. She graduated from the Minneapolis College of Art and Design in 2003 with a BFA in furniture design. Since then she has worked on products for Target Corporation and Caldrea. Currently, she lives in New York City, where she works in lifestyle and home product design.

Gary Brown is a professor at the University of California Santa Barbara, where he teaches journaling classes and has developed an extensive collection of artist journals and sketchbooks. Brown is currently editing four decade's worth of journals into artist book–digital printed constructions. His work has been featured in *Male Nude Now, New Visions for the 21st Century* (Rizzoli, 2001).

Primarily known as the musician who cofounded the group Talking Heads (1976–88), **David Byrne** has also directed films (*True Stories*), scored films (notably, *The Last Emperor*, for which he won an Oscar), and a ballet (*The Catherine Wheel*). He is also an accomplished visual artist who has several books and numerous exhibitions to his credit. Byrne's recent work includes the album *Grown Backwards* (Nonesuch, 2004) and a digital display entitled *Trees, Tombstones, & Bullet Points* at the George Eastman House.

John Clapp is the illustrator of five books for children, including books written by Robin McKinley, Liz Rosenberg, and Bruce Coville. His latest book, *Shining*, by Julius Lester, is a Book Sense 76 Pick and was selected for inclusion in the Society of Illustrators' annual show representing the Best Picture Book Art of 2003. A graduate of Art Center College of Design in Pasadena, he now teaches drawing and painting at San Jose State University.

John Copeland received a BFA from San Francisco's California College of Arts in 1998. He has appeared in numerous group shows and had a solo exhibition at 31 Grand in Brooklyn, New York, in Fall 2004, where he is represented. Copeland's journals can be viewed on his web site at johncopeland.com.

Mike Figgis is a writer/director/composer whose 1996 feature film *Leaving Las Vegas* was nominated for four Academy Awards. Figgis joined England's foremost avant-garde theater group, The People Show, in the early 1970s. He recently directed an episode of the Martin Scorsese-produced series, *The Blues*, and completed an installation, *The Museum of the Imperfect Past*, at the 2003 Valencia Biennale.

Hannah Hinchman is a writer/illustrator best known for her books about illustrated journals. She teaches summer workshops on that subject throughout the country. Her most recent title is *Little Things in A Big Country: An Artist and Her Dog on the Rocky Mountain Front* (W. W. Norton, 2004). Currently she is a graduate student in graphic design at Indiana University in Bloomington.

Rick Hoblitt is staff geologist at the Hawaiian Volcano Observatory in Hawaii National Park. He was a member of VDAP for ten years, during which time he was based at the David A. Johnston Cascades Volcano Observatory in Vancouver, Washington. Hoblitt received his MS in chemistry in 1970 and his Ph.D in geology in 1978, both from the University of Colorado in Boulder. He lives in Hawaii National Park with his wife.

Steven Holl founded Steven Holl Architects in New York in 1976. He is a tenured faculty member at Columbia University, where he has taught since 1981, and was named America's Best Architect for "buildings that satisfy the spirit as well as the eye" by *Time* magazine. He was honored by the Smithsonian Institution with the 2002 Cooper-Hewitt National Design Award in Architecture.

Maira Kalman is the author of thirteen children's books and is a frequent contributor to *The New Yorker.* In conjunction with M&Co., the design studio founded by her late husband, Tibor Kalman, she has designed sets for Mark Morris, fabrics for Isaac Mizrahi, handbags for Kate Spade, and watches for the Museum of Modern Art.

Jenny Keller is a professor in the science illustration program at the University of California Santa Cruz. She began keeping illustrated field journals in 1981. Her special interests include studies of skeletal anatomy and describing movement through animated sequences. She was the sole illustrator for *Dolphin Days* (by Kenneth S. Norris, W. W. Norton, 1991), which won the John Burroughs Award for best book of the year in natural history.

Anderson Kenny received his MArch from the University of Tennessee, Knoxville, in 1998. He currently lives in Connecticut, where he works for Centerbrook Architects and divides his time between painting, installations, and architecture. The aesthetic of rural settings combined with urban landscapes and contemporary design is a continuing influence in Kenny's work.

Marcy Kentz grew up in suburban Los Angeles and is now attending California College of the Arts in Oakland. She hopes to major in printmaking and book arts.

Christopher Leitch is an artist and designer who lives and works in Kansas City. His works emerge from chance processes and randomly selected materials, and, he says, "I never know what anything is going to look like. This uncertainty is liberating and invigorating." His drawing and textile designs have been exhibited and published around the world.

Nakano Masayoshi, 103, is retired from Hitachi Industries, where he worked as an engineer and, in later years, as vice president of the company's junior college. He resides in Tokyo with his family.

Thomas Oslund, the principal design director of oslund.and.assoc., is one of the leading design landscape architects in the U.S. He has received awards from the American Society of Landscape Architects, American Institute of Architects, and in 1992 was awarded the prestigious Rome Prize from the American Academy in Rome. He teaches and lectures at various colleges and universities and lives in Minneapolis with his wife and children.

Lyle Owerko works as a photographer and art director in New York and has received multiple awards and recognition, including from the New York Art Directors Club, the Cannes Advertising Festival, and American Photography. Most notably, his photography was seen around the globe when it was featured on the cover of *Time* magazine's special edition published on September 13th, 2001.

Robert ParkeHarrison received a BFA from the Kansas City Art Institute in 1990 and an MFA from the University of New Mexico in Albuquerque in 1994. He and his wife Shana began officially collaborating in 2001. Their traveling exhibition, *The Architect's Brother*, was originally shown at George Eastman House in 2002. ParkeHarrison is represented by Bonni Benrubi Gallery in New York.

Michael Roberts is known for his highly realistic portrait cutouts on wood, which have made their way into many collections, including the Congressional Portrait Collection. His subjects have included well-known political or historical figures as well as ordinary citizens. Based in Iowa City, where he lives with his wife and two daughters, Roberts is represented by the Iowa Artisan's Gallery.

A former graphic designer and graduate of Rhode Island School of Design, **Denyse Schmidt** has been sewing since her mother taught her as a child. As a professional seamstress, she has worked on everything from tutus and bishop's mitres to fine clothing. She has a gift line, *What a Bunch of Squares,* and a how-to book, both published by Chronicle Books.

Tucker Shaw is a writer who lives and eats in downtown Manhattan. Author of several books for young adults, including the award-winning *Flavor of the Week* (Hyperion, 2003), Tucker is an avid traveler and lifelong food freak who has been photographing his meals for years.

Brian Singer is the Creative Director at Altitude, a San Francisco–based design firm. He is the creator of The 1000 Journals Project, a global collaborative art experiment reaching over thirty-five countries and every U.S. state. Singer's design work has been recognized by the American Institute of Graphic Arts 365, the San Francisco Museum of Modern Art, *Communication Arts*, *Print*, *Graphis*, *Step*, *How*, the Society of Publication Designers, and the Western Art Directors Club.

Andrew Swift received his BS in biology in 1990 from Presbyterian College in Clinton, South Carolina, and then taught environmental education on the coast of Georgia. He served three years in the Peace Corps in Ecuador and later attended Augusta State University and the Art Students League of New York. In 1999, Swift earned his MS in medical illustration from the Medical College of Georgia, where he is currently an assistant professor.

Renato Umali was born in the Philippines but grew up in Jersey City, New Jersey. He currently lives in Milwaukee, Wisconsin, where he teaches video production and is an active musician, writing and performing the music for the found-text band The Paragraphs.

Idelle Weber attended Scripps College in Claremont, California, and the University of California, Los Angeles, receiving a BA in 1954 and an MA in 1955. She has been in numerous solo and group exhibitions and is represented in a large number of public and private collections. Weber taught painting at Harvard University and New York University and was also as an artist in residence at the Victoria School of the Arts in Melbourne, Australia. Her work can be viewed at idelleweber.com.

Martin Wilner is an artist living and working in New York City. Represented by Pierogi in Brooklyn, he has been in several group and solo shows. His ongoing subway diary, "The Journal of Evidence Weekly," is available online at www.tjew.com. "Making History: July 2004" appeared on the cover of *Pierogi Press* #11. He is also a clinical assistant professor of psychiatry at Weill Cornell Medical College and has a private practice in Manhattan.

road, looking at stratigraphy. The section at the Charcoal site sampled yesterday is:

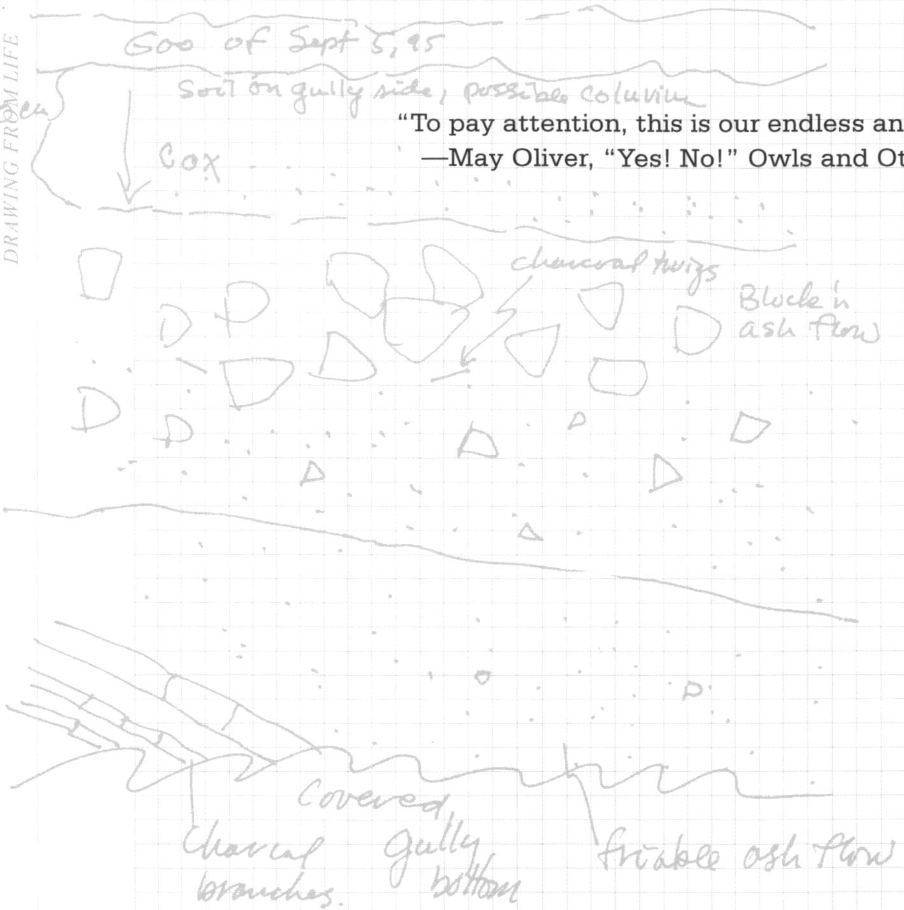

"To pay attention, this is our endless and proper work."
—May Oliver, "Yes! No!" Owls and Other Fantasies

Generalized stratigraphy down gully is: